RIGOR REDEFINED

Ten Teaching Habits *for* Surface, Deep, *and* Transfer Learning

MICHAEL McDOWELL

FOREWORD BY JOHN HATTIE

Solution Tree | Press

Copyright © 2024 by Solution Tree Press

Materials appearing here are copyrighted. With one exception, all rights are reserved. Readers may reproduce only those pages marked "Reproducible." Otherwise, no part of this book may be reproduced or transmitted in any form or by any means (electronic, photocopying, recording, or otherwise) without prior written permission of the publisher.

555 North Morton Street
Bloomington, IN 47404
800.733.6786 (toll free) / 812.336.7700
FAX: 812.336.7790

email: info@SolutionTree.com
SolutionTree.com

Printed in the United States of America

Library of Congress Cataloging-in-Publication Data

Names: McDowell, Michael (Michael P.), author.
Title: Rigor redefined : ten teaching habits for surface, deep, and transfer learning / Michael McDowell.
Description: Bloomington, IN : Solution Tree Press, [2024] | Includes bibliographical references and index.
Identifiers: LCCN 2023055139 (print) | LCCN 2023055140 (ebook) | ISBN 9781960574664 (paperback) | ISBN 9781960574671 (ebook)
Subjects: LCSH: Effective teaching. | Teacher effectiveness. | Transfer of training. | Student-centered learning. | Learning strategies.
Classification: LCC LB1025.3 .M353 2024 (print) | LCC LB1025.3 (ebook) | DDC 371.102--dc23/eng/20240208
LC record available at https://lccn.loc.gov/2023055139
LC ebook record available at https://lccn.loc.gov/2023055140

Solution Tree
Jeffrey C. Jones, CEO
Edmund M. Ackerman, President

Solution Tree Press
President and Publisher: Douglas M. Rife
Associate Publishers: Todd Brakke and Kendra Slayton
Editorial Director: Laurel Hecker
Art Director: Rian Anderson
Copy Chief: Jessi Finn
Production Editor: Kate St. Ives
Text Designer: Julie Csizmadia
Cover Designer: Abigail Bowen
Acquisitions Editors: Carol Collins and Hilary Goff
Assistant Acquisitions Editor: Elijah Oates
Content Development Specialist: Amy Rubenstein
Associate Editor: Sarah Ludwig
Editorial Assistant: Anne Marie Watkins

Acknowledgments

I am deeply grateful to the students and educators whose insights, feedback, and daily interactions have played a pivotal role in the development of this book. Your commitment to the pursuit of knowledge and your passion for teaching and learning have been a constant source of inspiration and a driver in my pursuit to improve the learning lives of students and find ways to improve education through pragmatism and innovation.

I extend my heartfelt thanks to Professor John Hattie for his unwavering influence on my thinking about teaching, learning, and leadership. His guidance and wisdom have been invaluable, shaping the very foundation of this work. I am fortunate to have had the privilege of learning from such a distinguished educator.

To the Solution Tree Press team, I express my sincere appreciation for your continued support and professionalism throughout the publishing process. Your dedication to excellence has been instrumental in bringing this project to fruition. I would like to particularly thank my editor Kate St. Ives for her calm approach, attention to detail, and sage advice.

To my family, I extend my deepest gratitude for your unyielding patience, unfiltered feedback, and unconditional love. Your unwavering support has been a constant source of strength, and I am profoundly grateful for the sacrifices you have made to make this journey possible. Our shared mission of improving the learning process and our shared values of hard work, curiosity, and kindness have enabled each key typed to be filled with both love for this field and passion for making it better for everyone.

This book stands as a testament to the collaborative efforts of a community dedicated to the advancement of education. Thank you all for your contributions, insights, and encouragement. May this work serve as a meaningful contribution to the field and inspire positive change in the lives of students and educators around the world.

Solution Tree Press would like to thank the following reviewers:

Erin Kruckenberg
Fifth-Grade Teacher
Jefferson Elementary School
Harvard, Illinois

Kory Taylor
Reading Interventionist
Arkansas Virtual Academy
Little Rock, Arkansas

Ian Landy
District Principal of Technology
School District 47
Powell River, British Columbia, Canada

Visit **go.SolutionTree.com/instruction** to download the free reproducibles in this book.

Table of Contents

Reproducibles are in italics.

About the Author ix

Foreword xi
by John Hattie

Introduction 1
    What Is Rigorous Learning? 2
    Why Is Rigorous Learning Important? 4
    What Dispositional Skills Can Enhance Student Rigorous Learning? 7
    How Can Educators Foster Rigorous Learning? 8
    How Do Educators Build Systems for Engaging Students in the Ten *Rigor Redefined* Habits? .. 11
    What Is in This Book? 13

1   Redefining Rigor 17
    Considering the Rigorous Learning Process 18
    Making the Ten Rigorous Learning Habits Habitual 28
    Conclusion 31
    Reflection Questions 32
    Next Steps 33
    What? So What? Now What? 34

2 Making Rigorous Learning Doable 35
Starting and Sustaining a Habit 36
Making Motion Matter 50
Inspecting the Motion Work 56
Conclusion 60
Reflection Questions 61
Next Steps 62

3 Developing Dispositional Habits 63
Starting With a Culture of *We Do* 64
Habit 1: Engage Metacognition 68
Habit 2: Navigate Challenge 77
Habit 3: Work Well With Others 83
Habit 4: Consolidate Learning 86
Incorporating Dispositional Habits Into a "We Do" Culture 90
Conclusion 91
Reflection Questions 92
Next Steps 93

4 Making Surface Learning a Habit 95
Mutual Learning 96
Habit 5: Build Knowledge Together 97
Habit 6: Check and Respond to Current Understanding Together 109
Conclusion 115
Reflection Questions 116
Next Steps 117

5 Developing the Habits of Deep Learning 119
Defining Deep Learning 120
Developing Deep Learning Habits 121
Habit 7: Develop Conceptual Understanding 123
Habit 8: Apply Conceptual Understanding 151
Making Deep Learning Feedback Social 161
Making Deep Learning Feedback Routine 165
Conclusion 166
Reflection Questions 167
Next Steps 168

6 Developing Transfer Learning Habits 169
Learning to Transfer 170
Habit 9: Build Contextual Understanding 171
Habit 10: Solve Complex Problems 181
Conclusion 198
Reflection Questions 199
Next Steps 200

Epilogue 201

Appendix 203
Consultancy Dilemma 204
Tuning Protocol 204
Affinity Mapping 205

References and Resources 207

Index 215

About the Author

Michael McDowell, EdD, has been a public school educator for the past eighteen years serving in the roles of classroom teacher, academic and athletic coach, school principal, assistant superintendent of personnel and instruction, and superintendent. During his tenure as a superintendent, Ross School District in California received state and national accolades, including the National Blue Ribbon Schools award, which recognized their work for student performance and mental health and well-being in the midst of the COVID-19 pandemic.

Dr. McDowell serves on numerous boards, served as a college professor, and worked for nonprofit organizations to enhance student learning around the world. Over the course of his career, Dr. McDowell has authored best-selling books, including *Teaching for Transfer: A Guide for Designing Learning With Real-World Application*, *The Lead Learner: Improving Clarity, Coherence, and Capacity for All*, *The Project Habit: Making Rigorous PBL Doable*, *Rigorous PBL by Design: Three Shifts for Developing Confident and Competent Learners*, *The Busy Teacher: Differentiation for Every Classroom*, and *Navigating Leadership Drift: Observable Impact on Rigorous Learning*. He has also created professional learning programs and workbooks, provided keynotes and workshops, and provided practical tools and resources for thousands of teachers and leaders on almost every continent around the world. A prolific author and consultant, Dr. McDowell is recognized as one of the leading authorities on integrating innovative and impactful practices into schools. Offering keynotes and executive coaching to heads of schools around the world, he partners with educational leaders to implement high-leverage strategies that will enhance teaching and learning in classrooms, schools, and systems.

Dr. McDowell received a bachelor's degree in environmental science and a master's in curriculum and instruction from University of Redlands and his doctorate in education in organizational leadership from the University of La Verne.

To learn more about Dr. McDowell's work, visit hingeeducation.org or follow him on X (formerly Twitter) @mmcdowell13.

To book Michael McDowell for professional development, contact pd@SolutionTree.com.

Foreword
by John Hattie

It is fascinating to shadow a high school student for a day. Attend the classes; sit, watch, and listen; talk to them at the beginning and end of class about their experiences and thoughts; and then share their excitement and exhaustion when the school day is over. You hear various teachers proclaim school rules that contradict the last teacher, you listen to teachers talking (about 90 percent of the time), you see teachers asking so many questions requiring less than a three-word answer, and you see the *doing* (worksheets, textbook questions, doodling). In a lot of this doing, there can be little learning. Students are asked to work alone or assigned to group work—and they typically detest group work, as it is often poorly constructed, invites those who can to *do* while the others watch, and offers credit that is often poorly ascribed. The school day is littered with facts, content, and knowledge—these are the currency of the day—and the above-average students prefer to have facts, as that is the game they are winners in. The dominant emotion in a class like this is often boredom caused by too many incoming facts (we can only hold four to six facts in our head at once, so the daze comes quickly), and when I and others like me become bored, sleepiness is the outcome. Many students learn to look engaged. They *do* the work, and scurry to the next episode of this same recipe.

Not all classes are like the class I've described, but I invite you to show this description to students, and most can recognize days like this. What keeps me going is that I do see many excellent teachers who can motivate and engage students in both the facts and the deeper conceptual understanding and the skills of transferring what they learn to new situations. Excellence is all around us. So how do we make all students experience great teachers by design, and not by chance?

Michael McDowell tackles this question throughout *Rigor Redefined: Ten Teaching Habits for Surface, Deep, and Transfer Learning*. Using the notion of *rigorous learning*, he outlines the breadth and depth of knowing, shows why it is motivating (all students like to be appropriately challenged), and offers many ways for educators to build systems for engaging students in his ten rigor habits. He notes that the task of achieving rigorous learning is a matter of the teacher not merely changing their performance but teaching the skills of learning at the breadth, depth, and transfer of understanding.

Rather than the more well-known Bloom's taxonomy, which mixes breadth and depth (although the 2001 revision did add cognitive complexity notions, to be ignored by most), Michael uses surface, deep, and transfer or what is commonly referred to as the SOLO taxonomy (also the basis for my own work). This taxonomy makes it easier for teachers and students to discriminate between the surface (background knowledge and skills), deep (related ideas or deeper learning), and transfer (application in diverse contexts). It asks for different teaching, learning strategies, success criteria, tasks, assignments, and feedback aimed at each of the three levels (the minute you put them together, the students will revert to believing that is the surface understanding you really want).

Michael also introduces the three pillars of rigorous learning: (1) balance (having the right proportion at the right time for the right tasks), (2) fluidity (making the levels discrete but also emphasizing balance across them), and (3) inclusion (giving all students the opportunity for rigor). Too often, those working below average are assigned work with fewer facts to learn and no depth—thus, they fall even further behind their peers.

Lessons and tasks need to include the three levels of surface, deep, and transfer with the right balance, and the ten disposition habits need to be taught. This approach assists teachers and students in making the learning exciting and turns students on to learning what we want them to know, understand, be able to do, and care about. We must also be clear about the nature of success, making the success criteria appropriately challenging, teaching students to work with others, ensuring teaching is devoted to not only the topic but also consolidating the learning, checking for understanding, building contextual understanding, and developing and applying the conceptual understanding. Michael's pinwheel metaphor helps bring these together more seamlessly, and the supporting content provides specific and workable suggestions for implementation in every classroom.

When I shadow a student experiencing classrooms where these habits are required and there is the optimal proportion of surface, depth, and transfer, I feel the learning. You see students who spike up with anticipation and feel the frustration that they do not know and cannot get it but then experience the "aha" when they appreciate that the frustration was worth it. You hear the quest to know more and go deeper, and you see and live the love of learning. This is why we all came into teaching, to enable all our students to develop a love of learning; this is what we recall when we sift back through our memories of the best experiences when we were at school; and this is what this book aims to encourage and engender.

Rigor is the catchword in the title and throughout the book. It implies thoroughness and meticulousness. It involves a level of diligence and development of competence. It ensures that the teaching and learning can withstand scrutiny and that the highest standards are maintained. It is rigor not in the sense of *rigor mortis* (the stillness of the body) but in the sense of *studii alacritas* (an enthusiasm or zealousness in learning).

Introduction

*I believe in the balance
between dreaming and building.*
—*Neri Oxman*

Did you ever play with a pinwheel when you were a child?

You know what I mean, don't you? That toy—maybe it's considered old-fashioned now, maybe a bit simple—with those colored vanes on a stick. They twirl in the wind, but *only* if you hold the stick just right, and only if you blow air into the vanes with the right amount of force. The pinwheel is a toy that asks the person who plays with it to find and apply balance. This book is about finding balance. Specifically, in a world in which trends in education often change as quickly as the weather, in which transient choices and expectations can feel dizzying for teachers, it offers K–12 educators clear, research-supported guidance that asks them to balance the core values of teaching with an innovative mindset—for instance, students must be competent in core academic knowledge and skills while also applying their knowledge and skills to real-world problems. Moreover, students must develop the skills to confidently learn how to learn while also ensuring they are learning the foundations of a discipline. In achieving this balance, teachers give their students the tools to find and apply balance in their own learning and therein to recognize rigor, seek rigor, and learn rigorously. The word *rigor* likely does not conjure ideas of hope, creativity, or enthusiasm. A pinwheel is likely not the first image that comes to mind. Instead, perhaps the word *rigor* brings to mind the haunting phrase *rigor mortis*: the postmortem process by which the body's muscles stiffen, resulting in rigidity, as a result of a variety of chemical changes in the muscle structure.

Educators often think of rigor as a linear process in which students must traverse certain levels of learning prior to accessing higher levels of learning. For instance, before we can apply ideas of how carbon molecules contribute to greenhouse gas, we must first recognize and recall facts. In addition, education systems consider rigorous learning hierarchical by nature, prioritizing certain levels of learning over other levels of learning: a student's ability to evaluate (that is, judge the values of information or ideas) is more important than the student's ability to understand (or determine what specific facts mean). Moreover, *rigor* is often conflated with the complexity of learning something new and the amount of work that students are required to complete within a given amount of time without consideration of the level of complexity. A mathematics homework assignment of a hundred procedural fluency problems each night may be considered "rigorous" by many.

However, as we will see, rigorous learning is far from stiff or rigid and is, in fact, a learning process that centers on fluidity, balance, and inclusion. In this book, the pinwheel serves as a metaphor for balancing key components of rigorous learning: effective habits, a recognition of the various types of complex learning—which I call *surface*, *deep*, and *transfer*; and the ability to move across these types of learning to address problems that exist in the classroom and the world beyond school. It is my hope and belief that this book will offer teachers ways to help their students take ownership of their learning and, through that learning, thrive in whatever contexts they may find themselves experiencing.

What Is Rigorous Learning?

Rigorous learning is the ongoing development and application of core academic knowledge and skills within and across disciplines. Put differently, rigorous learning is the integration of three categories of learning: surface, deep, and transfer learning with equal intensity (Biggs & Collis, 1982). Surface learning is defined as building background knowledge and skills. Here, students are defining ideas or using specific discrete skills. Deep learning is associated with relating ideas or concepts and connecting discrete skills together within a discipline. Transfer learning is associated with applying ideas or skills in different situations. Figure I.1 illustrates these three categories.

SURFACE	DEEP	TRANSFER

Source: Adapted from McDowell & Miller, 2022. Used with permission.
Figure I.1: Surface, deep, and transfer learning.

Table I.1 compares examples of surface, deep, and transfer learning expectations for students in elementary school and high school. Notice how surface learning is concentrated on defining, listing, and labeling whereas deep learning is focused on comparing content and transfer learning is focused on comparing and contrasting contexts.

Table I.1: Elementary and Secondary Examples of Surface, Deep, and Transfer Learning

	Surface	Deep	Transfer
Elementary Example	Defining the concepts of sunlight, wind, snow, rain, and temperature	Showing cause and effect between temperature and sunlight, wind, snow, or rain	Producing and presenting solutions to various challenges, which may include heat waves, hurricanes, or season changes
Secondary Example	Examining the demand for labor between 1400 and 1750 Investigating the conditions and treatment of enslaved Africans during the Middle Passage to the Americas	Comparing and contrasting the relationship between exploitation, death, and creation of wealth between 1400 and 1750 Evaluating the relationship between the decimation of Indigenous populations in the Americas and the growth of the Atlantic slave trade	Evaluating trends and patterns of the slave trades today around the world Developing a proposal for disrupting established patterns

Rigorous learning is based on three key pillars.

1. **Balance:** All three levels of complex learning are of equal importance and are required for students to develop and apply complex thinking. The levels of learning are not hierarchical but taxonomical.

2. **Fluidity:** All three levels of complex learning can and should be accessed in a variety of unit and lesson sequences. Teachers can and should provide students with different entry points for starting units and lessons that illustrate the fluid nature of rigorous learning and the importance of balance across each level, and to ensure that each level of learning is a routine part of a student's learning and not a monthly, quarterly, or yearly event.

3. **Inclusion:** All students must have the opportunity and support to learn across all three levels of learning. All students must have access to surface, deep, and transfer learning in each and every classroom. Surface-level knowledge is essential in a gifted and talented classroom just as transfer learning is essential in a special education classroom. These levels are not privileged to certain students but are essential for respecting each individual student and meeting the demands of rigorous teaching and learning.

Why Is Rigorous Learning Important?

Rigorous learning is important because students will be required to engage in both routine and nonroutine problems throughout their lifetime. Anton Korinek, Martin Schindler, and Joseph Stiglitz (2021) illustrate that the number of nonroutine jobs has substantially risen in the past decade in part due to automation and offshoring jobs to other parts of the world. However, students need to have the knowledge and skills for all sorts of jobs, both routine and nonroutine, as they may have multiple jobs during their lifetime that require various types of knowledge and skills. Take, for example, the later baby boomers, born in the years 1957 to 1964, who have held an average of twelve to thirteen jobs during their lifetime (Toossi, 2002). As such, rigorous learning prepares students with a diverse set of knowledge and skills to navigate the dynamic future job market and the multiple careers that lie ahead.

Rigorous learning also prepares students to face both kind and wicked problems. Picture this: the escape room—a perfectly thrilling time-bound immersive adventure experience that challenges the mind, body, and spirit. Escaperoom.com (2024) defines the experience in this way: "You and your team are locked in a room and are tasked with finding a way to escape." For example, you may have to solve a murder mystery, find someone who is missing, or select which door leads to a life of pleasure and which leads to pain. Before you enter an escape room, you are briefed on a mission of your choice. Once inside, you and your team are required to work together to discover hidden clues and hints, decode passwords, search for key items essential to the case, or escape. The beauty of this process is that everything is programmed, scheduled, and routine. While challenging, escape rooms are what David Epstein (2019) would call "kind environments." A *kind environment* is one in which all relevant information is readily available, you see the consequences, the consequences are completely immediate and accurate, and you adjust accordingly. In golf, you may hit the ball down the fairway, or you may go right into the woods. The beauty of golf is that you know the consequences of your actions. In the classroom, students may use the step-by-step process of solving a long-division problem and can evaluate their work from a sample in the textbook or receive direct feedback from a teacher and know immediately whether they are right or wrong. Escape rooms are similar. You learn *immediately* whether you have made the right decision in your selection of certain choices, and from that knowledge, you figure out next steps. Kind environments cultivate learning because they are a structured, routine, well-designed, and easily predictable environment.

Similarly, kind problems are challenges or situations in which feedback links outcomes directly to the appropriate actions or judgments and is both accurate and plentiful (Hogarth, Lejarraga, & Soyer, 2015). Kind problems give us the light bulb moments when we figure out a small shift in our practice or thinking that enables us to increase performance. An adjustment to a tennis racket, for example, or a change in tactics in using a clue in an escape room gives us immediate feedback, and we can adjust, improve, and do so contemporaneously.

What is challenging is that real life is not golf or escape rooms or even long-division problems. People play golf and go to escape rooms for bonding and retreat. They escape reality. Much in the real world and in traditional classrooms is not kind but wicked. By *wicked*, I mean, as Thomas Gilovich (1991) wrote, "The world does not play fair. Instead of providing us with clear information that would enable us to 'know' better, it presents us with messy data that are random, incomplete, unrepresentative, ambiguous, inconsistent, unpalatable, or secondhand" (p. 3).

Wicked problems are challenges or situations in which feedback in the form of outcomes from actions or observations is poor, misleading, or even missing (Hogarth et al., 2015). Wicked problems provide anti–light bulb moments because our actions are filled with unclear reactions, delays in improvement, and even inaccurate (or absent) feedback. Will sanctions work on reducing Russia's invasion of Ukraine? Will an increase in interest rates reduce inflation? To what extent will teaching students metacognitive strategies improve their learning this year?

While kind environments can be challenging, more of the world consists of wicked environments, and it is the world we must prepare students for. Andreas Schleicher (2019), director of the Organisation for Economic Co-operation and Development (OECD) Directorate for Education and Skills, argues in the *OECD Learning Compass 2030* that "education today must be focused on teaching students how to navigate an increasingly complex, volatile and uncertain world . . . it's about curiosity, compassion and the courage to put our cognitive, social and emotional resources into action. This will also be our best weapon against the biggest threats of our times: ignorance, hate, and fear." OECD has been working on enhancing student learning in both kind and wicked environments. One way is in developing adaptive problem solving for children and adults. Adaptive problem solving may be defined as a problem in which people are solving a problem for which a method of solution is not immediately available in a constantly changing environment (Greiff et al., 2017).

For instance, in one battery of assessments, there is a financial simulation problem that adult learners face that requires them to buy and sell stocks from a number of companies to maximize profit. The challenge is that as they begin making decisions, the computer program begins making changes, forcing the problem solvers to continuously adapt their solutions to the latest evolution of the problem environment. The changes in the task align to what Benjamin S. Bloom and colleagues described as application or transfer in the taxonomy of the cognitive domain in 1956. Specifically, they state, "If the situations . . . are to involve application as we are defining it here, then they must either be situations new to the student or situations containing new elements as compared to the situation in which the abstraction was learned" (Bloom et al., 1956, p. 125). Here, students are receiving not only a new situation but also new elements of change as compared to the way the problem was originally presented.

Another example, geared to younger student learners, shown in figure I.2 (page 6), focuses on baking cookies after school, an everyday-life scenario in which the problem solver has to plan and accomplish different goals over the course of a day. Here, as in the previous situation, learners would need to continually adapt their initial plans to changing circumstances and upcoming impasses by analyzing and evaluating new information.

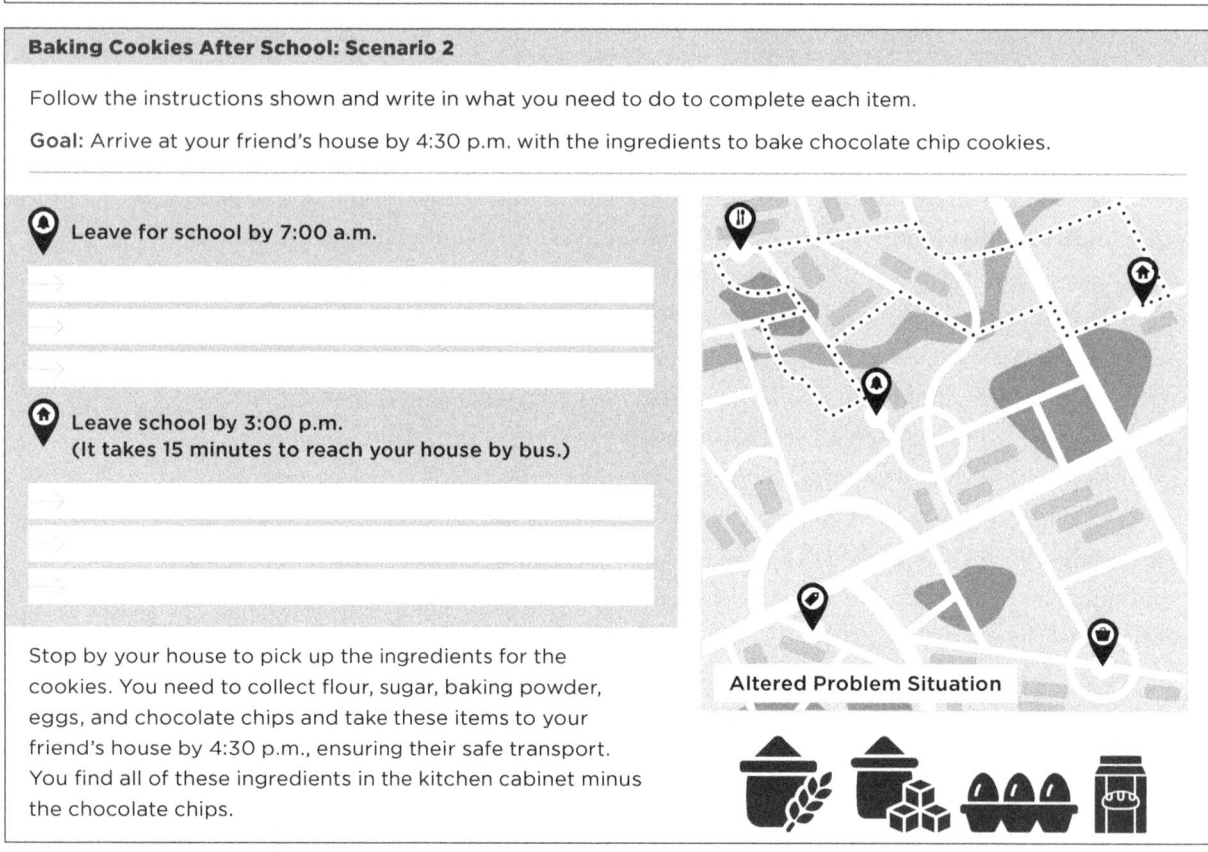

Baking Cookies After School: Scenario 1

Follow the instructions shown and write in what you need to do to complete each item.

Goal: Arrive at your friend's house by 4:30 p.m. with the ingredients to bake chocolate chip cookies.

- Leave for school by 7:00 a.m.

- Leave school by 3:00 p.m.
  (It takes 15 minutes to reach your house by bus.)

Stop by your house to pick up the ingredients for the cookies. You need to collect flour, sugar, baking powder, eggs, and chocolate chips and take these items to your friend's house by 4:30 p.m., ensuring their safe transport. You find all of the needed ingredients in the kitchen cabinet. (Your friend lives 20 minutes from you by bicycle.)

Original Problem Situation

Baking Cookies After School: Scenario 2

Follow the instructions shown and write in what you need to do to complete each item.

Goal: Arrive at your friend's house by 4:30 p.m. with the ingredients to bake chocolate chip cookies.

- Leave for school by 7:00 a.m.

- Leave school by 3:00 p.m.
  (It takes 15 minutes to reach your house by bus.)

Stop by your house to pick up the ingredients for the cookies. You need to collect flour, sugar, baking powder, eggs, and chocolate chips and take these items to your friend's house by 4:30 p.m., ensuring their safe transport. You find all of these ingredients in the kitchen cabinet minus the chocolate chips.

Altered Problem Situation

Figure I.2: Baking cookies after school: two scenarios.

To solve the baking cookies after school questions, students need to have surface, deep, and transfer learning. For instance, in both situations, students need to understand certain surface- and deep-level knowledge, including understanding and relating addition, telling time, and understanding elapsed time. In the first example, students are given a "kind" transfer problem whereby they need to find a solution with a few given constraints. In the second example, students are given a "wicked" problem whereby they need to recognize and address new circumstances to address the problem. In summary, both situations require students possess surface, deep, and transfer learning.

Students need to prepare for the types of kind and wicked problems that they will inevitably face in the workforce along with engaging with all facets of life. The ability to fluidly move across the taxonomical levels of learning, possess a balanced understanding of each level, and have access to continuing to build such levels of learning will be critical for students to be prepared for their future.

What Dispositional Skills Can Enhance Student Rigorous Learning?

Rigorous learning requires a set of dispositional skills that make such learning possible. Dispositional skills enable students to move across various levels of surface, deep, and transfer learning with ease. Dispositional skills are akin to motor oil, which lubricates the moving parts of a car engine, enhancing performance and preventing the damage that friction causes on a car. For students to learn new ideas, tackle kind and wicked application problems, and understand the core tenets of a subject, they need a set of dispositional habits that, like oil, allow the complex moving parts of rigorous learning to glide easily. This book presents four dispositional habits.

1. Engage metacognition
2. Navigate challenge
3. Work well with others
4. Consolidate learning

Research shows that a student's ability to actively engage their metacognition is one of the most powerful influences on student learning. Alex Quigley, Daniel Muijs, and Eleanor Stringer (2018) find that "evidence suggests the use of 'metacognitive strategies—which get pupils to think about their own learning—can be worth the equivalent of an additional +7 months' progress when used well." Engaging in metacognition is related to a student's ability to plan, monitor, and evaluate the goals of learning, their current progress, and what next steps they need to take to be successful. This requires learners to understand the goals of learning, recognize the gap between their own performance and goals, and identify what strategies they will take to complete tasks and move toward goals of learning.

Additionally, students need to develop skills of navigating the challenges presented within wicked and kind environments. Here, students must work through the emotional and cognitive dimensions of handling setbacks, receiving correct feedback, and navigating building systems to continually improve on a daily basis. While each of these factors yields a high impact on student learning, students must learn how to separate their identity or ego when facing setbacks and corrective feedback from the actual work of improving their learning in both kind and wicked environments (Hattie, 2023b).

Students must also routinely act as learning resources for one another (Wiliam, 2018). The ability to collaboratively develop clear expectations and build knowledge together through activities such as quizzing, working through problem-solving tasks, and giving and receiving feedback is critical for student learning. Moreover, deep learning requires that students engage in classroom discussions and seek help from peers (Hattie & Donoghue, 2016).

As students acquire new knowledge and skills, they must spend time and energy to reinforce or consolidate new learning. As students develop the knowledge of the various U.S. state capitals, how to use American Psychological Association citations, and the core tenets of the cell theory, they need to practice their learning so that the ideas and skills are remembered and can be easily retrieved. The skills students develop here include focused attention on improving learning within the context of a goal.

How Can Educators Foster Rigorous Learning?

Developing rigorous learning is nothing more than a set of small and doable daily habits within the classroom. Educators have an opportunity to foster rigorous learning by leaning on the power of habit science. Habits are typically developed in a three-step process: (1) a cue (to begin a habit), (2) a routine (the actual behavior), and (3) a reward (the satisfaction for completing the task; Duhigg, 2014). When we are first learning a habit, we must concentrate, but over time, the habit becomes tacit, and we simply engage in the routine each time a cue is presented.

James Clear (2018) writes that people never rise to their goals; they fall to their systems. By systems, Clear is referring to *actions* or *practices* people engage in each and every day. Goals are *motions* or *preparations* for actions; it is helpful to set an aim, but that does not materialize results. Educators and students must be aware of when they are in motion, which is planning, building, and strategizing as opposed to engaging in daily practices that create results. For instance, if a teacher works through a challenging word problem and students are taking notes, the teacher is then in *action* while the students are in *motion*. Students are watching teachers engage in the habit, but they are not engaging in the action as well. This is like a group of students setting a goal to lose weight and taking notes while a teacher runs by them. The students are not in action. To ensure students develop the operational habits associated with surface, deep, and transfer learning and to develop enabling habits that ensure students can fluidly move across levels of complexity, I recommend the following ten habits for educators to develop with K–12 students.

Rigorous Learning Dispositional Habits

1. **Engage metacognition:** Students will develop the habit to routinely clarify the learning goals they are pursuing, recognize their current performance relative to learning goals, and identify strategies they need to take to improve their learning.

2. **Navigate challenge:** Students will develop the habit to routinely accept and use feedback to improve their learning, handle setbacks when faced with conflicting or changing information, and employ strategies to manage their emotional state during times of change.

3. **Work well with others:** Students will develop the habit to routinely seek and provide feedback from others, understand multiple perspectives, and listen, ask questions, and advocate ideas when problem solving.

4. **Consolidate learning:** Students will develop the habit to routinely engage in deliberate practice across surface, deep, and transfer learning to improve retrieval of information, minimize forgetting, and enhance their ability to solve routine and nonroutine problems across disciplines.

Rigorous Learning Competency-Based Habits

Surface

5. **Build knowledge together:** Students will develop the habit to routinely learn new ideas and skills by engaging in practices that activate prior knowledge and require practices that are oftentimes redundant.

6. **Check and respond to current understanding together:** Students will develop the habit to routinely proactively seek out and use targeted and corrective feedback to improve learning.

Deep

7. **Develop conceptual understanding:** Students will develop the habit to routinely use skills to determine themes, patterns, and links between and across ideas within a discipline.

8. **Apply conceptual understanding:** Students will develop the habit to routinely apply knowledge and skills of themes, patterns, and links between and across ideas to address routine and nonroutine questions within a discipline.

Transfer

9. **Build contextual understanding:** Students will develop the habit to routinely determine themes, patterns, and links between and across ideas within one or more contexts and/or one or more disciplines.

10. **Solve complex problems:** Students will develop the habit to routinely apply their knowledge and skills of themes, patterns, and links between and across ideas within one or more contexts and/or one or more disciplines to solve routine and nonroutine problems.

The ten competency and dispositional habits make up the vanes of the pinwheel. The first four enable students to fully navigate the six habits of surface, deep, and transfer learning. When placed together, they form a set of rigorous learning habits that enable students to thrive in their learning. The pinwheel, of course, requires the right amount of force to move. Habits are the force that moves the pinwheel and enables both students and teachers to work together daily to live rigorous teaching and learning. See figure I.3.

Figure I.3: The learning habits.

Table I.2 shows the ten habits divided into dispositional and competency habits.

Table I.2: Rigorous Learning Dispositional and Competency Habits

Rigorous Learning Dispositional Habits	Rigorous Learning Competency Habits
An approach to moving across levels of complexity to meet the needs of a learner, a task, or content	A set of skills that enable learners to proactively engage metacognition, navigate change, and collaborate with others to solve problems
Habit 1: Engage metacognition	**Habit 5:** Build knowledge together
Habit 2: Navigate challenge	**Habit 6:** Check and respond to current understanding together
Habit 3: Work well with others	**Habit 7:** Develop conceptual understanding
Habit 4: Consolidate learning	**Habit 8:** Apply conceptual understanding
	Habit 9: Build contextual understanding
	Habit 10: Solve complex problems

How Do Educators Build Systems for Engaging Students in the Ten *Rigor Redefined* Habits?

Educators should begin the journey of deploying the ten *Rigor Redefined* habits by recognizing the power of agility or flexibility in the instructional practices required for rigorous teaching and learning. The current implementation of these ten habits is mixed across schools and school systems. For instance, the competency habits across surface, deep, and transfer learning vary significantly based on the level of expertise teachers possess. Research indicates that expert teachers spend a majority of their time and energy at the deep level of learning whereas teachers who lack expertise spend a majority of their time at surface learning (Hattie, 2003). Figure I.4 (page 12) illustrates that expert teachers spend a majority of their time and energy at the deep level of learning whereas teachers who lack expertise spend a majority of their time at surface learning.

Interestingly, expert teachers also appear to be nimbler in their use of instructional strategies to meet the surface, deep, and transfer learning needs of students. In one of the largest meta-summaries conducted on teacher expertise, Jason Anderson and Gülden Taner (2023) find that expert teachers regularly use a range of strategies from collaborative learning (that is, group work) as well as teacher-led activities such as whole-class direct instruction. Nonexpert teachers lacked the ability to either recognize student needs or use the right strategy to meet their learning needs. The ability to both recognize and address the learning needs of students across each level of learning is critical because researchers have found that different strategies are required across surface, deep, and transfer levels of learning (Hattie & Donoghue, 2016; Marzano, 2017).

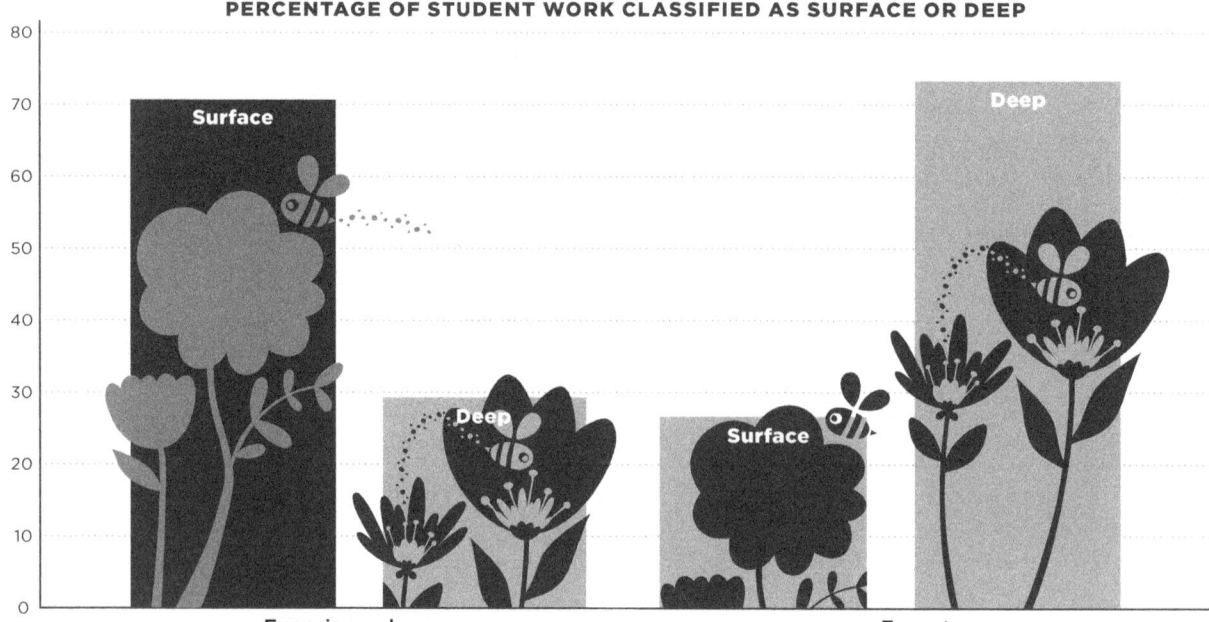

Source: *Adapted from Hattie, 2003. Used with permission.*
Figure I.4: Percentage of student work classified as surface or deep learning.

In addition, expert teachers leverage habit science to improve their routines. Like the wind pushing the pinwheel, small and doable routines make a lasting difference for students across surface, deep, and transfer learning. Expert teachers find balance between the levels of rigorous learning and pursue dispositional habits to support students in developing ownership over their own learning. For instance, one study showed that as students encountered complex problem solving, nonexpert teachers usually broke down the tasks to make them easier, resulting in a lack of challenging material for students (Epstein, 2019). Not surprisingly, only 8 percent of students around the world could successfully address transfer-level mathematics problems (Greiff et al., 2017). Experts typically support students in leveraging the dispositional habits and using strategies at transfer to problem-solve rather than overscaffold (Anderson & Taner, 2023).

Expert teachers also have a powerful mindset whereby they think pinwheels, not pendulums. The educational system is riddled with pendulum thinking whereby the amount of time and the priority educators place on specific levels of learning create shifting priorities. For instance, in a synthesis of studies around the world that incorporated a sample size of over a quarter of a billion students, 90 percent of the instruction privileged surface learning (Hattie, 2009). In addition, an analysis of 17,000 classrooms shows that students are not receiving any instruction in how to engage in application-based problems in any and all disciplines (Hattie, 2021). Experts must hold the tension between such competing forces. The pendulum is skewed to privilege one level of learning.

In an educational system that privileges surface learning and the demands of the work that require transfer, teachers need to seek balance. When the pressure for deep and transfer learning mounts because of the privileging of surface knowledge, schools reactively demand discovery-based learning and project-based learning, which work for certain levels of learning while lacking substantial impact on other levels of learning (Hattie, 2023b). Experts see this problem as a need for balancing learning across levels of learning and not reprioritization of complexity. All levels of learning have value in the system of habits to ensure students are prepared for rigorous learning. The task of this book is to calmly build a system of habits to ensure teachers develop small, doable, and flexible strategies that can be sustained by leveraging habit science and doing the same for students so that they learn at the surface, deep, and transfer levels and employ dispositional habits that fluidly move across each level. This book proposes that small shifts in educators' practices and in the practices of students can make all the difference in unlocking rigorous learning in classrooms every day and guides teachers in making these shifts to foster ten habits that students must develop to engage fully in rigorous learning.

What Is in This Book?

The practices illustrated in this book are well researched, field-tested, relatable, and realistic for the classrooms of today. This book has been designed to support classroom teachers, instructional coaches, site principals, and directors of curriculum and instruction in understanding, building, engaging in, and applying the ten *Rigor Redefined* habits in their classrooms, schools, and systems. Designed over the past several decades, including the past three years, the practices in this book come from the trials, tribulations, and triumphs of teachers working together to ensure rigorous learning through a balanced pedagogy that comes to life for their students.

The book contains six chapters , a conclusion, and numerous templates and other tools to guide educators through developing and consolidating the ten *Rigor Redefined* habits in their practices.

Chapter 1 (page 17) opens by discussing rigorous learning and the ways in which it is fluid (despite also being hierarchical), given the way in which learners move between different kinds of complex learning to meet their needs. It also further defines surface, deep, and transfer learning and charts a movement in thinking about learning in terms of taxonomies rather than hierarchies. It examines types of knowledge and their importance, and it shifts into exploring how to develop first dispositional habits and then competency habits.

Chapter 2 (page 35) centers on habit science and the practices teachers and students employ to ensure the ten habits take shape in the context of the classroom. The chapter outlines key strategies for starting and sustaining habits, developing plans for implementing new practices, exploring strategies to effectively plan for practice, and inspecting habits along the way. It examines the importance of *process* and the need for monitoring systems of practice.

Chapter 3 (page 63) explores the dispositional habits that serve as a catalyst for the competency habits of surface, deep, and transfer learning. The chapter provides specific practices that teachers and students can employ to engage metacognition, navigate challenge, work well with others, and consolidate learning.

Chapter 4 (page 95) examines the importance of developing surface-level knowledge and skills. Here we discuss specific strategies for building background knowledge and checking for understanding. The chapter embeds the central message that the work is socially constructed and that guided practice is a key lever for students to develop and consolidate learning. The chapter provides a large number of concise strategies that when routinely embedded build students' habits of building background knowledge together with others and checking and responding to understanding.

Chapter 5 (page 119) delves into the world of developing deep learning habits. The chapter provides an overview of two key habits of developing and applying conceptual understanding. The chapter offers a number of strategies that enable students to compare and contrast ideas within a field of study. The chapter focuses heavily on the use of structured protocols to build students' reading, writing, and talking skills at the deep level of learning.

Chapter 6 (page 169) expands on the habits of transfer-level learning by focusing on two key habits of developing and applying contextual understanding. As with other chapters, chapter 6 provides applicable strategies; these relate to comparing and contrasting ideas across contexts and disciplines. In addition, this chapter walks teachers through a series of habits that enable students to engage in problem solving at the transfer level, as well as protocols to build students' reading, writing, and talking skills at the transfer level of learning.

Over the rest of the book, readers engage six key questions that drive the development of teaching the ten habits to learners. These questions are meant for teachers to initially reflect and then monitor over time as they develop and consolidate habits of practice with students. These questions are as follows.

1. How do I balance ten key habits of rigorous teaching and learning in my classroom?

2. How do I leverage habit science to enhance rigorous teaching and learning in my classroom?

3. How do I build a system of dispositional habits in my classroom?

4. How do I build a system of surface-level teaching and learning habits in my classroom?

5. How do I build a system of deep-level teaching and learning habits in my classroom?

6. How do I build a system of transfer-level teaching and learning habits in my classroom?

With each revolution of the pinwheel, a beautiful cascade of colors illuminates before our eyes. Those revolutions are caused by a slight breeze. Our work is to calmly progress toward growth in student rigorous learning and overall empowerment. Let's harness the power of habit science, shed the myths of hierarchies and linear and binary thinking, and slowly but surely make a substantial difference in the learning lives of students. Let's approach this work from a place of calm progress and balance, fluidity, and inclusion.

Redefining Rigor

Humans like to consider everything as linear, when in reality everything is cyclic. . . . They are obsessed with straight lines. Straight roads, straight houses, straight pieces of steel, glass, and timber.

—**Robert Black**

When we mentally frame sides to an argument, we delve into either-or thinking. Thinking of learning as a hierarchy, in which specific levels of learning are privileged, is an example of either-or. The pendulum serves as a powerful metaphor of either-or thinking. On the other hand, the pinwheel is a countermetaphor serving as a powerful reminder of the balance between various levels of learning. The pinwheel centers on both-and thinking, requiring us to hold two seemingly opposite concepts or ideas in our mind at the same time. How do you approach thinking about the process of learning? Do you think of learning as a pendulum prioritizing specific levels of learning and centering on engaging in a linear process of teaching certain levels before other levels? Or, do you think of learning as a pinwheel integrating different levels of learning and engaging in mixed process of teaching across levels of learning?

In turns out that pinwheel thinking is critical for how educators engage with students in the classroom. Pooja K. Agarwal (2019) finds that when students engage in simultaneous practice involving surface, deep, and transfer learning, they increase their learning, whereas when students approach learning through a more hierarchical approach with retrieval first, they are less successful in engaging in deep- and transfer-level learning. Interestingly, the most effective practice was not to shift to teaching higher-order thinking but rather to mix practice across surface, deep, and transfer learning. That is, the most effective way to engage learners in thinking across levels of learning is to teach and assess across all levels simultaneously.

This chapter provides an overview of the rigorous learning process. Initially, the chapter discusses the differences between hierarchies and taxonomies and how those differences should be reflected in language, assessments, and unit and lesson sequences. The chapter then focuses on the importance of the types of knowledge and skills that students are learning and how identifying such knowledge is critical to supporting students in their learning. Finally, the chapter provides an overview of the important habits that enable students to develop rigorous knowledge and skill.

Considering the Rigorous Learning Process

As you read this book and start to engage in thinking about rigorous learning, you will likely go back and forth between different levels of learning (surface, deep, and transfer) in your own mind. There will be times when you will learn a completely new definition of a term (*surface learning*, as you learned in the introduction, page 1, or *building knowledge*, as you'll learn in chapter 4, page 95), construct a mental model of how the terms fit with your own mental schema (*deep learning* or *making meaning*), and begin planning ways to apply some of the strategies from this book in your own classroom (*transfer learning* or *applying understanding*).

A *schema* is a mental structure to help us understand how things work. It has to do with how we organize knowledge. As we take in new information, we connect it to other things we know, believe, or have experienced. And those connections form a figurative structure in the brain. While we are engaging in surface learning, we are typically learning new separate pieces of information. Deep learning is associated with connecting that knowledge. As people develop a greater schema, surface learning more effectively and efficiently connects to that schema (Donovan & Bransford, 2005). In other words, "cognitive scientists think of deep learning—or what you might call 'learning for understanding'—as the ability to organize discrete pieces of knowledge into a larger schema of understanding" (Meta & Fine, 2019).

Moreover, you won't do this in exactly the same sequence. In other words, you won't learn in this book via a linear sequence of surface, deep, and transfer learning each time. The order in which the components are addressed will vary. Alas, you do not follow a straight line when you learn. Rigorous learning is fluid and integrated across a range of equally valuable levels of learning.

The changing order of use of each level of learning you engage in is due to the fact that one's process for learning is not beholden to a hierarchy. Let's define some important terms before we go on.

- **Hierarchy:** A system or structure in which people, objects, or concepts are ranked or ordered in a series of levels or grades based on their relative importance, authority, or power. For instance, this book has established a set of chapters (chapters 4, 5, and 6) that sequence surface, deep, and transfer learning in a linear order, denoting a hierarchy.

- **Learning taxonomy:** A system or structure for categorizing and organizing different types of learning objectives and outcomes. For example, this book illustrates a range of teaching and learning strategies at the surface level (chapter 4, page 95), the deep level (chapter 5, page 119), and at the transfer level (chapter 6, page 169). This is an example of a taxonomy.

- **Process:** The steps or actions needed to achieve a specific goal. It involves the execution of a plan, which may include research, planning, implementation, and evaluation. Process is dynamic and may change based on feedback, results, or new information. This book provides strategies teachers and students may take to effectively engage in the process of planning, implementing, and evaluating habits in chapter 2 (page 35).

To summarize, hierarchies are about ranking, taxonomies are about categorization, and processes are about actions toward a goal. Let's further consider how these concepts connect by using metaphors.

A taxonomy is like a restaurant menu. Dishes are grouped into different sections based on their cuisine, ingredients, or dietary requirements. For example, a menu might have sections for appetizers, entrées, desserts, and vegetarian options. Within each section, there could be further subdivisions based on cooking style or flavor profile. Each dish can be classified into one or more categories, and the categories may not have a specific order or relationship to each other. On the other hand, a hierarchy is like the order of those categories on a menu. For instance, appetizers are often located at the beginning of the menu, followed by entrées, and then desserts. This order is due to customs of how people are expected to eat at a restaurant. In education, taxonomies are formed by categories of learning based on theoretical models of learning such as Bloom's taxonomy (Bloom, 1956) and Webb's Depth of Knowledge (Webb, 1997). The way in which curricular resources define the scope and sequence of units and lessons for students and the way in which schools or districts prioritize specific levels of learning influence the order and importance of each type of complex learning.

Process is how we order and enjoy our dinner. While many people follow the way in which a hierarchy is presented, others may enjoy dishes in different orders. Who hasn't started with a bit of dessert or, after eating a main course, ordered an appetizer? As such, people don't always follow the hierarchical nature of the menu.

As you read this book and implement practices, you will naturally find yourself going back and forth between different levels of learning (that is, the learning taxonomy).

Some of you are new to the teaching profession and will likely have more surface knowledge to develop, but this doesn't preclude you from moving to the other levels, deep and transfer. Some of you are experts and are spending your time at the deep and transfer levels but may move to the surface level to collect a few new ideas or review previously learned material and search for small changes in the research or to consolidate previously learned material. For example, a novice student may share ideas on how to solve climate change while still learning about how compounds are formed, while expert students may use flash cards to review their understanding of compounds while applying their knowledge to solving a climate change issue. Just like inexperienced and expert chefs, we will use the recipe book, but we may not follow it with fidelity. We will skip around, both building our knowledge and dreaming, to make a dish that's from a different section. This is how humans learn.

Since, as a learning process, rigorous learning focuses on three types of learning that are of equal importance, encouraging various entry and exit points across those kinds of learning throughout a unit or lesson ensures all students are a part of the conversation of rigorous learning. One school that fully encapsulates the living and breathing definition of rigorous learning is Stonefields School in New Zealand (see figure 1.1).

Stonefields School (2024) shares their perspective on the learning process in the following way:

> The learning process helps learners investigate, problem-solve, make informed decisions, and advance their learning. It steps them through three key stages of learning—Build Knowledge, Make Meaning and Apply Understanding. Doing so aims to demystify the learning process, helping learners know what to do next. We teach specific thinking skills to draw upon at each of the three stages.

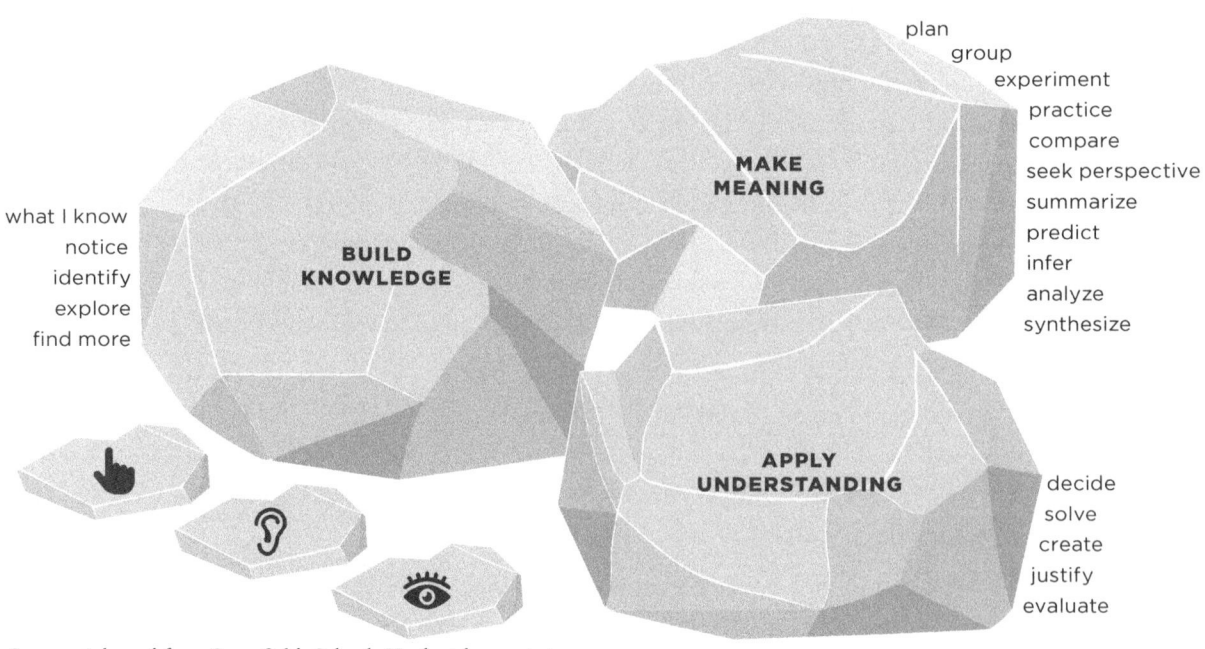

Source: Adapted from Stonefields School. Used with permission.
Figure 1.1: The learning process.

The learning process is the way in which students encounter and interact with rigorous learning (Hook & Casse, 2013). While this school uses terms such as *building knowledge*, *making meaning*, and *applying understanding* in lieu of *surface*, *deep*, and *transfer*, the important shared element is the fluidity across different levels of learning. Figure 1.2 depicts a pollinator (the bee) traveling from one plant (surface) to another similar plant (deep) and across different plant species (transfer). Notice how the arrows point in all directions symbolizing the fluid nature of learning.

Source: Adapted from McDowell & Miller, 2022. Used with permission.
Figure 1.2: Sample visualization of surface, deep, and transfer learning.

Shifting From Hierarchies to Taxonomies

In the rigorous learning process, students may enter learning at any of the three levels. For instance, students may begin the learning of local, tribal, state, and national governmental institutions at the transfer, deep, or surface level. Imagine a teacher starts students off with a real-world issue that involves an increase in local taxes, or the challenges of eminent domain related to a tribal government. Known as a problem- or project-based approach, starting at transfer would position students to need surface and deep learning and likely would engage students to see very quickly the real-world implication of such learning. Of course, a more traditional approach would require students to learn critical vocabulary about the various branches of government, followed by comparing and contrasting those bodies. Lastly, a teacher may start students off with a conversation associated with conceptual understanding or deep learning. The teacher may ask students to discuss why parents pay taxes, why there is a speed limit, or why the teacher is required to serve jury duty.

In all situations, learning is occurring fluidly between different levels of learning (that is, taxonomy). There is not a specific linear navigation path to learn (that is, hierarchy). Many of the cognitive models that have been developed for educators and students are misinterpreted in this sense. However, in Bloom's *Taxonomy of Educational Objectives* (Bloom et al., 1956), original writing about levels of learning, each level was distinct and important rather than a prerequisite for another level. Dylan Wiliam (2023) shares that "Bloom and his committee proposed a taxonomy of educational objectives, not a hierarchy." This framework for learning is not called *Bloom's hierarchy*; it's called *Bloom's taxonomy*. Every level is of equal importance. As such, we don't have to use the words *lower-order* or *higher-order thinking* and can focus more on thinking across multiple levels. Unfortunately, the visual pyramids that were constructed in 1956 and revised in 2001 position people to think of learning as a linear process that is hierarchical and prioritizes certain levels over others.

The confusion and, at times, fixation with prioritizing hierarchies over taxonomies has influenced the ways in which we assess students. We need to find better models that move us away from dichotomies. In the words of Stephen Jay Gould (1990), "I strongly reject any conceptual scheme that places our options on a line, and holds that the only alternative to a pair of extreme positions lies somewhere between them. More fruitful perspectives often require that we step off the line to sit outside the dichotomy" (p. 51). While all models have some limitations to the actualization of a concept, they can signal our values. In this book, the pinwheel is used as an integrated model that illustrates the interconnectedness of surface, deep, and transfer learning along with dispositional habits that support students in moving across each categorical level with ease.

Beyond visual representations of learning taxonomies, popular scoring rubrics illustrate hierarchies over taxonomies. For instance, in table 1.1, the left-hand column illustrates a standard 4.0 scale that prioritizes simple to more complex aspects of a learning goal rather than recognizing the importance of balancing all levels of learning. The right-hand column shows a slight adjustment in the scoring that prioritizes the balance of taxonomical levels over hierarchies. This scoring scheme is derived from the important work of Robert J. Marzano (2010).

Table 1.1: Transitioning Standards-Based Reporting From a Hierarchical to a Taxonomical Approach

Hierarchy-Centered Rubrics			Taxonomy-Centered Rubrics		
Score 4.0	More complex learning goal		Score 4.0	Meets all three levels of learning (surface, deep, and transfer)	
	Score 3.5	In addition to score 3.0 performance, partial success at score 4.0 content		Score 3.5	In addition to score 3.0 performance, partial success at score 4.0 content
Score 3.0	Target learning goal		Score 3.0	Meets two levels of learning	
	Score 2.5			Score 2.5	
Score 2.0	Simpler learning goal		Score 2.0	Meets one level of learning	
	Score 1.5			Score 1.5	
Score 1.0	With help, partial success at score 2.0 content and score 3.0 content		Score 1.0	With help, partial success at score 2.0 content and score 3.0 content	
	Score 0.5	With help, partial success at score 2.0 content, but not at score 3.0 content		Score 0.5	With help, partial success at score 2.0 content, but not at score 3.0 content
Score 0.0	Even with help, no success		Score 0.0	Even with help, no success	

Source: Adapted from Marzano, 2010.

When we free ourselves from hierarchical thinking, we can begin to see the flexibility in how units start and end. In my previous book, *Teaching for Transfer* (McDowell, 2020), a number of different pathways of how students may encounter each level of learning along their learning process (see figure 1.3) were presented. Students could start off a lesson at the transfer level exploring the challenges of microplastics in the ocean followed by a surface-level lesson on ecosystems. Of course, the lesson could have started off at the deep level whereby students were tasked with discussing the reasons underpinning healthy ecosystems. The unit could have also started at the surface level with students learning core vocabulary and taking notes on the various types of ecosystems that exist on the planet. The sequencing can vary; the important part of rigorous learning is to treat each level as distinct and equally important. As one first-grade student shared with me, "Rigorous learning is like a well-balanced meal. You need your meat, potatoes, and cake. You have to have cake!"

Pathway	PHASE I: Entry Point	PHASE II: Connecting	PHASE III: Integrating
Traditional Pathway	Surface	Surface ⟷ Deep	Surface, Deep, Transfer (cyclical)

Source: McDowell, 2020, p. 104.
Figure 1.3: Pathways for ensuring surface, deep, and transfer learning.

continued →

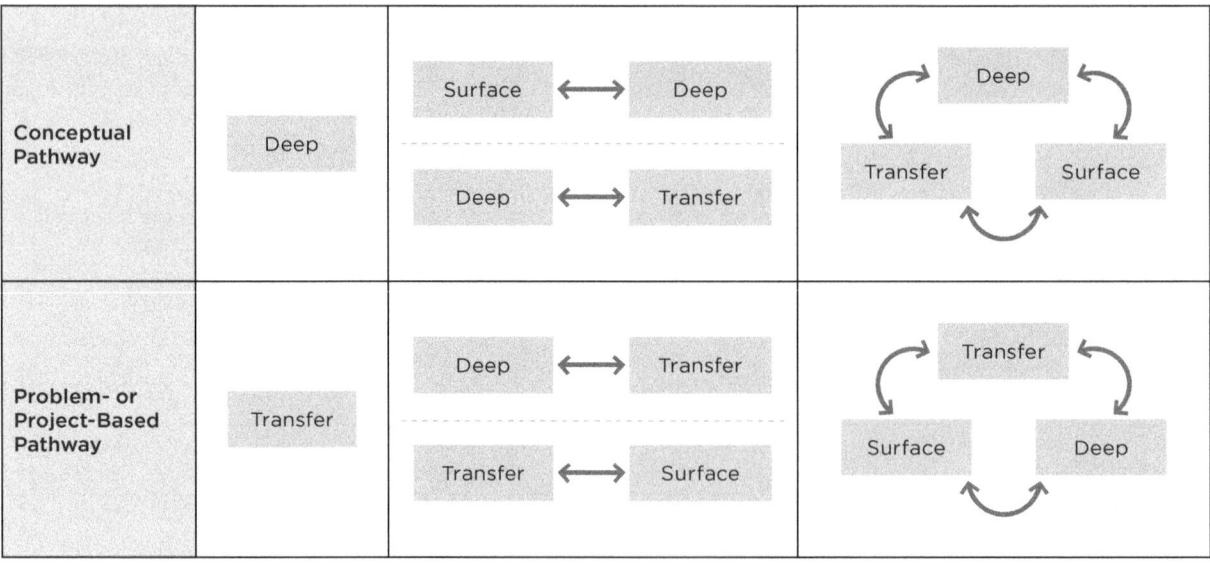

Examining Categories of Knowledge and Skill

Take a minute and read the following recap of a sporting event:

> **Jordan Silk chipped in with 23 before falling in the second last over. With Sydney needing seven from six deliveries, Hughes put the result beyond doubt with a towering leg-side six off Nathan Ellis. Tom Curran then iced the game with a boundary through the covers. (ESPN cricinfo, 2023)**

What happened in the game? Do you have enough background knowledge to apply your skills of reading to make sense of the passage?

Now, read the following:

> **Flacco threw two TD passes in the first half to Njoku and then completed a 41-yarder to wide receiver David Bell in the fourth quarter when the Jaguars gambled with an all-out blitz on fourth down. As Bell streaked to the end zone, Flacco did his best to keep up—for an old guy. (CBSNews, 2023)**

What happened in the game? Do you have enough background knowledge to apply your skills of reading to make sense of the passage?

The first passage was related to a game of cricket, a sport unfamiliar to many in the United States, whereas the second passage was related to American football, a much more familiar game in the United States. Your ability to understand the passages is largely dependent on your background knowledge on the games of cricket and American football.

Similarly, researchers Donna R. Recht and Lauren Leslie (1988) interviewed 64 students with varying levels of reading ability and asked them to read a play-by-play of half an inning of a baseball game. What they found was students' prior knowledge of baseball was much more impactful on student's understanding of the passage than their reading ability. The students who were the most successful had declarative knowledge, which is the background knowledge about baseball needed to understand what was occurring in the passage.

More recently, David Grissmer and colleagues (2023) tracked the progress of more than 2,000 students in a content-rich curriculum for four to seven years, starting in kindergarten. These students substantially outperformed students who spent most of their time on standardized reading comprehension skills. Natalie Wexler (2023) states that the results of the study were so significant for the treatment group that if the results translated to all American students, the United States would move from a rank of fifteenth to fifth in education. More concretely, the gains for fifth graders were so large that "according to the researchers, they *eliminated* the gaps on Colorado tests between students from low- and high-income families" (Wexler, 2023).

Such research is backed further by findings that a sustained content literacy intervention that aligns content and instruction across grades can help students transfer knowledge to novel reading comprehension tasks (Kim et al., 2023). Students who engage in knowledge-rich curriculum as opposed to a skill-focused curriculum scored 18 percentage points higher on general reading comprehension. Again, background knowledge is a critical scaffold that builds and supports deeper learning and enables effective transfer.

However, we must remember that learning is a balancing act between various levels of learning. Agarwal (2019) argued that mixing practice across levels of learning was more potent for building students' knowledge. In addition, Guy Claxton (2021) shares that students must learn and experience transfer-level learning and learn the procedural skills to handle confidently the variety of learning challenges that can be expected throughout life. As such, students need to develop skills and be exposed to multiple contexts in order to learn across all levels of learning. In this way, educators need to be mindful of the categories of knowledge and skills students are learning, which include declarative knowledge, contextual knowledge, and procedural knowledge. Each is defined as follows.

- **Declarative knowledge** is associated with understanding concepts, ideas, facts, themes, or principles.
- **Procedural knowledge** is associated with understanding how to engage in a specific process or procedure.
- **Contextual knowledge** is associated with the examples, situations, and tasks through which students experience declarative and procedural knowledge.

One way to think of these categories of knowledge and skills is that declarative knowledge is about facts and conceptual understanding that comes from the relationship between two or more facts whereas procedural knowledge is all about skills and the coordination between those skills. For instance, learning the steps in the scientific method is procedural whereas learning about prokaryotic and eukaryotic cells is declarative. While both levels of learning are critical, a student's ability to transfer procedural knowledge is largely dependent on the student's declarative knowledge. Contextual understanding is what students are learning the declarative and procedural content through. For instance, imagine students are making slime as a way to understand the transitional states of matter. In this example, slime is the context, transitional states of matter are declarative knowledge, and following the steps of the science experiment is procedural knowledge.

One example of combining declarative, procedural, and contextual knowledge comes from an elementary curriculum designed by EL Education (2024), a nonprofit professional development and curriculum developer. The program has designed an English language arts (ELA) curriculum that expects students to learn both core knowledge, known as declarative knowledge in science, such as understanding photosynthesis as well as procedural skills in writing. For example, one of the third-grade units of study requires that students learn about animal adaptations (that is, declarative knowledge) and information writing (that is, procedural knowledge), and they do this through the context of frogs (that is, contextual knowledge). In this situation, students and teachers must be able to discern the declarative knowledge that they are expected to learn from the contextual knowledge they are being exposed to in the unit of study. If students are unable to separate the context (that is, frogs) from the declarative knowledge (animal adaptations), then they likely will lack clarity of expectations and will be unable to develop deep and transfer levels of learning. Discerning these categories of knowledge and skills for both teachers and students is critical.

As we teach students declarative and procedural knowledge, we have to make sure students can understand the distinction between declarative and procedural knowledge with the contextual knowledge that enriches the lesson and engages the learner. Table 1.2 illustrates each category of knowledge and skill.

Table 1.2: Description and Examples of Declarative, Procedural, and Contextual Knowledge

	Declarative	**Procedural**	**Contextual**
Defined as . . .	Concept or idea	Process, skill, or procedure	Situations and examples
Questions	Questions that are centered on who, what, when, where, and why	Questions that are primarily centered on how	Questions that are primarily focused on examples of declarative and procedural content
Type	Facts, thesis, themes, principles	Rules, tactics, procedures	Examples, situations
Example	Photosynthesis, colonialism, transitional states of matter	Scientific method, writing process	Fossils, slime, scramble for Africa, writing about school uniforms
Example Learning Intentions	Students will understand the events that led to the Civil War.	Students will be able to determine breathing rate and heart rate.	Students will create slime.

Once they identify the categories of knowledge and skill, teachers are able to identify the type of learning expected for students across the surface, deep, and transfer levels. Table 1.3 illustrates additional examples of each learning level, applicable at both the elementary and secondary level.

Table 1.3: Declarative, Procedural, and Contextual Knowledge Across Surface, Deep, and Transfer Learning

Example	Surface	Deep	Transfer
Declarative knowledge example	Define photosynthesis.	Compare and contrast photosynthesis and glycolysis.	Solve real-world problems that involve photosynthesis.
Declarative knowledge example	Identify different types of matter.	Relate temperature to different kinds of matter. Evaluate non-Newtonian liquids from other states of matter.	Hypothesize solutions to problems across contexts.
Procedural knowledge example	Respond to who, what, when, where, and how questions. Follow one-step written instructions.	Confirm predictions about what will happen next in a text by identifying key words (that is, signpost words). Relate prior knowledge to textual information. Retell the central ideas of simple expository or narrative passages.	Use context to resolve ambiguities about word and sentence meanings.
Procedural knowledge example	Identify key messages from a text. State key ideas and messages from a text. Identify examples and textual evidence from generated interpretations from a text.	Develop an interpretation exhibiting careful reading, understanding, and insight. Organize the selected interpretation around several clear ideas, premises, or images. Develop and justify the selected interpretation through sustained use of examples and textual evidence.	Apply interpretations with textual evidence around central ideas across multiple texts.
Contextual knowledge example	Identify different types of dinosaurs (for example, Deinocheirus).	Compare and contrast the myths and truths about dinosaurs.	Develop strategies for informing the public of myths and truths about dinosaurs.
Contextual knowledge example	Identify different leaders in the United States (for example, George Washington).	Compare and contrast various leaders based on attributes of heroism.	Draw conclusions on whether leaders will remain heroes in the eyes of Americans over time.

The preceding table illustrates the important distinction between declarative, procedural, and contextual knowledge as well as the importance of ensuring a balance between each.

Making the Ten Rigorous Learning Habits Habitual

For people to improve, they must have a system or process of improvement (Clear, 2018). If we want to improve our health, we need to eat well and exercise on a routine basis. Merely setting a goal won't do the trick. Learning the different categories of knowledge and skills across the surface, deep, and transfer levels also requires a system of small and doable practices that occur on a daily or at least several-days-a-week basis.

As mentioned in the introduction (page 1), this book proposes a set of ten habits that provides students with the right skills and knowledge to engage in wicked and kind problems with others. The ten habits are divided into two categories. The first category is a set of dispositional habits that focus on how to approach learning. Specifically, dispositional strategies center on a student's ability to engage metacognition, navigate challenge, work well with others, and consolidate learning. The second category of habits is a set of routines that ensure students learn across the surface, deep, and transfer levels. These competency habits ensure students' progress through and across every level and build, refine, and sustain knowledge and skills across the varying categories of knowledge (declarative, procedural, and contextual).

Dispositional Habits

Students need to have a certain set of tools to navigate the learning requirements of the surface, deep, and transfer levels, aided by a set of cognitive, emotional, and behavioral tools. These cognitive, emotional, and behavioral tools aim to meet each level of engagement. Cognitive engagement is centered on whether students are experiencing the learning that they are intended to learn from an experience. This is where students see a discrepancy between their current understanding and work to alleviate the gap between an ideal state and their current understanding. Behavioral engagement is focused on whether students are doing what they are supposed to do to learn. Emotional engagement is centered on whether students are interested in the learning, feel they belong in their school, are physically and psychologically safe, engage in positive and meaningful experiences at school, have friends, and have hope (Knight, 2022). When teachers support students in becoming aware of their own engagement levels and how to handle situations of boredom, monitor their own behavior when times are challenging, and respond to gaps in their learning, students become owners of their own learning and work in partnership with teachers.

While there are a number of dispositional habits that support students and some very good books on the subject (see James Nottingham's 2017 book *The Learning Challenge* and John Almarode and Kara Vandas's 2018 book *Clarity for Learning*), the following four habits have been found to have a positive and substantial impact on learning (Hattie, 2023b).

- **Engage metacognition:** Students have the wherewithal to know the goals of learning, their current level of understanding, and what next steps they need to take in their learning across levels of learning.

- **Navigate challenge:** Students have the tools to be aware of their current emotional, cognitive, and behavioral habits to move their work forward in a productive way.
- **Work well with others:** Students have the tools to be aware of peer dynamics and to move their work forward in a productive way.
- **Consolidate learning:** Students have the tools to ensure the learning process and learner qualities become routine patterns in their lives.

To ensure each learning quality habit is enacted with fidelity, this book provides success criteria for each habit. Much like lifting a weight, there is a proper technique to ensure maximum benefit and minimize poor performance when picking up a new learning habit. In addition, table 1.4 lists a number of teaching practices that can be used to enable students to engage in each habit. While this list is not exhaustive, the strategies serve as potential habits for teachers to ensure students are making learner qualities and the learning process routine.

The dispositional habits serve as a lubricant that enables students to smoothly move across levels of learning and navigate the challenges they will inevitably face in both kind and wicked environments. As students develop and refine their dispositional habits, they develop a great ownership over their own learning. The power of the pinwheel metaphor is that such habits should be employed in conjunction with the competency habits of surface, deep, and transfer learning.

Table 1.4: Dispositional Habits

Habit	Success Criteria
HABIT 1: Engage Metacognition	*Students will . . .* • Routinely use evidence to determine expectations and current levels of understanding • Take action when receiving feedback and tracking progress
HABIT 2: Navigate Challenge	*Students will . . .* • Routinely use strategies to navigate negative thinking • Use routines for maintaining focus and generating curiosity when facing boredom, setbacks, and new situations
HABIT 3: Work Well With Others	*Students will . . .* • Have the tools to be aware of peer dynamics and to move their work forward in a productive way
HABIT 4: Consolidate Learning	*Students will . . .* • Rehearse and reflect on learner qualities and the learning process

Competency Habits

Hattie and Donoghue (2016) show that the positive impact of learning strategies is related to how well matched they are to the level of learning. For example, when students engage in practice testing at the surface level, the impact is substantial, whereas seeing patterns in new situations has a much more powerful effect at the transfer level. The same matching phenomenon occurs with instruction: Whereas direct instruction is a powerful influence at the surface level, problem solving is less impactful at the surface level but shows positive effects at both the deep and transfer levels of learning (Hattie, 2023b). In this way, students and teachers need to develop a set of habits that build learning across the surface, deep, and transfer levels. Table 1.5 shares a set of success criteria to ensure each learning quality habit is engaged in with a degree of fidelity. Similar to table 1.4 (page 29), table 1.5 lists a number of teaching practices that can be used to enable students to engage in each habit. While this list is not exhaustive, the strategies serve as potential habits for teachers to ensure students are making learner qualities and the learning process routine.

Table 1.5: Competency Habits

Level of Learning	Habit	Success Criteria
Surface Learning	**HABIT 5:** Build Knowledge Together	*Students will . . .* • Actively engage with small bits of new information • Routinely elaborate and summarize new information to solidify understanding
	HABIT 6: Check and Respond to Current Understanding Together	*Students will . . .* • Be prepared to respond to questions and actively engage with new material at any time • Engage with corrective feedback
Deep Learning	**HABIT 7:** Develop Conceptual Understanding	*Students will . . .* • Compare and contrast concepts through reading, writing, and talking • Develop conceptual understanding across multiple facts and ideas by following through on structured reading, writing, and talking protocols
	HABIT 8: Apply Conceptual Understanding	*Students will . . .* • Create and back up claims with credible sources and anchored to core content • Develop, discuss, and challenge ideas with others
Transfer Learning	**HABIT 9:** Build Contextual Understanding	*Students will . . .* • Scan multiple contexts to find common patterns and unique differences
	HABIT 10: Solve Complex Problems	*Students will . . .* • Employ problem-solving processes that integrate divergent and convergent thinking routines • Engage with authentic audiences to solve problems • Address setbacks and changes in the contextual problems

Competency habits are the driving practices for building and applying learning that addresses problems in both kind and wicked environments. As students develop and refine their competency habits, they develop a stronger level of competency and flexibility to move across each level. The power of the pinwheel metaphor, as previously noted, is that such habits should be employed in conjunction with the dispositional habits.

Conclusion

This chapter began with the ideas of approaching learning from various paradigms. The first paradigm was represented by the pendulum: a metaphor for the either-or approach as it illustrates choosing sides or priorities among the different levels of learning and dispositions. The second paradigm was illustrated by the pinwheel because it represents the idea of integrating all levels of learning simultaneously. The holistic paradigm of learning frees students and teachers from following a rigid path of learning and allows them to explore different pathways to learn across levels of learning. The power of this integrated approach is catalyzed by developing students' dispositions as well as aligning teaching and learning across each level of learning. This is realized using small and doable habits that teachers and students can engage in daily.

Before you embark on the remaining chapters of this book, reflect on how routine each of the dispositional and competency habits are for you and your students right now. To support you in this reflection, consider taking the *Rigor Redefined* survey (see the reproducible for "Next Steps," page 33) and plan for how you will start or sustain certain practices in your classroom. Once you have completed the survey, share the data with colleagues and discuss themes and patterns and potential next steps. Consider using chapter 2 to support yourself in implementing new practices, and leverage chapters 3–6 (pages 63, 95, 119, and 169) to find with concrete strategies to enhance your practice and impact student learning.

The ten *Rigor Redefined* habits are the central focus of the remaining chapters of this book. We will explore how to start and embed habits and then look at how we can engage in dispositional and competency habits to ensure students are prepared for each class period and the world that awaits them when they graduate. In the next several chapters, the questions, processes, and tools are laid out to start, sustain, and close units to ensure students not only learn but learn at high levels.

Reflection Questions

1. How do you, your students, and your school define rigorous learning?

2. Does the pendulum or pinwheel metaphor have a stronger connection to your practice? Or, put differently, to what extent do you agree that the shift from hierarchies to taxonomies is critical for enhancing student learning over time?

3. To what extent do you incorporate all levels of learning across your units and lessons?

4. To what extent do you categorize learning goals by the category of knowledge and skill (that is, declarative, procedural, and contextual knowledge)?

5. When thinking about your own students, what dispositional habits stand out for you as the greatest opportunity for improvement?

6. When thinking about your own students, what competency habits stand out to you as the greatest opportunity for improvement?

Rigor Redefined © 2024 Solution Tree Press • SolutionTree.com
Visit **go.SolutionTree.com/instruction** to download this free reproducible.

Next Steps

1. Take the *Rigor Redefined* survey by accessing the QR code. Evaluate your level and your students' level of implementation. The survey will ask you questions about the frequency of the habit rather than the impact of the habit. The survey will ask you to select from one of the following options for each habit.

    a. Routinely engage in this habit without prompting

    b. Routinely engage in this habit with prompting

    c. Occasionally engage in this habit

    d. Plan to engage in this habit

2. After reviewing the survey, conduct the What? So What? Now What? (page 34) protocol with colleagues to identify potential next steps.

3. Home in on a key habit and the success criteria by selecting the chapters of the book that are a critical need for your students.

4. Once a habit or set of habits have been identified, read chapter 2 (page 35) and devise a plan of action for acquiring and consolidating the habit.

What? So What? Now What?

This protocol was developed by Gene Thompson-Grove (2012). It allows educators to collectively give and receive feedback. Once educators have taken the *Rigor Redefined* survey (page 33), share the results with colleagues to review and then follow the specific steps of the protocol.

Introduction

Review all steps of the protocol before beginning. The group should be divided into subgroups of three or four. All participants take turns facilitating and presenting.

Process

1. Individually outline a challenge or success from the data in the *Rigor Redefined* survey. Participants should each answer the following questions:

   What? (What did I do? What am I working on?) and So What? (Why is this important to me?) (5 min.)

2. In rounds:

   a. Each participant goes through this process. First, they explain what they've written and then they ask a focus question. Those not presenting take notes and write down questions.

   b. Each group member asks clarifying questions.

   c. Participants talk, taking up each of the following questions along with any focus questions that have emerged. The presenter listens to the conversation, considering the perspectives and insights, taking notes.

      i. "What I heard the presenter say was . . ."

      ii. "Why this seems important to the presenter is . . ."

      iii. "What I wonder is . . ." or "The questions this raises for me are . . ."

      iv. "What this means to me is . . ."

      v. "What I might suggest is . . ."

   d. The presenter leads a group discussion reflecting on how to respond to insights the group members have come up with—Now What?

3. Debrief

Source: Adapted from Thompson-Grove, G. (2012). What? So what? Now what? Center for Leadership & Educational Equity.

Making Rigorous Learning Doable

> *"Why does San Francisco have such a visible homelessness problem, compared to other places?"*
> *"It is a housing problem."*
> —**Ezra Klein and Scott Weiner**

In philosophy, the law of parsimony or, as it's more commonly known, *Occam's razor*, dictates that the simplest explanation is preferable to one that is more complex. For instance, while people debate about the various reasons for homelessness in California, often the solution is the simplest—build homes. In education, the problem of getting students to learn how to read, for example, turns out to be fairly straightforward, though difficult to implement: teach students to practice letter-sound relationships in specific sequences and to do that over and over (Moats, 2020).

When it comes to improving our practice, the simplest approach is to make small shifts in practice to get better. Often in our pursuit of rigorous learning we focus on end-of-unit activities or events rather than focusing on small and doable habits throughout a unit. For instance, in project-based learning, the idea is that students work on culminating products at the end of the unit rather than weaving in small surface, deep, and transfer routines. Events don't lead to habits. Daily routines lead to habits, and habits are a cornerstone of teaching practice that leads to rigorous learning because rigorous learning is developed through routine practice.

Additionally, one of the confounding challenges of implementing habits is that we can sometimes confuse planning with practice. Steve Blank (2009) calls planning habits *motion habits* and practice habits *action habits*. For instance, when we plan to go to the gym, we are in motion, whereas when we lift weights in the gym, we are in action. In teaching, when we are designing a unit, we are in motion; when we are engaging in a questioning technique with students, we are in action.

This chapter provides concrete steps that you can take for starting and sustaining habits in your classroom. The chapter looks at the strategies you can use to make habits easy to implement in your classroom and strategies for maintaining habits over the course of your career. It focuses on the critical importance of making the instructional core observable by articulating habits of practices for students, offering a menu of routines for teachers to use across each level of learning to ensure students develop the right habits, and giving guidance on the tasks through which students engage with each level of rigor. The chapter also focuses on the means to inspect and grow habits of practice. Finally, the chapter lays out a set of motion habits that can amplify the action habits laid out in the book. The chapter includes a conclusion with reflection questions and next steps.

Starting and Sustaining a Habit

People are creatures of habit. We wake up every day and follow a sequence of habits we have built over time. Making changes can cause stress, even when the decision to make them is made willingly, even eagerly. This stress results from the fact that changing requires people to alter the very habits that enabled them to survive up to the point of change. While those habits may have been suboptimal, they did represent survival and therefore stability—change can make people feel unbalanced and temporarily unsafe (Clear, 2018). When people are expected to make changes in short durations of time, the stress of change can be even greater (Huberman, 2022a, 2022b). Classrooms are change-making spaces. Akin to a weight room or a track, when someone steps into a classroom, they realize that they are about to be tasked with making changes to their habits. The reason is that the purpose of the classroom is for growth or change in our status. And there is that moment at the beginning of the class where everyone, teachers and students alike, want to stick with what they know and not push through to something new, like to a new habit. We must move from what is familiar to use, or "roaming the known," to slightly outside of our current understanding to develop new knowledge and skill, or "nudging the known."

To support students in engaging in the ten *Rigor Redefined* habits, teachers need aligned and consistent routines, with corresponding habits of practice that are small and doable. Figure 2.1 illustrates a number of success criteria and guideposts that will also be explored more fully in chapters 3–6 (pages 63, 95, 119, and 169, respectively).

Habit	Success Criteria	Guideposts for Success Criteria	Teacher Routines
HABIT 1: Engage Metacognition	Use evidence of learning to inform next steps	Co-construct expectations of learning	Entry Events Silent Protocol Work Sample Scramble Error Analysis Assessment Scramble Matrix Approach Clues Approach Hexagonal Approach (See these strategies in further detail in table 3.2, page 70.)
		Engage in clarity checks	Known/Nuance/Novel To and Through I Used to Think . . . Now I Think . . . Summarize Key Learning (See these strategies in further detail in table 3.3, page 72.)
		Process check with leveled success criteria	Entrance and Exit Tickets 3-2-1 KWL (Know, Want to Know, Learned) Chart K/NTK (Know/Need to Know) Error Analysis (See these strategies in further detail in table 3.5, page 74.)
	Take action to improve learning	Determine next steps	Learning GPS Third Teacher References Four Corners ABCD/1234 (See these strategies in further detail in table 3.6, page 74.)
		Take action from feedback	30:5 Camera 1/Camera 2 On the Move (See these strategies in further detail in chapter 3, page 75.)
HABIT 2: Navigate Challenge	Manage negative thinking	Monitor orientation	Cups Zones of Learning Orientation Reflection on Progress Gratitude Prompts Monitor Your Mood Compass Points (See these strategies in further detail in table 3.7, page 79.)
		Implement structured protocols	TAG Protocol Tuning Protocol Consultancy Dilemma (See these strategies in further detail in table 3.8, page 81.)
	Cultivate curiosity	Employ routines for building curiosity	Think Again Scaffold the Start Praise the Pause

Figure 2.1: The learning habits success criteria and teacher routine checklist.

continued →

Habit	Success Criteria	Guideposts for Success Criteria	Teacher Routines
			In2out
			Pass the Questions Around
			Four Corners
			Present-Deepening Prompts
			Keep-Inquiry-Going Prompts
			Cue Transfer Prompts
			Ask Students to Think About Their Thinking
			(See these strategies in further detail in chapter 3, pages 82 and 83.)
HABIT 3: Work Well With Others	Develop relationships	Establish and implement expectations for collaborative work	Setting Up and Using Agreements
			Creating Roles for Process
			Build Upon
			Think and Wonder
			Think, Feel, Care
			Appreciation, Apology, Aha
			Feelings and Options
			(See these strategies in further detail in table 3.9, pages 83 and 84.)
	Solve problems together	Structure discourse	Affinity Mapping
			Tuning Protocol
			Consultancy Dilemma
			What? So What? Now What?
			(See these strategies in further detail in table 3.10, page 85.)
HABIT 4: Consolidate Learning	Slow things down		Wait for an Answer
			Flat Affect
			Rehearsal
			Quizzing
			(See these strategies in further detail in chapter 3, pages 86 and 87.)
	Space things out		Spaced Practice
			Backward Fading
			Interleaving
			Success Analysis Protocol
			What? So What? Now What?
			I Used to Think . . . Now I Think . . .
			Critical Friends Protocol
			Take Away, Take Back, Tension
			(See these strategies in further detail in chapter 3, pages 87 and 88.)
	Incorporate small changes in routines		Curveball Questions
			Bridging Levels of Learning
			(See these strategies in further detail in chapter 3, pages 89 and 90.)

Habit	Success Criteria	Guideposts for Success Criteria	Teacher Routines
HABIT 5: Build Knowledge Together	Interact with new information	Guide practice with new knowledge	Direct Modeling Backward Fading Zoom In, Zoom Out Examples and Nonexamples (See these strategies in further detail in chapter 4, pages 98–99.)
		Interact with surface learning	Making Predictions Choral and Echo Reading Cloze Activities Numberless Word Problems and Slow Reveal Graphs Close Read Vocabulary Development Use Mnemonics I Describe, You Draw (See these strategies in further detail in chapter 4, pages 102 and 107.)
	Elaborate and summarize new information	Elaborate on new information	Full-Sentence and Academic Vocabulary Responses What Makes You Say That? Clear and Muddy (See these strategies in further detail in table 4.2, page 107.)
		Summarize new information	Getting the Gist Summarize the Story So Far Think-Pair-Share (See these strategies in further detail in table 4.2, page 107.)
HABIT 6: Check and Respond to Current Understanding Together	Respond to surface questions		Nonvolunteer Strategies (Popsicle Sticks, Numbers on Chairs, Name Generator) (See these strategies in further detail in chapter 4, page 110.) Probing and Process Questions (See table 4.3, page 110 for further detail.) True or False Agree or Disagree Four Corners ABCD or 1234 (See these strategies in further detail in chapter 4, page 111.)
	Act upon corrective feedback		Four-Quarter Marking Sticky Note Technique Quizzing and Correcting Deliberate Practice (See these strategies in further detail in chapter 4, page 113.)
HABIT 7: Develop Conceptual Understanding	Compare and contrast concepts	Build complex dialogue gradually	Three- and Five-Interval Turn and Talks (Conjunctions, Subordinating Conjunctions, and Appositives) Fronted Adverbial Drills Picture Worth 1,000 Words Backward Fading Sentence Development Revisiting Cloze Activities

continued →

Habit	Success Criteria	Guideposts for Success Criteria	Teacher Routines
			Extended Think-Pair-Share
			Elaborative Interrogation
			Final Word
			In2out
			Wagon Wheel
			Socratic Seminar
			Jigsaw
			Text-to-Text, Text-to-Self, Text-to-World
			World Cafe
			Open Space Technology (OST)
			Chalk Talk
			Chat Station
			(See these strategies in further detail in table 5.1, page 124.)
		Infuse daily deep learning thinking routines	Frayer Model
			2 Box Induction
			Sentence Stems
			+1 Routines
			Generate-Sort-Connect-Elaborate
			Parts, Purpose, and Complexity
			Same Surface, Different Depth (SSDD)
			Graphic Organizers
			(See these strategies in further detail in table 5.4, page 142.)
			Sentence Stem Comparisons
			Question Stem Comparisons
			Analogies
			Sequential
			(See these strategies in further detail in table 5.5, page 146.)
HABIT 8: Apply Conceptual Understanding	Create and inspect claims, evidence, and reasoning (CER)		Claim, Support, Question
			Connect, Extend, and Challenge
			Imagine If . . .
			Think-Puzzle-Explore
			Kick the Tires
			(See these strategies in further detail in table 5.1, page 124.)
	Develop, discuss, and challenge ideas with others	Challenge ideas with complex discourse	Four As
			Elaborative Interrogation
			Friendly Controversy
			Perspective Analysis (with/without artificial intelligence [AI])
			Town Hall Meetings
			Lincoln-Douglas Debates
			Chalk Talk
			Red Team
			(See these strategies in further detail in table 5.1, page 124.)
			Circle of Viewpoints
			(See this strategy in further detail in table 6.6, page 193.)

Habit	Success Criteria	Guideposts for Success Criteria	Teacher Routines
			Critical Friends
			(See this strategy in further detail in chapter 3, page 88.)
			Issaquah
			(See this strategy in further detail in chapter 5, page 161.)
		Make deep learning feedback social	Harkness Protocol (Discussion Mapping)
			Consultancy Dilemma
			What? So What? Now What?
			(See this strategy in further detail in table 5.11, page 162.)
			Tuning Protocol
			(See this strategy in further detail in chapter 3, pages 58, 81, and 85.)
			Talk Detectives
			(See this strategy in further detail in chapter 5, page 163.)
			Odd One Out
			(See this strategy in further detail in chapter 4, page 112.)
			Sticky Note Technique
			(See this strategy in further detail in chapter 4, page 113.)
			Sort It Out Protocol
			Dots Strategy
			Questions Before Comments
			Out of Many
			(See these strategies in further detail in table 5.15, page 165.)
HABIT 9: Build Contextual Understanding	Compare contexts	Similarities and differences	Matrix
			Assessment Scramble
			(See these strategies in further detail in table 6.1, pages 172 and 173.)
			Quick Checks (To and Through)
			(See this strategy in further detail in table 3.3, page 73.)
			Graphic Organizers (T-Chart and Venn Diagrams)
			(See this strategy in further detail in table 5.6, page 150.)
			Semantic Analysis
			Three- and Five-Interval Turn and Talks
			Analogies and Metaphors
			Whip-Around
			(See these strategies in further detail in chapter 6, pages 172 and 178.)
		Make predictions	Generating Hypotheses
			Predict and Verify
			SCCG
			Plan Scenarios
			3 Cs
			(See these strategies in further detail in chapter 6, pages 178–180.)

continued →

Habit	Success Criteria	Guideposts for Success Criteria	Teacher Routines
HABIT 10: **Solve Complex Problems**	Employ problem-solving processes	Define the problem: Understanding the root cause	Fishbone Five Whys Realm of Concern Portable Surprises Gap Analysis Circles of Action (See these strategies in further detail in table 6.5, page 184.) Open Space Technology (OST) Skunkworks Socratic Seminar
		Define the problem: Solution criteria	Chalk Talk Step In, Step Out, Step Back (See this strategy in further detail in table 6.5, page 184.)
		Searching for information: Possible solutions	SWOT Option Explosion Revise Carousel Brainstorm Orchard Cove Scenario Planning SCCG Creative Comparisons (See these strategies in further detail in table 6.5, page 184.)
		Searching for information: Solution choice	Affinity Mapping Friendly Controversy Nominal Group Techniques Town Hall Meeting SCCG (See these strategies in further detail in chapter 6, page 184.)
		Applying a solution: Implementation	Gallery Walk What? So What? Now What? Critical Friends Charette (See these strategies in further detail in chapter 6, page 184.)
	Engage with authentic audiences		Empathy Interviews True for Whom? Three Stories Thinking Hats Think, Feel, Care (See these strategies in further detail in table 6.6, page 193.)
	Address setbacks and changes		Curveballs Dynamic Presentations Open the Success Criteria Situation Room (Types 1, 2, and 3) Sequels Skunkworks (See these strategies in further detail in table 6.7, page 194.)

The routines or habits that teachers engage in for meeting surface, deep, and transfer learning needs in their students vary based on the nature of each taxonomic level of learning. The checklist illustrates different routines that teachers can incorporate into their lessons to help surface, deep, and transfer learning become a common experience in the classroom and a long-term habit for students and teachers. The routines vary based on the levels of learning because they each serve a different purpose for enhancing student learning. As discussed earlier, Hattie and Donoghue (2016) identify a wide range of learning strategies that students need at each level (see table 2.1, for a list of strategies). This research is supported by others, including Marzano (2018) who shows that instructional strategies are more effective when they are aligned to the level of learning they were originally designed to enhance. For instance, while problem- and project-based learning (PBL) can yield more than one year's growth on student learning, but its impact is sensitive to the level of learning. PBL has an impact on surface learning that is almost negligible, has an average influence at transfer, and significantly improves student learning at the deep level (Hattie, 2023b). As such, the alignment of teaching and learning strategies to levels of learning is critical for student learning.

Table 2.1: Influences on Student Learning Across Levels of Rigor

Influence	Surface	Deep	Transfer
Outlining	X		
Evaluating similarities and differences across contexts			X
Seeking help from peers		X	
Classroom discussion		X	
Mnemonics	X		
Seeing patterns in new situations			X
Strategies to integrate prior knowledge (for example, KWL)	X		
Evaluation and reflection		X	
Solving problems in new situations			X

Source: Hattie & Donoghue, 2016.

The teaching routines for building student learning processes in this book are based around strategies that substantially enhance student learning at each categorical level of learning. What can make them successful is that the strategies are small, doable, and sustained over time. Research has shown that deep and transfer learning are often not given the same time, energy, and effort as surface learning (Epstein, 2019; Hattie, 2021). For instance, in 2020 Hattie shared, "We've just looked at 17,000 transcripts of teachers teaching classes and we could not find any teaching of transfer." The challenge for teachers is how to encounter transfer learning in small and doable ways and sustain those practices over time.

So how do we make the ten *Redefining Rigor* habits routine in our classrooms? Are there ways that we can shrink the change to make it feasible for busy teachers in the classroom? The good news is yes! Six specific approaches for teachers to engage in the ten habits are suggested here to serve as a catalyst for implementation.

1. **Sustain:** Make the habit a daily routine as opposed to an event.
2. **Small:** Make the routine manageable for you within the habits you are already using in the classroom.
3. **Stack:** Link a new habit to your current practices in the classroom.
4. **Shelter:** Protect this work by not adding other habits so that you remain focused on only a few new practices at a time.
5. **Sprint:** Start by implementing a habit in one class, one discipline area, or one small group of students before you broaden your use to all your students.
6. **Share:** Make sure to collect evidence of the impact of your implementation of a habit and determine next steps.

The following sections expand on each strategy before discussing motion habits versus action habits.

Sustain—Make It Routine

A core part of choosing any habit that we want to work on is to ensure that the habits we choose are those that we will engage with every day. Picking a new habit that occurs once a month or once a week is more like picking an event than a routine. Launching an entry event at the beginning of a unit is an event that illustrates the start of a problem or project. Randomly checking student understanding using popsicle sticks when asking the class questions each day is a habit.

Consider these key checks on the sustainability of a habit.

- Is this a habit (as opposed to an event)?
- Will I engage in this habit every day of the week?
- Will students engage in this habit every day of the week?

Small—Make It Manageable

When selecting one of the ten habits in this book, it is important to consider what change you will make, what change will be expected of students, and what change will be made to the specific content you are teaching and expecting students to learn. These key considerations are known as the instructional core (City, Elmore, Fiarman, & Teitel, 2009). The instructional core consists of the following three elements.

1. **Teacher:** The specific routines utilized to enhance student engagement and improvement in learning
2. **Student:** The specific routines that link to learning qualities and the learning process
3. **Content:** The specific surface, deep, and transfer learning or dispositional activities and tasks students and teachers are working through

Once a habit is selected, the grain size of the habit we select to employ is important. When we attempt to take on boulder-sized habits, we are doomed to fatigue after a few attempts. Imagine you want to reduce the amount of calories that you consume each day. You notice that you consume about 3,000 calories per day and enjoy two diet soft drinks during the day and a candy bar after dinner. You decide that you will no longer eat breakfast, cut from your diet all sugary drinks, and no longer eat chocolate. That's likely not going to work after a few days because the change is too big to stick with. You'll be going after a boulder-size habit rather than a pebble.

The idea is to effectively manage a new habit rather than aim for a large change. In the case of making a dietary change, for example, start with consuming half of the number of sodas you usually have and see how it goes. Begin reducing intake and making small changes in your behavior. Over time, you will make the types of improvements you desire in a sustainable way. This is taking aim at a pebble-sized habit. Over time, you can begin putting pebble-sized habits together to form a rock-sized habit and ultimately combine rocks into boulders (see table 2.2).

Table 2.2: Grain Size of Habit Development

	Boulder	Rock	Pebble
Definition	A sequence of five or more complex habits	Three or four new habits that are connected to current habits	One or two new habits that are nestled in between current habits
Example	When I take attendance, students will engage in three short conversations. During the first conversation, students will compare two ideas. Next, they will add academic language into the conversation. Finally, they will incorporate conjunctions. They will then write down three sentences and give each other feedback using a rubric.	When I take attendance, students will engage in a turn and talk that incorporates three short conversations. During the first conversation, students will compare two ideas. Next, they will add academic language into the conversation. Finally, they will incorporate conjunctions.	Students will repeat key vocabulary words after I state them during a presentation.

The same behaviors in the formation of habits in dieting can be incorporated into teaching and learning. For example, before you attempt to implement ten new formative assessment practices, work on one for several weeks. Before using strategies in this book for surface, deep, and transfer learning all at once, pick one habit and learn about it. To guide you in making the decision of where to start, consider the specific learning needs of students and which habit is most motivating for you to implement. Your motivation may be drawn by the ease of implementation or by your interest in exploring a new approach to teaching and learning. Allow that motivation to influence your decision. Ensure that you buoy your decision with the observations you are witnessing in class with students.

When starting the process of implementing a new habit, make sure to stay at the pebble-sized routine. For instance, if students are struggling with speaking to other students, then consider having students engage as a class in echoing or repeating what you say. Repeat this process for a number of days and perhaps weeks before moving toward more complicated, rock- or boulder-sized routines. Over time, as the habit becomes tacit, the class can move from echo recall to talking with one another by comparing ideas using conjunctions, subordinating conjunctions, fronted adverbials, and appositives.

Stack—Link It to Your Current Practice

Habit stacking or habit anchoring is the process of linking old habits together with a new habit (Clear, 2018; Fogg, 2021). Imagine a chain that has one chain link locked to the next chain link and then the next chain link—all in succession. A chain is a great metaphor for our habits. When we wake up, we start our daily habits. We brush our teeth, take a shower, put our clothes on, and eat breakfast. Each habit leads to the next habit. If we want to change our habits, we need to think about inserting a new chain link into the chain.

When we stack or link a habit between two already familiar and common habits, we have a better chance of implementing and sustaining it if we treat the habit as something separate from our current practice. Often, however, we tend to struggle with the timing of implementation and begin to treat the habit as "another thing" we must do.

Imagine a teacher wants to increase student dialogue. The first step would be to review their current habits that underpin their interactions with students and that they stack or link together, such as this following sequence.

> Greet students at the door—direct students to an opening activity—take attendance—ask students questions about the opener.

Next, they would identify the habit. In this case, the teacher may determine that students need to improve in deep learning and so may decide to include a pair-share to encourage student dialogue. Next, the teacher selects a place in their current sequence of classroom habits where the new routine may fit. Once they have identified the habit and where it will fit, they insert it in the chain.

> Greet students at the door—direct students to an opening activity—take attendance—ask students to do a brief pair-share about their responses—ask students questions about the opener.

Andrew Huberman (2022b), a neuroscientist and professor at Stanford University School of Medicine, recommends stacking new habits by scheduling the time and day one intends to implement a habit. The argument is that phases of the day will invoke a shift in mood and mindset that is more conducive to building and keeping habits. Table 2.3 illustrates a suggested pathway for when teachers may want to stack new habits into their practice and when they should reflect on practices.

Table 2.3: Creating a Schedule for Habits

Phases	PHASE 1: 0–8 hours after waking up	PHASE 2: 9–15 hours after waking up	PHASE 3: 16–24 hours after waking up
Time Frame	6:00 a.m.–2:00 p.m.	2:00 p.m.–8:00 p.m.	8:00 p.m.–6:00 a.m.
Description	This is when you want to take on new habits and behaviors that are challenging for you—you are naturally more readily able to engage.	This is when you want to taper your stress level and take on habits and things you are already doing that don't require a lot of override of limbic friction—for example, journaling or music.	Deep sleep is critical to wiring neural circuits required for building habits.
Tag line	*Sprint here.* Pick a small doable habit (routine) and implement with a small group of students or one class.	*Inspect here.* Use evidence to reflect on progress and determine next steps.	*Rest here.* Pause your commitment to this work and relax.

Stacking is a helpful influencer of habit formation because it anchors new habits to existing patterns and behaviors that teachers have cultivated over years of practice. By stacking a new routine in the classroom, you and your students will likely stick to the new behavior, and the new practice will feel not like "another thing" to do but rather like a "connected thing" to do. Even more, if we can time new habit formation to the time of day that our brains are prepared to learn new ideas and then reflect on implementation, we are better prepared for new learning and long-term habit formation.

Shelter—Protect This Work by Not Adding Other Changes

When adding a link to the chain, it is critical that you do not add too many habits. We can become a bit overzealous when we are planning new practices, but it is the implementation that counts for results. Let's revisit the earlier example: wake up—brush teeth—shower—put on clothes—eat breakfast. Imagine suddenly changing that routine to this: wake up—brush teeth—*run—lift—do yoga*—shower—put on clothes—eat breakfast—*drink coffee (wait to eat until after 2:00 p.m.)—listen to a podcast on self-discipline—walk to work—meet three new people.* The amount of new activities that are involved will likely be difficult to initiate because there is a tremendous amount of upfront learning along with the difficulty of monitoring and maintaining so many new practices at a high-quality level in the long term. Now imagine adding many habits at once to a routine in your classroom. What if greet students at the door—direct students to an opening activity—take attendance—ask students questions about the opener became greet students at the door—*give each student a unique handshake*—direct students to an opening activity—take attendance—*ask students to do a brief pair-share about their responses*—ask students questions about the opener—*rank work samples in small groups and co-construct success criteria*? Within the parameters of the teacher day, you would probably feel even more overwhelmed by adding too many habits at once than you would when adding habits to your personal routines. If we attempt to add too many new habits and fail to stack them to our current routines, the chances of making these parts part of our daily practice are slim. The idea here is to be like the tortoise in Aesop's fable. Go slow to go far.

Sprint—Start With a Small Group Before You Scale

No new habit stands the test of children. When we learn of a new strategy in a book, at a conference, or from a colleague next door, we have to remember that it will not be exactly replicable in our classroom. Remember context matters. Dylan Wiliam (2018) once shared that "everything works somewhere and nothing works everywhere" (p. 1). Everything needs to be modified to work in our classrooms. As such, we must learn how our new habits and students' habits interact with each other in a small setting before we look to scale and expand any new practice. We do this by selecting one group or setting in which we will practice the habit for a few weeks. After a few weeks, we can then reflect on the implementation, inspiration, and impact of the work in a relatively controlled setting. Consider table 2.4 for this reflection.

Table 2.4: Implementation, Inspiration, and Impact Questions

Implementation	Inspiration	Impact
Is this practice doable?	Is this practice interesting to me and to the students (or is it a slog)?	Did this habit make a noticeable difference to student learning?

The key takeaway here is to test out new practices and learn how challenging they are to implement and how they impact students before spreading a practice to more students and potentially different content areas. The idea here is to learn from earlier attempts to better understand the exact changes that are required as more students and contexts are encountered.

Share—Measure Your Impact, Discuss Findings, Determine Next Steps

As we engage in a new habit, we need to have some degree of support and guidance along the way. When we are working hard to get back into shape, a coach can provide encouragement, guidance, and accountability for ensuring we show up each morning to meet our goals. Having someone by our side doesn't mean we have to perform for them; rather, we learn with and from them. This form of accountability is what I call *lowercase accountability*, an informal way of holding people responsible for their actions. This approach to accountability is in contrast to *uppercase Accountability*, which is a formal way of evaluating others in their efficacy of particular actions. When engaging in habit formation, teachers should find a colleague with whom to share their progress of implementing a new habit using lowercase accountability. This is not a means to prove your success but rather a way to learn about the impact of your habits and the journey you and students are going through as everyone is trying something new. The learning should be messy with lots of learning about what worked, what hasn't worked yet, what doesn't work, and what you are still curious about.

There are several approaches that teachers can take to support one another in engaging in lowercase accountability. First, teachers can simply use a set of questions to support each other in thinking through the approach to engaging in the habit as well as the impact of the habit on students. Suggested questions include the following.

- How did you decide on the specific habit you are trialing in your classroom right now?
- To what extent have you been able to ensure that the habit is sustainable?
- What have you learned from implementing this practice in your classroom? Or, how was following this practice similar to and different from what you have implemented before?
- What is your hunch about the future of this work for you and your students?
- What was your intention when you implemented this practice? To what extent have you met your initial intention?
- What evidence exists that the practice is making an impact on student learning?
- What are your next steps?
- Does the amount of your effort balance with the impact you are finding with students?
- Does the practice need to shift to better meet your context?
- What are specific steps you will take to continue this practice?

In addition to using a series of questions, teachers may want to engage in structured protocols to give and receive feedback from colleagues. One suggested protocol is the Consultancy Dilemma (see the appendix, page 204). In the Consultancy Dilemma protocol, teachers share challenges they are currently facing with a small group of colleagues. The small group asks a teacher clarifying questions to better understand the dilemma. Clarifying questions (National School Reform Faculty, n.d.a) may include the following.

- Why is this a dilemma for you?
- Why is this dilemma important to you?
- If you could take a snapshot of this dilemma, what would you/we see?
- What have you done already to try to remedy or manage the dilemma?

Once the clarifying questions have been addressed, the group has a conversation about potential next steps the teacher may take to address the dilemma. The teacher receiving feedback listens and does not engage in the discussion and takes notes to promote their own thinking and crafting of next steps.

Other check-ins with staff on whether specific practices should be continued or changed are important. Finally, after reviewing your progress and that of your students, determine whether you should continue to pursue the current practice. When teachers work together to share their learning and receive lowercase accountability support, everyone can learn from taking action on student learning.

Making Motion Matter

While implementing action habits is critical, motion habits can serve as a catalyst to lower the threshold for taking action. Motion habits are related to planning and strategy. They prepare us for action. When I write out my lesson plan for the day, print out all the materials that I need, and ensure that every student has the materials they need that day (motion habits), it is much easier for me to implement my lesson and try out a new practice (action habits). As such, planning to engage in surface, deep, and transfer learning can serve as an accelerant for the action habits described in detail in chapters 3–6 (pages 63, 95, 119, and 169, respectively). The motion habits that are helpful for realizing rigorous learning in the classroom include the following.

- Construct learning intentions
- Develop leveled success criteria
- Create tasks
- Construct curveballs
- Launch the work

Each of these motion habits is detailed in the subsequent section.

Construct Learning Intentions

Teachers need to identify the category of knowledge and skills that are expected with each local, state, or national standard. Often, procedural and declarative knowledge are integrated within one standard. In addition, contextual knowledge is often referenced within or after a learning outcome is presented in the curricular resources teachers and students are using. The suggestion here is to discern the categories of knowledge to ensure both students and teachers are clear on the procedural, declarative, and contextual knowledge they will be learning. One way to do this is to answer the following questions while considering a standard such as this one.

- What core factual knowledge are students learning? This is declarative knowledge.
- What specific skills-based knowledge are students learning? This is procedural knowledge.
- Through what means are students learning declarative and procedural knowledge? This is contextual knowledge.

While it may be easy to define categories of knowledge and skill when thinking of learning more generally, or when considering contexts, it can be more difficult within the framework of a specific unit or lesson. For example, figure 2.2 shows two examples of the procedural, declarative, and contextual knowledge students are going to learn about in school. In the first example, students are learning about the internal and external structures of an organism to understand how they survive, grow, adapt, and reproduce. This declarative knowledge will be learned through various contexts, including examining armadillos and basilisk lizards. In addition, students will be learning how to develop their informational writing.

Example	Procedural	Declarative	Contextual
Example 1	Informational writing	Plants and animals have both internal and external structures to survive, grow, adapt, and reproduce	Armadillo Basilisk lizard
Example 2	Narrative writing	Interaction between geosphere, biosphere, or atmosphere	Rainforest Taiga

Figure 2.2: Tagging the categories of knowledge and skill.

It can be a little more difficult to identify categories of knowledge within the formal structure of a standard. For instance, one science standard in New York state requires students to investigate how senses can detect light, sound, and vibrations even when they come from far away and to use the collected evidence to develop and support an explanation. This standard includes declarative knowledge (understanding how to define, relate, and apply light, sound, and vibrations) and procedural knowledge (investigating, collecting evidence, and developing and supporting an explanation).

Develop Leveled Success Criteria

As teachers design units, it is critical that success criteria are created for surface, deep, and transfer learning. One way to begin this work is to create leveled success criteria using verbs that are typically assigned to each phase of surface, deep, and transfer learning. Table 2.5 provides sample verbs that are often associated with each level of complexity.

Table 2.5: Success Criteria Verb Rhetoric

Surface	Deep	Transfer
Name	Compare [concepts]	Compare [contexts]
Tell	Contrast [concepts]	Contrast [contexts]
Restate	Synthesize [concepts]	Synthesize [contexts]
Define	Analyze [concepts]	Analyze [contexts]
Describe	Evaluate [concepts]	Evaluate [contexts]
Recognize	Draw conclusions [concepts]	Draw conclusions [contexts]
Label	Predict	Predict
Match	Solve nonroutine problems	Formulate
Model	Show cause and effect	Hypothesize
Use rules	Infer [concepts]	Critique
Perform a procedure		Infer [contexts]

The verbs in table 2.5 can be used for both procedural and declarative knowledge and skills. Verb phrases, including *use rules, perform a procedure, solve nonroutine problems,* and *produce and present* are typically used when developing procedural knowledge and skills. Verbs such as *describe, label, match,* and *critique* are typically used when developing declarative knowledge.

The success criteria should be created for declarative and procedural knowledge separately. This allows students to focus on each category of knowledge and skill when they are tracking their growth and giving and receiving feedback. Success criteria do not necessarily need to be developed for contextual knowledge because contextual knowledge is not typically required on state, national, and international assessments. In addition, the transfer level requires that students apply their declarative and procedural learning across contexts, which reinforces the learning of contextual information. For instance, in kindergarten, students need to learn declarative knowledge associated with the relationship between weather and temperature (see figure 2.3). Notice how in the transfer-level category the contextual knowledge (in this case, heat wave, hurricanes, season changes, eclipse, and surfing conditions) has been struck out of the rubric. The reason for this is to support students in staying focused on the declarative knowledge they need to apply in multiple contexts rather than focusing on one or a few contexts.

Example	Procedural	Declarative	Contextual
Example 1	Define and identify sunlight, wind, snow, or rain and temperature.	Show why weather is the combination of sunlight, wind, snow, or rain and temperature.	Produce and present solutions to various challenges.
Example 2	Describe the sun, moon, and stars in the sky.	Evaluate why patterns of the sun, moon, and stars in the sky can be observed, described, and predicted.	

Figure 2.3: Learning intentions and success criteria across multiple goals.

When you are teaching multiple goals, the success criteria should be separated for surface and deep learning but then integrated at the transfer level to support students in applying knowledge and skills across standards and contexts. Figure 2.4 illustrates an example of integrating learning intentions and success criteria.

Example	Surface	Deep	Transfer
Example 1	Define and identify sunlight, wind, snow, or rain and temperature.	Show why weather is the combination of sunlight, wind, snow, or rain and temperature.	Produce and present solutions to various challenges.
Example 2	Describe the sun, moon, and stars in the sky.	Evaluate why patterns of the sun, moon, and stars in the sky can be observed, described, and predicted.	Create a critique of proposed solutions to a problem.

Figure 2.4: Learning intentions and success criteria across multiple goals within the same unit.

Framing success criteria as questions enables teachers to plan for the types of questions that can be used to start and end lessons, and move the learning forward by igniting it or reflecting on it. These questions are typically written at the transfer level of learning and are associated with applying learning within and across contexts. At the deep level of learning, questions are typically overarching questions that enable conceptual thinking. These types of questions are often called *essential questions*. Essential questions typically require students to compare and contrast content found within surface learning to answer open-ended questions that require synthesis, analysis, evaluation, and prediction of surface- and transfer-level learning. An example question could be one such as this middle- to high-school-level question: *Who wins and who loses when technology changes?*

Similar to essential questions, *driving questions* typically require students to compare and contrast contexts and require a combination of surface and deep learning to develop. The main difference is that whereas essential questions focus on the relationship across content, driving questions focus on the relationship across contexts. For example, who wins and who loses when ChatGPT is used in schools? To fully address such a question requires students to develop surface-level, deep-level, and contextual knowledge within transfer learning as well. Table 2.6 displays question types and examples.

Table 2.6: Question Types and Examples

Example	Surface	Deep	Transfer
Question Type	Foundational	Essential	Driving
Example	What countries played a major role in starting World War II?	Why does studying conflict give us insights into preventing another war?	Should the United States take actions in armed conflict without North Atlantic Treaty Organization (NATO) support?

As driving questions are being constructed, teachers should ensure that the questions require students to take action or make a contribution to a problem within one or more contexts. When we ask a question such as "Why does studying war give us insights into preventing future wars?" students are less likely to discuss what they would do in a real-world situation. When we ask, "Should the United States send missiles to Ukraine to aid in its war with Russia?" we task students with making claims, providing evidence, and requiring reasoning for their answers (see table 2.7).

Table 2.7: Crafting Driving Questions

Steps	Meta-question	Question
STEP 1: Surface level	What do we need to learn?	What were the implications of World War II for the establishment of the new world order?
STEP 2: Deep level	So what does this mean for our lives?	Why does studying war give us insights into preventing future wars?
STEP 3: Transfer level	Now what can I do with this information?	To what extent can we take action to prevent another war? Should Biden send missiles to Ukraine?

To support the design of driving questions, teachers should draft a question and then use a set of meta-questions to ensure that students are having to determine next steps to address a real-world problem. The core meta-question for determining next steps is to determine what students will do with the information once they learn the knowledge and the context. Table 2.7 illustrates a set of meta-questions that support teachers in refining their driving questions. In addition, teachers should consider using question stems such as *Should . . .* and *To what extent . . .* when designing driving questions. In addition, teachers should consider using the prompt *Why?* for essential questions and *What?* and *How?* for foundation questions.

Success criteria enable students to develop clarity of what they are learning across types of learning and a rationale for learning content through the answering of foundational, essential, and driving questions.

Create Tasks

Mike Schmoker (2018) argues that reading, writing, and talking tasks are the critical element for students to develop high-quality understanding of key outcomes. As tasks are being designed across curriculum, classifications of knowledge (procedural, declarative, and contextual), and classifications of learning (surface, deep, and transfer), reading, writing, and talking tasks should be incorporated. Table 2.8 illustrates a sample of such tasks across the surface, deep, and transfer levels.

Table 2.8: Reading, Writing, and Talking Tasks Across Surface, Deep, and Transfer Learning

Example	Surface	Deep	Transfer
Reading	Preview a passage and highlight key ideas.	Place annotations when key inferences about relationships and principles become apparent.	Find other texts that draw on similar inferences and principles from a different context.
Writing	List and describe key ideas.	Construct a thesis statement that depicts the relationships of key ideas.	Write an opinion piece.
Talking	Recite key ideas.	Argue the key principles and inferences from a passage.	Argue how the key principles and inferences from the class-based passage relate to a next context in front of a panel.

Construct Curveballs

While the discussion of curveballs is explored more extensively in chapter 6 (page 194), I share a brief overview of the design work here. Curveballs are small subtle shifts in student work that bring about a student's ability to develop transfer-level thinking. For instance, imagine a student who is exploring an analogy (for example, waving flag versus coiled spring) that was generated from an AI chatbot and comparing transverse and longitudinal waves to determine the strengths and weaknesses of the analogy. As the students are working on that analogy, the teacher changes the analogy on the students and asks them to compare a different analogy (for example, ripple in water versus compression in a spring).

The curveball is the change in analogy that broadens students ability to transfer across multiple contexts. Tables 3.11 (page 89) and 6.7 (page 194) provide a number of ways for teachers to engage students in using curveballs in the classroom. The suggestion here is to specifically plan for when curveballs would be implemented with students.

Launch the Work

Finally, teachers should plan ways in which they will start their units of study with students. At the transfer level, students often begin with exploring multiple contexts and attempting to identify the connection between the contexts or engaging in a complex problem that they will need to solve during the unit of study. At the deep level, students often begin by exploring the rationale for a particular phenomenon, or the reason an author wrote an article. At the surface level, students often begin by reviewing key terms or working through a procedure. Table 2.9 provides an elementary and secondary example, respectively.

Table 2.9: Launching the Work Across Surface, Deep, and Transfer Learning

	Elementary	Secondary
Starting at Surface	Students will be tasked with writing down the procedures to a mathematics problem by observing the teacher solve a mathematics problem. The teacher will not speak while demonstrating how to solve the addition of two fractions. The teacher will then compare student procedures to their own and discuss next steps for everyone to solve a mathematics problem.	Students will begin with examining an introductory paragraph to an argumentative essay on Truman's decision to drop the atomic bomb. The teacher will place a dot on the essay and ask students to identify what the dot might mean and what they may be learning in class.
Starting at Deep	A class will observe a basketball game, and the teacher will ask students to observe the defense of a team. Next, the students will observe a coach call a time-out and then observe the defense change. The teacher will ask the students to turn and talk on why the coach made that decision.	Students will begin with exploring the painting of Guernica and discussing the potential reasons why Picasso created this painting. Next, students will begin reading *For Whom the Bell Tolls*.
Starting at Transfer	Students are given short videos that are all related to volume (for example, filling up a pool, releasing air in a balloon, observing ice melt in a cup). Students are tasked with identifying what they may be learning as well as constructing an analogy.	Students are presented with two real-world problems. One group of students is tasked with solving the homelessness crisis in California (for example, to what extent can we create short-term and long-term solutions to solve the homelessness crisis?), and another group is tasked with finding alternative transportation options for urban centers to minimize carbon emissions and disenfranchise vulnerable communities worldwide (for example, to what extent can we create short-term and long-term solutions to minimize carbon emissions and disenfranchise vulnerable communities worldwide?).

Inspecting the Motion Work

As you design and inspect units of study, develop routines for ensuring that rigorous learning is embedded in the work. The following five steps are helpful for checking for rigorous learning in any and all curricular resources you are using.

Take the following steps to inspect the units of study you've created.

- Tag categories of knowledge
- Determine rigor sequences
- Create a range of assessments
- Ensure task incorporate reading, writing, and talking across surface, deep, and transfer learning
- Follow through via feedback

Tag Categories of Knowledge

As we review our plans, we need to ensure that we include procedural, declarative, and contextual knowledge, and confirm whether we have incorporated the levels of rigor within those areas of knowledge. As a reminder, procedural knowledge is related to skills, declarative knowledge is conceptual, and contextual knowledge is topical. As discussed earlier, declarative knowledge is required for procedural knowledge to effectively transfer across different situations. As such, teachers need to make sure that declarative knowledge is present in their unit plan development and overall instruction.

In addition, students should understand the difference between declarative knowledge and contextual knowledge so they can effectively transfer declarative knowledge across contexts. One way to inspect this work is to review the learning intentions and success criteria and ensure that both have been created for declarative and for procedural knowledge. Most state standards and curricular frameworks omit contextual information and, as such, contextual information should not be included in learning intentions and success criteria. This is important because students are expected to transfer their declarative knowledge and procedural knowledge across contexts.

In addition, teachers should infuse contextual information into driving questions so that students see the need for applying or transferring their declarative knowledge and procedural knowledge. Finally, teachers should ensure that tasks have been created for declarative and procedural across surface, deep, and transfer level learning.

Determine Rigor Sequences

Teachers should determine the best sequence for ensuring surface, deep, and transfer learning. The more teachers consider varying the sequence, the better chance students will have to experience the fluidity of surface, deep, and transfer learning.

This can be accomplished by changing the way in which teachers begin and end units of study. For instance, in a traditional pathway, teachers begin by teaching surface level learning, then connect the surface learning to deep learning and finally apply that learning to one or more real-world situations. An example of this would be the study of the body systems in which students first learn the various body systems and then move towards understanding the concept of homeostasis and the relationship between organ systems. Finally, students are given a set of problems to solve that jeopardize the homeostatic nature of the human body. Those problems may include sending humans to outerspace, or deep underwater, or getting a disease such as malaria, COVID-19, or cancer.

In contrast to the traditional pathway, students may begin at either a conceptual or problem-based pathway. A conceptual pathway would present students with a discussion on the nature of the consistent temperature of the body and then move towards learning about the body system and then addressing potential ailments of the body. In a problem-based approach, students would begin with the various scenarios and then learn the core content so they may make an informed diagnosis and prognosis to the situations they face.

During this time, teachers may review whether or not curveballs have been embedded and if there may be opportunities to include curveballs at the transfer level of learning. In the situation above, a curveball may include new lab results that create increase complications of the situation (for example, the patient is having kidney failure, the patient is pregnant) or, perhaps, the lab results were mixed up and each student has just received word that some of their results for their patient are inaccurate. These curveballs bring a sense of relevance and interest into the transfer level setting. More information on how to apply curveballs in the classroom is discussed in chapter 6 (page 194).

Create a Range of Assessments

While the most important part of assessment is using assessments with students to inform practice, teachers need to plan how to use assessments throughout a unit. The assessments that are developed are designed to inform teachers and students of progress across surface, deep, and transfer learning within the different types of knowledge students are expected to learn. Consider the following types of assessments.

- **Unobtrusive:** An assessment in which we don't interrupt the learning (for example, watching a student throw a football, observing students working in a group, or a student solving a problem)

- **Obtrusive:** An assessment in which we stop the learning and determine a student's level of performance (for example, a quiz)

- **Student constructed:** An assessment that is generated by students (for example, a student designs a project that demonstrates mastery of the standards in a specific unit)

The question is, do teachers balance their use of assessment types (that is, unobtrusive, obtrusive, and student constructed) across surface, deep, and transfer learning? Reflect on the following questions.

- **Unobtrusive:** What percentage of time do I use this form of assessment in my practice? What would be a small shift to deepen this practice?
- **Obtrusive:** What percentage of time do I use this form of assessment in my practice? What would be a small shift to deepen this practice?
- **Student constructed:** What percentage of time do I use this form of assessment in my practice? What would be a small shift to deepen this practice?

Ensure Tasks Incorporate Reading, Writing, and Talking Across Surface, Deep, and Transfer Learning

As students transcend different levels of learning, there is a tendency at the transfer level to shift to presentations, dioramas, posters, and Pinterest-style pieces of work. While these types of tasks add a degree of engagement, they should be used in moderation, because for students to gain knowledge, they need to read, write, and talk across levels of surface, deep, and transfer learning. A quick check that students are reading, writing, and talking is all that is needed here. A quick check would consist of reviewing each task across surface, deep, and transfer learning and ensuring that students are required to read text at grade level, write a response at the correct complexity level, and engage discussion at the appropriate type of learning. For instance, if students are learning about rhetorical analysis, tasks we would encounter may include reading Letters from a Birmingham City Jail by Martin Luther King Jr. (surface learning), writing a rhetorical analysis of the letter (deep learning), discussing the strengths and weaknesses of several AI-generated responses (for example, ChatGPT, Gemini, Perplexity, and Claude), of a rhetorical analysis in class (deep learning), and then writing a response a letter from a school today using King's rhetorical strategies in a unique context and presenting that letter to an authentic audience (transfer learning).

While the incorporation of activities that require cutting, pasting, and scrolling can incorporate a degree of emotional engagement, the inclusion of reading, writing, and talking ensure that students are cognitively engaged across surface, deep, and transfer levels. If tasks are missing these elements, teachers should simply infuse an article or book passage for students to read, a prompt to write, and leverage a discussion protocol to discuss the passages or their own writing and that of their peers. There are a number of strategies discussed across chapters 3–6 (pages 63, 95, 119, and 169) that teachers may use for tasks across each type of learning.

Now, as John Wooden (Wooden & Jamison, 2009) has argued, achievement should not be mistaken for activity. As such, we must remember that just because we are busy preparing our lessons doesn't mean we are making an impact on student learning.

Follow Through Via Feedback

As you are designing your units of study, you should receive feedback from your colleagues. It is important to receive feedback early and often. The longer you work on something, the less you will use new feedback. Higher solo initial investment equals less incorporation of feedback from others.

As such, when you are creating a unit of study, build the habit of receiving feedback after less than thirty minutes of work. Then, repeat it an hour later. The process of integrating feedback in this way is called the Tuning Protocol. The Tuning Protocol is a way to structure informal feedback that is short and sharp. See the appendix (page 204) for detailed instructions.

Monica Ready—Napa Valley Unified School District: Director III Curriculum, Instruction, & English Learner Services – Secondary—Doable Changes

Stay small, stay focused, keep it doable.

The daily challenge I face personally—and bear witness to professionally—is the politics of distraction. Early in my career I adopted the mantra: stay small, stay focused. More recently, I have added the last part: keep it doable. I work with middle and high school building leaders and teachers, and the most important problem of practice is: How do we support educators with small, doable habits that have a high impact on student learning? How do we inspect our impact on student growth when implementing small, doable habits? Two years ago, we began to center our instructional support toward these problems of practice.

We started with building leaders. My elementary counterpart and I began to work with principals to implement learning sprints. Teachers chose their instructional strategy based on student need. They monitored the progress of a small group of students over a 3-4 week time period. Throughout the year, every teacher was expected to engage in three learning sprints. During each learning sprint, department or professional learning community leaders met to develop the sprint, check progress, course correct, and finally reflect on evidence of student growth.

Throughout this change management process, I have learned three important leadership lessons.

First, it takes more than permission to stay small and focused. When we launched learning sprints, we encouraged educators to stay small and focused on one instructional practice. They could use the same instructional practice for all students, but they only had to inspect the impact it had on a small group. In reviewing learning sprints and meeting with teacher leaders, we quickly realized that our ability to engage in small, doable habits of practice was inhibited by our tendency to mix multiple strategies and measure their impact on entire classrooms. We learned how to get even smaller by providing training and support on specific instructional strategies. For example, teachers monitored how many times their multilingual learners spoke during a class discussion and set goals to increase that over a three-week period. We modeled and provided examples of learning sprints that identified methods for gathering evidence from a small group in a doable way.

Second, when everything works in education, educators need support staying small and focused on what works best. During our first learning sprint we focused on teachers learning the process. As we moved through the second learning sprint, we realized that the strategies selected were not those that would yield the highest results. We realized that teachers need support with pre-assessment data in order to determine the best strategies. As we use proficiency scales, we are learning how to align strategies to students' levels of learning based on the scales.

Third, it is essential to sit in the mess. Learning is messy and often uncomfortable. Educators are often esteemed as those who have the knowledge. Positioning leaders and teachers as learners is a paradigm shift. Keeping leaders in the "learning zone" requires showing up on site, creating space for them to share their challenges and championing them as they identify their next best step in the learning process.

Where are we now? The temptation to conclude our story with a resounding climax is strong. But I've learned that the greatest impact on student learning doesn't happen through a single event. It is educators' daily commitment to engage in small, doable habits and inspect student growth that has the highest impact. It requires playing the long game. As a leader responsible for 9,000 students every day, it requires giving myself and the educators around me the permission to stay small, stay focused, and make it doable.

Conclusion

In this chapter, we laid out a menu of strategic options for teachers to pursue, inspect, and improve habits of practice for both students and teachers. In addition, this chapter laid out specific areas of focus for designing and inspecting units of study. Remember that habits take time to implement. The tortoise in Aesop's fable is a good reminder that most success is built over time. Think of calm progress as you go.

Reflection Questions

1. How does your approach to developing new habits relate to what has been described in this chapter?

2. What are key questions that emerge for you regarding your implementation of current habits?

3. What motion habits stand out as critical for you to develop in your class, department, or school?

4. To what extent do your grade-level or department teams reflect on practices in regard to progress toward habit development and consolidation?

5. Which of the ten *Rigor Redefined* habits stand out as a critical need for you and your team right now?

Next Steps

1. To begin fostering students' development of each habit, teachers need to work either individually or together to identify an area of focus, implement the practice, and inspect the impact. The recommendation here is to use the *Need It—See It—Start It—Show It* process to engage students in the ten *Rigor Redefined* habits. Work with colleagues to answer the following four questions.

    a. **Need it:** What is compelling to you and your team right now? Bring evidence of student tasks, interactions, or assessments that support the answers to this question.

    b. **See it:** How will you make what you want to improve observable in the next six weeks? Identify one specific routine that you and your students will engage in over the next several weeks. Identify what the routine will look like for you and your students.

    c. **Start it:** How can you lower the threshold to move from evidence and ideas into action and from action into evidence and ideas? Review the specific elements of making habits doable in this chapter (small, stack, sustain, shelter, sprint, share) and determine steps you will take to ensure your routines meet these criteria.

    d. **Show it:** How will you demonstrate your impact to others? Determine who will implement the practice, when the practice will be implemented, and when you will show your progress to others.

2. Work in teams to design the following motion habits across a school year and across school years. As John Hattie (2023a) shares, "The greatest single issue facing the further enhancement of students is the need for teachers to have common conceptions of progress and standards. Moderating standards and expectations across teachers (and schools) is essential to student growth." One of the most powerful things we can do as teachers is design the following elements to ensure students' progress at high levels as they engage in the ten *Rigor Redefined* habits.

    a. Constructing learning intentions

    b. Developing leveled success criteria

    c. Creating tasks

    d. Constructing curveballs

    e. Launching the work

Developing Dispositional Habits

*If you're not prepared to be wrong,
you will never produce anything original.*
—**Sir Ken Robinson**

In the early 2000s, Green Day was one of the top bands in the world. They had sold millions of records and sold out stadiums. Their recipe worked. But when they went to record a new album they found they were exhausted and out of ideas. The studio they were about to begin recording in caught fire. They even contemplated breaking up. So what did they do?

They began experimenting with polka music, salsa, and dirty versions of Christmas songs. Instead of demonstrating anger and angst in their speed and sound, they shifted to juxtaposing a typical pop sound with anger and angst baked into the big ideas of each song. During this time, they ended up creating the album *American Idiot*, which turned out to be one of their best-selling records of all time.

As Apple Music (n.d.) states, Green Day was "ambitious, anthemic, a little clunky, but committed to the big ideas." Their commitment created a great punk album, and that album went on to form the basis of the 2010 Broadway musical, *American Idiot*. Green Day knew what to do when they didn't know what to do. They faced external challenges from fires and internal challenges between each other and their own ideas and, in doing so, triggered and channeled creativity. Green Day leaned into learning. They focused on what they wanted to do—they wanted to create a whole new form of punk that was more "Bohemian Rhapsody" than Ramones. The members of Green Day navigate challenges by experimenting with new ideas, work together, and play off the strengths of each person. And, they continue to practice and refine current and new skills. Green Day are expert learners.

Expert learners know what to do when they don't know what to do. They lean on their habits of learning and make lemonade out of lemons. General Electric engineers were given a modest budget and a short time frame to improve rural health care and ended up developing an electrocardiogram device that costs less than $1 per scan and is lightweight and battery operated (Acar, Tarakci, & Knippenberg, 2019). Teachers invented innovative ways to check for understanding with students on Zoom during the COVID-19 outbreak. Constraints require people to engage in practices or habits that are conducive to change in situations. People who have had routine experiences in engaging in both kind and wicked environments have the habits to excel in those situations. Interestingly, people who have developed dispositional habits for changing circumstances not only succeed in the situations but often end up producing creative solutions. As such, students need to learn the dispositional habits of handling change and facing setbacks so that they may produce creative solutions. How people respond to constraints delineates the learners from the watchers.

How do we cultivate the habits of learning for our students? We start by showing them how we, as educators, learn, and teach from there. Teachers are expert learners. The key challenge is for teachers to embrace and teach students the habits they use to learn. When we ensure students become their own teachers over time through short and sharp routines, habits of expert learning emerge.

In this chapter, teachers will learn about the key dispositional habits that enable students to develop a sense of personal and social responsibility over their own learning, routines for navigating challenge in both kind and wicked environments, the practices that produce effective collaborative working relationships, and processes for consolidating previously learned and new material. When students develop these dispositional habits in the aggregate, they develop a sense of confidence and humility as leaders and learners working to solve both in-class and real-world problems. This process begins with creating a classroom culture that is anchored to a collective approach to dispositional habit development.

Starting With a Culture of *We Do*

You don't change cultures by changing culture. You change cultures by changing the problems people within a culture routinely respond to. The routines, rules, and rituals that classrooms follow are all ways that groups of people *respond* to recurring problems. In Clayton M. Christensen and Kristin Shu's (2006) *What Is an Organization's Culture?*, they say, "When attempting to change an organization's culture . . . the fundamental unit of analysis, or the starting point, is the *task* [problem], not the process or culture—because processes, priorities and culture are a *response* to recurring tasks [problem]" (p. 8).

When you travel, you learn how people queue at airports, order food, and handle medical emergencies. When you start a new job, you learn how people ask for help, handle failures, and navigate the margin of error for being late to a meeting. These examples of "the way we do things around here" are all associated with routine problems. Classroom cultures are the same. How students and teachers respond to problems tells you about the culture. Who raises their hands in class? How do students handle mistakes? How do students talk with each other when they are in small groups? Classroom teachers are likely attempting to solve problems related to academic proficiency, building products or learning, ensuring appropriate comportment, or developing collective progress. Students in a rigorous classroom that develops dispositions and establishes a learning process focus on problems related to collective progress. In these classrooms, proficiency is viewed as a byproduct of growth.

To change a culture, a teacher must start with the problems they are solving. If teachers begin making changes to the ways people solve problems without changing the problems, then they will face tremendous pushback from the students, parents, administration, and colleagues. If you change the response without changing the problem, you are in trouble. Imagine you started to infuse growth mindset techniques in the classroom and talked about the importance of making mistakes. Yet at the same time, you left a grading policy linked to proficiency levels untouched. The real problem, then, is that you are evaluating your proficiency while telling everyone that you value progress. This inconsistency will keep everyone from engaging in the new strategies you are sharing.

In cultures that are focused on solving routine problems related to collective growth in learning, dichotomies about power become less relevant or interesting to teachers and pupils. The notion of a shared responsibility of learning or centering work as in *we do it* or *we do it together* makes a lot more sense to a community working together to solve problems of progress.

The lesson here is that the shifting responsibilities between "I do" and "you do" are underpinned by the shared responsibility of collective learning. The task then is collective progress and a sense of togetherness in learning, whereby everyone is in, as James Clear (2018) would say, action. Contemporary research supports this idea. Martella and colleagues (2024) found that the integration between active learning and lecture of approximately four-minute rotations led to higher achievement at surface- and deep-level learning as well as built higher confidence amongst students. Although the research of Martella and colleagues is taken at the collegiate level, the research gives us insight into the power of continued engagement with students and the power of moving between "I do" and "you do" through "we do."

Following are two broad action steps you can take as a teacher to create and maintain a classroom culture that is conducive to rigorous teaching and learning, and that is firmly set within a system that values shared responsibility for learning.

1. Build a collection of stories of shared growth.
2. Develop learner qualities.

Build a Collection of Stories of Shared Growth

First, change the narrative of your classroom problems. Marshall Ganz, a senior lecturer at Harvard and a leader in multiple social movements, argues that storytelling is a powerful way to begin shifting the problems cultures are solving. Ganz (2009) suggests the following three stories should be built within communities. Let's look at how these stories are developed with students (see table 3.1, page 66).

Table 3.1: Questions That Drive the Three Stories

The Story of Self	The Story of Us	The Story of Now
What are my values?	How will we work together?	How will we move forward to enhance our learning?
How have those values been shared?	What are our shared challenges?	What do we do to support each other as we face new challenges and opportunities?
How do I live those values?	What are some of our opportunities?	
How have I struggled to live those values?		How do we make this story a reality?

Source: Adapted from Ganz, 2009.

First is *the story of self:* Tell your personal story on the importance of pursuing growth over time. Talk about the importance of collectively pursuing growth through your own trials and tribulations. Answer these questions and share the answers with students.

- What challenges have I faced, and what choices have I made that show why I am moved to teach and enhance the learning of others?
- In this story, how do I describe the results of our choices and shed light on what gives us hope?

Second is *the story of us:* Here we connect our values together. We seek to learn the stories of our students, and we weave them together around the values that we share. As Ganz (2009) states, "One way we establish an 'us'—a shared identity—is through telling of shared stories, stories through which we can articulate the values we share, as well as the particularities that make us an 'us'" (p. 5).

Third is *the story of now:* What opportunities do we have to enhance our learning together? This is a place that intertwines our hopes and dreams. Here we look at the interconnection between behavior, emotions, and cognition to form a story that enables students to focus on learning. The story must illustrate that change is possible.

Develop Dispositional Habits

Students and their parents should know that the focus of the classroom is on progress and that is cultivated by four key learner quality habits and six learning process habits. All stakeholders need to know what such a culture looks like and sounds like and the learner qualities that enable students to successfully thrive in the learning process.

Ron Ritchhart (2012) has done an excellent job framing the need for developing a culture of thinking in the classroom. He argues for a set of routines that make thinking habitual. In addition, he is a strong advocate of bringing parents into the conversation of learning. For example, when I was a superintendent of a school district in the United States, I would provide parents with Ritchhart's resources to talk with their children at the dinner table, in the car or on the bus, and in the classroom. This resource was critical to invite and support parents in talking about learning with their children. Ritchhart's (2012) making-thinking-visible routines, paraphrased, follow.

- **Point out and notice thinking:** Note your child's thinking using the language of thinking. For instance, you might say, "That's an interesting idea" or "I like how you made that connection, I hadn't thought of that before."

- **Develop a growth mindset:** Embrace the belief that intelligence is an ability that changes, grows, and develops (Dweck, 2001). Praise your child's processes and efforts rather than fixed attributes. You might say, "I really like how you divided that project into sections to tackle it, what a great strategy" rather than "You're good at science."

- **Challenge instead of rescuing:** Allow your children to experience their mistakes. Instead of rescuing them, help guide them through the mistake as a learning opportunity. You might say, "What do you think led to this part of your project not working? Can you map out the steps you took and figure out where a step should change to create a different outcome?"

- **Encourage questions:** Help your child gain confidence in asking questions. Instead of focusing on asking them what they learned or heard focus on guiding them to develop and pursue curiosity. You might say, "What can you ask in this situation, what would you like to know?"

- **Focus on the learning instead of the work:** Always make learning the goal instead of fulfilling assignment. Discuss with your children the purpose of the assignment and what they think they may learn, and then focus on the learning. You might say, "What are you learning, how is it important, how does it connect to things you care about?"

In addition to understanding and being invested in developing the dispositional habits, parents need to have the language to discuss the competency-based habits. Beyond my own experience as a teacher, principal, and superintendent, I have found that in countless places around the world, the surface, deep, and transfer taxonomy appears to be the easiest to use. Five additional conversation starters to consider for parents related to competency-based habits follow. Recall that the six competency-based habits are explored extensively in chapters 4–6 (pages 95, 119, and 169, respectively).

1. **Tell me more:** Ask your child to extend their answers with examples and sources.

2. **Connect to context:** Ask your child to share an example of how the ideas in class connect to the real world.

3. **Connect to other ideas:** Ask your child if they have noticed any relationships across ideas within and across different subjects.

4. **Used to think:** Ask your child what has changed in their thinking after school. This could be a completely new concept or a change in their previous understanding. Simply listen.

5. **Show me the evidence:** Ask your child what they think about ideas shared in class. After they share, ask them what evidence they have to support their

ideas. Next, ask your child to share other perspectives and what evidence supports their ideas.

The aforementioned conversation starters with children are designed to be used by parents and their children in casual conversations to and from school. Parents can simply pick one and use it to support children in their learning how to learn (such as dispositional habits) or learning about core content and how it applies in the world (such as competency-based habits).

Collectively, teachers and parents work in a culture that is focused on growth. This is critical for the development and sustainability of dispositional habits. Develop the dispositional habits within a culture focused on progress. Change is associated with a system of teacher-led routine practices that occur Monday–Friday in class. The routines form habits that demonstrate the dispositional habits that produce students' abilities to know what to do when they don't know what to do. While there are a number of habits that could be a central focus, this text homes in on four key habits.

1. Engage metacognition.
2. Navigate challenge.
3. Work well with others.
4. Consolidate learning.

Habit 1: Engage Metacognition

In the book *The Practices of Adaptive Leadership: Tools and Tactics for Changing Your Organization and the World*, authors Ronald A. Heifetz, Marty Linsky, and Alexander Grashow (2009) argue that effective leaders step back and observe actions and reactions throughout the system they are working within. They do this to monitor and evaluate the impact of their leadership and make plans for making a positive impact on their organization. The authors use the term *getting on the balcony* to describe stepping out of their current actions, observing their own thinking, and determining next steps. This process of planning, monitoring, and evaluating our own thinking is known as metacognition.

When students learn to step back from their daily tasks and observe how they are progressing toward learning outcomes and identifying strategies to improve their learning, they can make a significant difference to their achievement levels. For instance, one set of studies found that metacognition produced the equivalent of an additional seven months of progress in learning (Education Endowment Foundation, n.d.). Beyond its overwhelming powerful influence on student learning, this is one of the least expensive ways to have a high impact on student learning, and it is the most robust influence studied in K–12 education.

Students who develop the habit of asking and answering questions such as "Where am I going in my learning?," "Where am I now in my learning?," and "What next steps will I take to improve my learning?" demonstrate the type of planning, monitoring, and evaluation of one's own learning. As students pursue the answers to these questions, they gain an understanding of the strategies they need to meet goals of learning, learn how to reflect on their current performance and the efficacy of their current strategy to meet goals, learn how to proactively seek feedback to improve, and begin developing ownership over their own learning. Some studies, including the largest synthesis of meta-analyses in education (Hattie, 2023b), show that the ability to conduct and act on a gap analysis between ideal performance, status of current performance, and next steps to improve has the potential to double a student's rate of learning. As a result, metacognition is an important habit to cultivate to improve overall achievement levels and to monitor their progress across the other nine habits.

To begin cultivating the habit of engaging in metacognition, students need to practice routines that enable them to identify the gap between ideal performance and current performance and then identify next steps to improve. Teachers should assist students in doing the following.

1. **Find the gap:** Determine the distance between current understanding and expectations of the lesson or unit.
2. **Take action:** Identify and implement the most effective strategies to move toward expectations.

As such, this habit has the following two key success criteria that teachers can use to work toward helping students meet: (1) use evidence of learning to inform next steps and (2) take action to improve learning.

The success criteria are guideposts to monitor the degree to which students are developing the habits of effectively engaging metacognition while they learn. When they use these criteria routinely, students develop the strategies to plan, monitor, and evaluate their learning. The following subsections illustrate strategies teachers can employ with students to develop the habit of engaging metacognition.

Success Criterion 1: Use Evidence of Learning to Inform Next Steps

Students have the wherewithal to know the goals of learning, and they can learn to gauge their current level of understanding and what next steps they need to take in their learning across levels of learning. This success criterion is defined by routinely using evidence to determine expectations and current levels of understanding. To enable students to develop the capabilities to routinely reach this success criterion, teachers work with students at the beginning of units and lessons to ensure that their attention is centered on the intentions of learning. Strategies that support students in developing this clarity include the following.

- **Co-construct expectations of learning:** Students engage in routines to determine the expectations of learning.
- **Engage in clarity checks:** Students are identifying the context of learning, the content of learning, and their current progress in meeting the content expectations of learning.

- **Monitor progress using leveled success criteria:** Students are identifying the type of learning (that is, surface, deep, and transfer) they are currently working through and the gap between their current progress and meeting all types of learning.

Co-Construct Expectations of Learning

When starting a unit, present students with activities that enable them to develop an understanding of the learning expectations. Students must be able to discern the following before teachers engage across the learning process.

- **Context:** Transfer-level knowledge
- **Content:** Procedural or declarative knowledge
- **Task:** The work that they are expected to complete
- **Setting:** The situation within which the learning process occurs

Telling students the differences between these factors doesn't create the level of clarity desired. Cognitive dissonance, a process in which we are confused by what we expect as compared to what has been presented, is a necessary ingredient. In a 2008 study, a researcher had students take a test and then observe a video that showed incorrect information, followed by the correct information (Muller, 2008). While the participants were confused by this experience, their scores on a physics test were significantly higher than those of students who simply were presented with the right information.

Using strategies that require students to wrestle with the goals of learning prior to explicitly presenting them is a process known as co-construction. Co-construction is the process of developing clarity of expectations together as a class. This process should be initiated at the beginning of every unit with students. Table 3.2 illustrates several strategies that teachers may use with students to prompt cognitive dissonance and co-construct clarity.

Table 3.2: Co-Construction Strategies

Strategy	Description	Example
Launch Entry Events	Provide a hook that establishes clarity of students' current learning and connects to deep and transfer learning.	Students are tasked with solving a local problem related to an increase of invasive species in their community.
Silent Protocol	Provide students with a step-by-step procedure without talking. Students then draft the steps and compare them with the teacher's description of the steps.	Students observe a teacher solving a mathematics problem and then attempt to write down the exact procedures. Students then evaluate their procedures with the teacher's explanation.
Work Sample Scramble	Provide students with multiple work samples and ask them to rank samples without and with a rubric. Next, students evaluate the differences in their ranking compared to the teacher's ranking.	Students attempt to rank six pieces of art without a rubric. Next, students receive a rubric and reorganize the samples. The teacher then shares the correct ranking, and the class discusses the differences across the three rounds of ranking.

Error Analysis	The teacher makes intentional mistakes and asks students to identify and correct the mistakes. As students correct mistakes, the class develops success criteria.	Students observe a teacher counting up to 10 and notice the teacher skips numbers repeatedly. The students correct the teacher's process and develop success criteria for future use.
Assessment Scramble	The teacher presents students with questions from an assessment that ranges across surface, deep, and transfer levels of learning. As students classify the assessment types, the teacher works with students to identify goals and criteria.	Students work in small groups to sort each question from an assessment across levels of complexity and identify the learning intentions and success criteria.
Matrix Approach	The teacher presents two to four different contextual examples of a learning intention and success criteria. The teacher then tasks students with identifying the potential learning goals and success criteria that connect the contexts.	Students use a Venn diagram and place contexts in the outside bubbles and work together to identify the potential goals that connect the various contexts.
Clues Approach	The teacher provides students with the learning intention and then a set of verbs for surface, deep, and transfer learning. Students attempt to create a set of success criteria and then evaluate their criteria with the teacher's rubric to identify differences.	Students craft a rubric and evaluate the rubric against the rubric developed by the teacher. They then determine the degree of discrepancy and why that discrepancy exists.
Hexagonal Approach	The teacher provides students with a list of words that are either contextual or declarative content on the board. Students place those words on one of two color hexagonal sticky notes. Next, students attempt to match the hexagons based on relationships between contexts and content.	Students work in small groups to fill out hexagons and then match hexagonal sticky notes to make meaning across each of the words. Next, students discuss what they think they will be learning.

The strategies mentioned in table 3.2 enable students to crystalize their understanding of the expectations of learning. For example, the Silent Protocol is a strategy where the teacher refrains from speaking, and students closely observe the teacher's actions to derive criteria for success.

1. Share the learning intention with students and ask them to write down the steps they notice as an example is provided in small steps. Share with them that each step will be presented without sound.

2. Pause after each step and ask students to write down a success. Have pairs of students share out similarities and differences for the success criteria of the demonstrated step.

3. Check student responses and then share the actual success criteria with the students. Ask students to briefly discuss the similarities and differences between the teacher's success criteria and the student's success criteria.

4. Repeat this process for the entire process or procedure. Once completed, ask students to reflect on the similarities and differences between the teacher's success criteria and the student's success criteria.

This approach places the onus on students to actively analyze and discern effective teaching methods. By fostering a student-centered approach, the Silent Protocol encourages critical thinking, observation skills, and collaborative learning as students collectively construct their understanding of what constitutes successful teaching practices.

Another example of co-constructing expectations of learning involves giving students written work samples and tasking them with identifying the learning goal and the success criteria and then ranking the samples without a teacher-developed rubric. Next, students are given a teacher-developed rubric and asked to re-rank the samples. Following the first two steps, the teacher walks students through their ranking. The teacher then asks students to reflect on what they got correct, where they were close, and where they were completely wrong.

For example, in one high school art class, students were given six pieces of art and asked to rank the pieces without a rubric. Students worked together to identify their own learning intentions and success criteria. Next, students were given the teacher's rubric and asked to re-rank the samples according to the rubric. Following this second step, the teacher walked students through their interpretation of the pieces using the rubric. Such strategies that combine student engagement with rubrics and work samples have a powerful impact on student learning. As Anastasiya Lipnevich, Ernesto Panadero, and Terrence Calistro (2023) state, "We conclude that teachers can encourage students to use both rubrics and exemplars to generate self-feedback and improve performance" (p. 136).

Engage in Clarity Checks

Ongoing checks for understanding throughout a lesson or unit should be brief and require only a few minutes of class time. Table 3.3 presents a few quick checks for understanding during a unit. Such checks should occur early and often during a lesson.

Table 3.3: Clarity Checks for Outcomes

Known/ Nuance /Novel	Students reflect on their initial thinking on a prompt by answering the following three questions: 1. **Known:** What did I/we get right? Why? 2. **Nuance:** Where was/were I/we close to the correct answer? Why? 3. **Novel:** Where was/were I/we completely wrong? Why?
To and Through	Students share with each other the context that they are learning the content through, the content they are learning, and the task they are expected to perform.
I Used to Think . . . Now I Think . . .	Students share with each other and the class what they used to think and what they now think regarding an idea.
Summarize Key Learning	Students write one to three sentences at the beginning of each class on the outcomes of the unit or lesson, success criteria, and their current progress from yesterday's lesson.

For students to see a shift in their level of understanding about the learning intention and to discern how their abilities align with the success criteria, the teacher may use a strategy called the *Known/Nuance/Novel protocol*. Students simply answer the following three questions. These questions could be answered through pair-share discussions, journal entries, or exit slips.

- **Known:** What did we get correct?
- **Nuance:** Where were we close?
- **Novel:** Where were we completely wrong?

One of the most important elements of habit formation is consistency. The changes that make a difference are small and sustaining. Clarity checks ensure that students are developing a consistent routine for determining where they are going in their learning.

Monitor Progress Using Leveled Success Criteria

Learning intentions and success criteria should be readily available for students after they work through the co-construction process. Remember the idea is for students to wrestle with what they think the expectations are of learning and then for teachers to illustrate the learning so they can work together or co-construct what the learning actually is for the unit or lesson. Leveled success criteria across surface, deep, and transfer learning lay out the pathway across the types of learning. This is important for students to monitor their learning before, during, and after a unit. Table 3.4 shows an example of learning intentions and success criteria. As discussed in chapter 2 (page 35), teachers should spend time up front designing rubrics across each level so that students can readily access and use these tools to monitor their learning.

When combining leveled success criteria with co-construction, students can determine the distance between their current understanding across each level of complexity and expectations of the lesson or unit. This process of finding the gap is critical for students to seek and use feedback. Several key routines that may be helpful for students appear in table 3.5 (page 74).

Table 3.4: Leveled Success Criteria

Learning Intention	Surface	Deep	Transfer
Elementary Example	Define executive branch, legislative branch, and judicial branch. Explain the process in which laws are made.	Relate the three branches of government. Relate the formation of laws with the three branches of government.	Critique the reasons particular laws failed or succeeded. Produce or present a solution to a local, state, or national problem.
Secondary Example	Define neutrons, protons, and electrons. Define bonding. Label neutrons, protons, and electrons. Explain molecule, compound, and element.	Compare and contrast neutrons, protons, and electrons. Relate neutrons, protons, and electrons to molecules, compounds, and elements. Evaluate the formation of compounds using bonding.	Hypothesize the formation of various compounds. Solve a problem using the understanding of the formation of compounds.

Table 3.5: Checks for Monitoring Progress

Entrance and Exit Tickets	Students submit responses to questions at the beginning and the end of class.
3-2-1	Students generate three words or thoughts, two questions, and one metaphor or simile considering their current progress in learning.
KWL Chart	Students reflect on what they know about this topic (K), what they want to know about this topic (W), and what they learned about this topic (L).
K/NTK	Students share what they know (K) and "need to know" (NTK) in their learning.
Error Analysis	Students reflect on current errors in their learning and reflect on the potential reason for the error and potential next steps to correct the error.

Success Criterion 2: Take Action to Improve Learning

Once students are clear on the expectations of learning and their current level of understanding, they need to develop the habit of using feedback to move their learning forward. They can do this through using the following strategies.

- **Determine next steps:** Students engage in routines to plot a course for action.

- **Take action from feedback:** Students engage in routines to take action to meet expectations in light of current progress.

- **Use differentiated feedback:** Students use feedback across surface, deep, and transfer learning.

Determine Next Steps

After students develop an understanding of current performance relative to learning expectations, they need to engage in routines that enable them to answer the question "What's next in my learning?" Table 3.6 offers a set of strategies that enable students to answer that question.

Table 3.6: Determining Next Steps

Strategy	Description
Learning GPS—Where am I going? Where am I now? What's next?	Students share out the goals of learning, their current progress, and what next steps they will take to improve their learning. This is often accomplished in pairs or small groups.
Third Teacher References	Students are tasked with finding a resource on the wall or in their resources that supports them in their learning and sharing that strategy with a partner and then taking action.
Four Corners	Students are tasked with answering a multiple-choice question and then physically moving to a corner of the room to demonstrate their choice. They then work with others at each corner to discuss whether they are correct or should move to another corner. The teacher then discusses the answer with the class and tasks students with planning a next step to improve their learning.
ABCD/1234	Students are tasked with answering a multiple-choice question and then showing their response using cards or a whiteboard that illustrates A, B, C, D or 1, 2, 3, 4. Students typically share their rationale before the teacher discusses the answer. The teacher then discusses the answer with the class and tasks students with planning a next step to improve their learning.

For example, inspired by the function of a GPS guiding individuals to their intended destinations, the Learning GPS strategy builds students' ability to develop a routine for assessing their progress toward learning goals. The process revolves around three potent questions.

1. **"Where are we going?"** prompts students to envision their educational destination, setting a clear trajectory for their learning. Provide students with the learning intention and success criteria along with a work sample of ideal work. Have students work in pairs to write a statement, create an image, or present the goal at the end of the unit. Ask probing questions to help them separate the content (What are we learning?) from the context (What means are we learning it through?).

2. **"Where are we?"** encourages students to gauge their current position, fostering self-awareness and reflective insights into their academic journey. Provide students with evidence of prior knowledge (for example, pencil-and-paper test, whiteboard responses). Ask students to determine the distance or gap between their current performance and the end of the unit. Model this step through self-talk. Give students process questions to stimulate their thinking and monitor your own reflection.

3. **"What's next?"** serves as a compass, guiding students toward the next steps required for continuous improvement. Students work in pairs to plot the next three steps they will take to improve. Have model steps presented for students and monitor the classroom asking questions of students to get them to ensure the next step is doable and center their focus on the goal.

After these three steps, use a fishbowl protocol to have pairs check in with each other on the three questions and their three next steps. Pose "I wonder" questions to guide students when the next steps are too broad or not aligned to the success criteria. Go step by step with students in pairs, asking students to ask one another each question and then randomly check for efficacy. Provide questions and corrective feedback each day as students check their progress.

Take Action From Feedback

Teaching students how to take action from feedback is critical. One way to build this habit is to give students specific durations of time in which they need to make changes to their current work and illustrate those changes to others. Teachers can offer the following.

- **30:5:** Students are tasked with making a change to their work thirty seconds after they receive feedback from others and then again after five minutes. The students then discuss the difference in their work.

- **Camera 1/Camera 2:** Students keep a copy of their original work and then compare it to a revised copy. Next, the students reflect on the difference with a peer and determine next steps within a specific duration of time.

- **On the Move:** The teacher walks around the classroom and provides brief directive feedback on what to change and then continually monitors changes on each rotation.

Each of the preceding strategies provides students with support in ensuring they understand the feedback as well as ensuring they act from the feedback they receive.

Use Differentiated Feedback

As students progress across surface, deep, and transfer learning, they will need different types of feedback (Hattie & Timperley, 2007). For instance, as students develop surface-level learning, they will likely need corrective feedback from a knowledgeable other. This feedback could be from a teacher or a peer. The key is that they receive direct feedback, make the change, and then reflect on the change in learning. As Stanislas Dehaene (2020) contests in *How We Learn: Why Brains Learn Better Than Any Machine . . . For Now*, pointing out errors to and then expecting students to correct the work is a critical ingredient of successful learning. For instance, a teacher may identify a mistake via a written comment or visually show the mistake and ask targeted questions to identify student understanding, which may prompt sharing exactly how to correct the error. Chapter 4 (page 95) provides several strategies to engage in corrective feedback.

On the other hand, as students engage in deep and transfer learning, the type of feedback they need to receive shifts from corrective feedback to approximate feedback. Akin to the traditional hot-and-cold game where someone uses cues such as "warm" and "cool" to direct others toward a desired destination, students need to receive feedback that points to an area that needs attention in lieu of giving specific corrective feedback. This approach emphasizes providing clear and immediate feedback by marking specific points in a student's performance while building assessment capabilities. One such approximate strategy includes the Dots strategy. The Dots strategy is a routine in which a teacher places a small dot on students' work as a visual indicator of an area of potential improvement or an area of identified strength. The teacher does not specify whether the dot is a strength or weakness, requiring students to reflect on their own work as well as the learning intentions, success criteria, and work samples that have been provided. Teachers monitor whether students use work samples, success criteria, or peers to evaluate their own work. Students then share their thinking in relation to the dot. Teachers then share the similarities and differences between their analysis and the students'.

Other strategies include giving students questions in lieu of specific direct feedback. For instance, if a student made a grammatical error, the teacher would ask, "What grammatical strengths and weaknesses stand out to you in this paragraph?" as opposed to stating, "Fix this dangling modifier." Or, imagine in a mathematics class, instead of telling students which answers were incorrect, we simply told them the number of items correct and the number missed and tasked them with identifying their own strengths and weaknesses and fixing the errors. Additional strategies that specifically target surface, deep, and transfer learning, including the routines for engaging in corrective and approximate feedback, are discussed in the chapters 4, 5 and 6 (pages 95, 119, and 169, respectively).

Ultimately, a student's ability to "get on the balcony" to monitor, evaluate, and plan next steps in their learning requires the formation of habits through small and doable daily routines. Those routines involve students establishing clear learning expectations and evaluating their current performance. Beyond using evidence of learning to inform next steps, students need to take actions to improve learning. Routines including receiving and using feedback to meet students' needs at each level of learning—surface, deep, and transfer—are critical. When such success criteria are combined, students can routinely step out of their current practice and answer the questions "Where am I going in my learning?," "Where am I now," and "What's next?"

Habit 2: Navigate Challenge

How do people handle setbacks such as receiving feedback that they need to correct their writing assignment, failed their test to receive the next belt in karate, or missed several questions on a chemistry exam? Research shows that some people face such setbacks by attributing errors to their identity. Those individuals have what researchers call an ego-oriented mindset and link feedback to who they are as a person. An ego orientation emphasizes a sense of competency relative to how other people perform rather than personal mastery in getting better (Nicholls, 1989; Smith, Cumming, & Smoll, 2008). If they fail, then they are to blame, and others are to be looked to from a place of comparison.

Other people face challenge by viewing setbacks and feedback as part of the process of improving. They separate their identity from the input they receive. Researchers call emphasis on improving learning, asking questions, and working with others a mastery orientation (Seifriz, Duda, & Chi, 1992). Those with a mastery orientation engage in routines that ensure they are thinking about how to improve from setbacks and feedback rather than focusing on their standing relative to other people's performance.

Beyond the orientation of how we perceive setbacks, facing challenge is also associated with how people face boredom and activities they lack interest in. No one initially loves playing the violin, swimming butterfly, or learning their multiplication tables. No one starts out being good at sounding out letters or lifting weights. Everyone will make a lot of errors and will likely do so in front of others, but to become good at something, you simply need to begin. An important part of rigorous learning is developing practices that support students in managing negative thinking and cultivating curiosity. As with the other habits in this book, it all starts with small and doable practices. The habit of embracing challenge incorporates the following two success criteria: (1) manage negative thinking and (2) cultivate curiosity.

Success Criterion 1: Manage Negative Thinking

One of the key elements of developing a mastery-oriented mindset is to engage in routines that enable students to learn how to navigate discomfort in learning. In the interview "The Parent of a Teenager is an Emotional-Garbage Collector," clinical psychologist Lisa Damour tells New Yorker writer Jessica Winter (2023) that "mental health is not about feeling good or calm or relaxed. . . . It's about having feelings that fit the circumstances you're in and then managing those feelings well, even if those feelings are negative or unpleasant." Students need the tools to be aware of their emotional and cognitive behavioral habits, and they can develop the ability to move their work forward in a productive way.

When we assign feedback to our identities, we begin a path on a downward spiral toward shame. Shame is based on one of the greatest fears that all people have: rejection. Brené Brown (2020), a psychologist and best-selling author, states that shame is:

> **basically the fear of being unlovable—it's the total opposite of owning your own story and feeling worthy.... Shame is the intensely painful feeling or experience of believing that we are flawed and therefore unworthy of love, belonging, and connection. (p. 52)**

Brown (2020) contrasts shame with guilt. She argues that shame is about who we are and guilt is about our behaviors. She says that while guilt is uncomfortable, it is a force for good. We can apologize, make amends, and change our behavior. Shame prevents us from believing in ourselves and making change for the better. In the classroom, not all errors should make us feel guilty, but they should make us see our errors and then change our behavior without the baggage of shame. We may still feel uncomfortable, but we do not attribute that lack of discomfort to ourselves or others.

Teachers can help students recognize that errors are about behaviors that can and need to be corrected rather than about identity by stating "this piece of work needs to include citations" rather than "you need to include citations." When students state incorrect things, they need to see that the incorrect things are simply ideas, not something that is tied to their identity. As such, students need to work on recognizing when they are in shame and when they are simply making errors or engaged in a behavior that was not appropriate or correct in the moment. Key strategies to use that enable students to manage negative thinking include the following.

- **Monitor orientation:** Students engage in specific routines for determining their current orientation (ego versus mastery) toward setbacks and feedback.
- **Structured protocols:** Students engage in specific procedures to reflect on using feedback and handling setbacks in their learning.

Monitor Orientation

Guy Claxton (2022) argues that our orientation toward our ego and mastery are omnipresent in our minds every day and can be shifted based on the situation we are in. That is, we operate under the demands of minimizing errors and engaging in near perfect performance. Attention is on others' assessments of our quality (am I going to get the mark or the applause I want?) and, at the same time, a mastery orientation of focusing on long-term competence through valuing errors and experimentation. He uses the metaphor of an amplifier to explain the presence of both orientations. He states that these orientations toward how we handle challenge are:

> **like the menu of sound modes that are built into an amplifier like a television sound bar. You can opt for drama or sports or music or documentary, and so on, and when you do, lots of small adjustments are made inside the amplifier that change the overall quality of the sound.**

To support students in spending more time in mastery orientation when they are in the classroom, teachers can work with students on recognizing their current orientation and determining next steps (see table 3.7). The modes we inhabit determine how we will operate in different settings.

Table 3.7: Strategies to Manage Negative Thinking

Strategy	Description
Cups	Students are provided with three different-colored cups that represent each learning zone. Students are tasked with showing their current zone in class.
Zones of Learning	Students are shown the zones on a chart in the room and are asked to turn and talk with a partner in their zone about what steps they can take to engage in the learning zone. Students then share their ideas.
Orientation Reflection on Progress	Students track their progress across the surface, deep, and transfer levels and address prompts related to their current orientation of learning.
Gratitude Prompts	Students answer several prompts through reflections that enable students to move toward a mastery orientation.
Monitor Your Mood	Students track their emotional fluctuations on the framework based on the work of Marc Brackett entitled RULER skills for five key skills (www.rulerapproach.org) also a process where students can track their emotional fluctuations throughout the day.
Compass Points	Students analyze their progress on a task and evaluate through four key prompts: East (exciting), West (worrisome), North (needs), and South (stance and suggestions).

One particular strategy to consider is to have students track their progress over time across the surface, deep, and transfer levels. In addition, students should reflect on their current orientation while working across each type of learning.

For instance, as students track their academic growth, teachers may ask students to reflect on the levels of learning they understand, are working through, and have not started. This can be accomplished by finishing three sentences:

- The levels I have confidently learned are . . .
- The levels I'm working through include . . .
- The levels I have not started include . . .

In addition, students should reflect on the orientation of learning they are experiencing at the moment and over the past few days. Students should write one or two steps they will take to center their focus on the learning zone.

- Over the past few days, I have been spending most of my time in the _____ orientation. My next steps include . . .
- The steps I will take today to spend time in focusing on my own learning include . . .
- My support I need to engage in mastery orientation include . . .

Another strategy includes having students' track their cognitive patience over time within a class, across the day within school, and across the day in its entirety. Maryanne

Wolf (2018) argues in her book *Reader, Come Home* that cognitive patience is our ability to stay focused within a task. Wolf specifically focuses on the idea of reading and our ability to reduce our novelty bias (the idea of chasing something new) and instead sitting with a book or an idea discussed in class. In the world of today, with countless distractions, a student's ability to monitor their patience in a task, especially in reading and writing, is a critical element of navigating the challenge of distraction. Strategies that may help students develop and track their cognitive patience include the following.

- Read a text to students, have them listen to the reading, and then discuss key takeaways from the text. After they discuss key takeaways, ask students to reflect on how well they were able to stay focused on the reading.

- Have students read a text in print each and every day and then reflect on the impulse of changing to other activities (including getting on their iPhone).

- Ask students to create a T-chart, listing in the left column the various activities they do that activate their novelty bias (for example, social media, texting) and then documenting in the right-hand column when they stuck with the activity and when they moved away from the activity.

Another strategy that can be helpful for students to center on a mastery orientation is to include reflection protocols that include being appreciative of the support we receive from our family, teachers, and community. Moreover, gratitude enables us to build a strong sense of self awareness. Gratitude reflections include brief discussions that focus on the abundance of what we have around us. Small, easy routines that teachers may implement with their students include the following. They may have students incorporate these gratitude reflections into their journals, use them as daily starters, or use them in exit tickets (Oppland, 2017).

- I'm grateful for these three things I hear _____.
- I'm grateful for these three things I see titled _____.
- I'm grateful for these three things I smell _____.
- I'm grateful for these three things I touch or feel _____.
- I'm grateful for these three things I taste _____.
- I'm grateful for these three blue things _____.
- I'm grateful for these three birds or other animals _____.
- I'm grateful for these three friends _____.
- I'm grateful for these three teachers _____.
- I'm grateful for these three family members _____.

Gratitude prompts are a great way to center students for the day and illustrate to them that we care about their social-emotional development as well as their cognitive development. Beyond using the aforementioned prompts, teachers may consider doing the following.

1. Look around the room and write down three things you are grateful for.

2. Write down those people that you are grateful for in your life.
3. Think about how you have overcome challenges, using the ubiquitous strengths you bring to the world. What are you grateful for today?

Implement Structured Protocols

Protocols are step-by-step activities that accomplish goals such as giving and receiving feedback, identifying the root cause of a problem, and developing possible solutions. Certain protocols are designed to ensure that students maintain a mastery-oriented mindset when they are receiving feedback on their performance. There are many structured protocols that support the development and maintenance of a mastery-oriented mindset, which include the TAG protocol, the Tuning Protocol, and the Consultancy Dilemma (see table 3.8).

Table 3.8: Structured Protocols for Mastery-Oriented Feedback

Protocol	Description
TAG Protocol	A feedback protocol that provides students with the opportunity to (1) tell them something they did well, (2) ask a question, and (3) give a suggestion.
Tuning Protocol	A feedback protocol that provides students with the opportunity to provide warm (that is, I like . . .) and cool feedback (that is, I wonder . . .).
Consultancy Dilemma	A feedback protocol that provides students with an opportunity to share a challenge and listen to others' thinking on how to solve the problem.

For instance, the TAG protocol is a structured way to give people feedback in a way that nurtures a mastery mindset. The TAG protocol requires that peers review a piece of student work and (1) tell the student something they did well, (2) ask a question, and (3) give a suggestion. Students ask questions in the form of "I wonder" statements that prompt students to think about their own changes that they need to make. For instance, a student may say, "I wonder how well this sentence meets the success criteria." This is in sharp contrast to giving suggestions under the guise of a question such as "I wonder if you can correct this sentence." Additionally, the suggestions students offer do not include personal pronouns and instead focus on how the work can and should change.

Success Criterion 2: Cultivate Curiosity

This success criterion is defined by using routines for maintaining focus and generating curiosity when facing boredom, setbacks, and new situations. Routines become habitual when we repeatedly engage with them. Do we engage the novelty bias as we encounter boredom and procrastinate or blame others when we face setbacks or encounter new situations? Or, do we engage with boredom to find the nuance, remain persistent, and understand our role in setbacks and encountering new situations? Employing the following strategies with students enables them to develop the right type of routines when they face boredom, setbacks, and new situations.

The following strategies prompt students to mentally plan before engaging in an activity.

- **Think Again:** Ask students to form one or more guesses to a prompt (for example, "What do you think is the answer to this problem?" or "What is your hunch on a potential solution to this problem?") before they start an activity, rank those guesses, and prepare to check their guesses in the middle and end of the activity. Then, they should compare their initial thinking with their current understanding.
- **Scaffold the Start:** Start with guided inquiry before open-ended questions. Lay out a number of questions up front, and ask students which one they want to ask or how they would change the question to be more interesting.
- **Praise the Pause:** State the following before you expect students to respond to a question: "I'm about to ask you about X—prepare to respond to the question with an answer, an answer and an example to support your idea, or a different question." Giving students an opportunity to process their thinking with you and their peers is helpful.
- **In2out:** Structure inquiry by following these steps.
    a. Students reflect on the question in writing ("in" = inward focus).
    b. Students turn and talk with a partner ("2" = pair-share).
    c. Students hold a discussion with the class (out).
- **Pass the Questions Around:** When you ask your class a question, make sure at least five students answer before you respond.
- **Four Corners:** When there is more than one answer that emerges from students, ask them to move to different parts of the room to identify their preference. They should discuss why they chose their selection and move around the room to the desired corner if they change their mind.
- **Present-Deepening Prompts:** Move questions outside the default "what" and "how" to "should," "to what extent," "where," and "when." For example, rather than just asking, "What is environmental racism?" you can ask where we see it occurring in our communities. In lieu of asking, "How do we address environmental racism?" you can ask, "When do solutions that mitigate environmental racism work effectively, and when do they fail?"
- **Keep-Inquiry-Going Prompts:** Prompting for deeper responses from students with "What makes you say that?" or "Where would I find out if you are correct?" pushes them to seek out their own rationale and precision in thinking.
- **Cue Transfer Prompts:** Prompting for transfer responses from students with questions like "Where do we see this in the real world?" or "To what extent can we see connections from this situation to another situation in your life (or our community or our world)?" or "Should we consider other perspectives?" pushes them to seek out different contexts and different perspectives.

- **Ask Students to Think About Their Thinking:** Questions may include "How does the process of questioning in this classroom extend to other environments?" and "How do you stay curious when things are hard or boring?"

Managing negative thought and building routines that cultivate curiosity will over time enable students to embrace the challenges they will inevitably face in life. The habit of embracing challenge must be more than platitudes decorated on walls or in quarterly assemblies. The habit of challenge must be built and curated each day. This is accomplished through small and doable routines.

Habit 3: Work Well With Others

The most successful collaborative work comes from the belief that everyone we engage with carries with them valuable information and that not everyone has the exact same information. As such, every member of a pair, group, or team has a desire to understand what others may see in a certain situation or problem and that they value any differences that emerge as opportunities to learn (Schwarz, 2013). In other words, a successful group cultivates a mastery orientation.

To successfully work well with others, students must engage in consistent routines that build relationships with peers and solve frequent problems of understanding perspectives, giving and receiving feedback, and making decisions. As such, this habit focuses on the following two success criteria: (1) develop relationships and (2) solve problems together.

Success Criterion 1: Develop Relationships

Relationships are a cornerstone to working with others. To develop strong relationships, students need to engage in small and doable habits with their peers. Table 3.9 illustrates a number of routines teachers should infuse into daily practice with students.

Table 3.9: Establish and Implement Expectations for Collaborative Work

Strategy	Description
Setting Up and Using Agreements	Set up communication norms for peers to give and receive feedback and solve problems.
Creating Roles for Process	Stimulate student conversations rather than focusing on task roles.
Build Upon	Support students in sharing out, paraphrasing statements, and then adding additional information to remarks from others.
Think and Wonder	Promote students generating and asking questions and then exploring the ideas of others.
Think, Feel, Care	Promote different viewpoints and consider the emotions and perspectives of others. Students are presented with a situation or scenario to consider. They are asked to "think" about the situation from a different perspective, "feel" about the situation from their perspective and another perspective, then "care" and consider why it matters to them.

continued →

Appreciation, Apology, Aha	Help students process their learning experiences and connect with themselves, their peers, and the content they encounter. Students share an "appreciation" of what they found valuable from the learning experience, they provide an "apology" or acknowledgement of any mistakes they made or opportunities missed (for example, not actively listening), then share an "aha" moment that brought clarity or a realization that emerged for them during the learning experience.
Feelings and Options	Help students engage with social and emotional dilemmas. It supports students in exploring different perspectives, considering their emotions, and practicing language for constructive and kind communication. This routine walks students through the process of identifying the dilemma, exploring feelings, generating options, choosing, and then taking action.

One strategy that can be immediately infused in a classroom routine is the establishment of collective agreements. Students should routinely use a set of conversational norms when working with peers to solve problems. Conversational norms focus on the quality and equality of discussion within a group. The conversation norms suggested here include the following.

- **Speak like you are right and listen like you are wrong:** Students should share opinions, ask questions to build on, challenge, or learn more from their ideas.

- **Check assumptions:** Students should look for the credibility and angles of their own ideas and those of their peers, and the sources they used.

- **Anchor your solutions to agreed-on criteria:** When getting ready to select a choice, students should go back and review the expectations for the solution as well as other solution options.

In addition to agreements, students should routinely create a set of roles that promote student dialogue and decision making. Roles that are likely helpful here include the following.

- **Credibility observer:** This role focuses on the degree to which sources are being checked and that the team is using sources correctly.

- **Process observer:** This role focuses on ensuring students are both sharing and listening to each other and that everyone is taking part in the discussion.

- **Viewpoint coach:** This role is primarily focused on determining the various ideas that are being shared and the similarities and differences between these ideas.

Once agreements and roles have been created, teachers should infuse routine practices that build students' use of agreements and roles in action. For instance, the build upon strategy supports students in sharing out, paraphrasing the previous statement, then adding an additional paraphrase while adding a connective. An example of this strategy can be implemented in four steps.

1. Place students in dyads or triads and provide them with a situation that you want students to reflect upon (for example, the role of AI in politics). Share that you will ask them questions and support them in building a conversation with others.

2. Prepare students to explain, build off, or counter other groups' statements. After they discuss the question, ask groups to share out. Once the first person or group shares out, the next group should paraphrase what the other group shared and then use a comparing or contrasting connective. For example, "What I heard from their group is that AI has a lot of potential benefits for voters. In addition . . ."

3. Once the second person or group shares out, the next group should paraphrase what the other group shared and then use a comparing or contrasting connective, such as "In contrast . . ."

4. Repeat this process across various activities.

Success Criterion 2: Solve Problems Together

Beyond setting up and using agreements and roles, teachers should routinely employ a set of protocols to ensure student dialogue is structured so that learning is moving toward meeting objectives. This dialogue could be focused on a myriad of topics, including giving and receiving feedback, developing an understanding of different perspectives, or making a decision.

Protocols leverage the established norms and roles to include each individual voice and enable the group's collective choice. Table 3.10 provides a number of protocols that meet the following goals. See the appendix for detailed steps to the protocols.

- Leverage protocols that ensure multiple perspectives.
- Utilize protocols that structure feedback so a student or group's idea is critiqued while their identity is separate and celebrated.
- Engage in protocols for students to make decisions.

Table 3.10: Group Protocols for Leveraging Voice and Choice

Strategy	Purpose	Description
Affinity Mapping	Multiple perspectives	Find similarities and differences amongst ideas.
Tuning Protocol	Feedback	Support students in receiving feedback by listening to positive remarks and questions to prompt their thinking.
Consultancy Dilemma	Feedback	Have small groups work through an individual's dilemma in learning.
What? So What? Now What?	Decision making	Support individuals in separating facts, inferences, and suggestions.

One example of the power of protocols is the Tuning Protocol. A *Tuning Protocol* is a structured process that tasks students with sharing their ideas and then listening to others give feedback on the ideas (page 204). During this time, the student receiving feedback doesn't share their opinions. They listen and learn. The power of the protocol is that it allows time and space to listen to the gifts of feedback. The protocol separates the identity of the ego of the receiver of feedback from the ideas proposed. This allows the receiver to fully engage in the process.

Habit 4: Consolidate Learning

To consolidate learning, teachers must engage in processes that enable students to make knowledge and skills *tacit*. Robert J. Sternberg and Joseph A. Horvath (1999) refer to engaging in using knowledge without awareness as "tacit knowledge." For instance, over time, we forget about our skills to drive a car, solve math problems, read a book, or tie our shoes. The practice has been consolidated or tacit.

The dispositional habits described in this chapter are themselves a type of learning that needs to be consolidated. The criterion for success with this practice is that students rehearse and reflect on the learner qualities. As students become familiar with them, teachers need to work with them on strategies that enable those routines to become consolidated into their practices without prompting or reminders. The success criterion for this habits is: rehearse and reflect on learner qualities and the learning process.

Success Criterion: Rehearse and Reflect on Learner Qualities and the Learning Process

Strategies recommended for rehearsing and reflecting on learner qualities are as follows.

- Slow things down.
- Space things out.
- Incorporate small changes in routines.

Slow Things Down

In the article "The Making of an Expert," the authors K. Anders Ericcson, Michael J. Prietula, and Edward T. Cokely (2007) argue that "the journey to truly superior performance is neither for the faint of heart nor for the impatient. The development of genuine expertise requires struggle, sacrifice, and honest, often painful self-assessment. There are no shortcuts." Teachers need to work with students on practicing and refining their learning. Following are several simple ways to slow things down.

- **Wait for an Answer:** Allowing time to think between asking a question and requiring an answer gives students the opportunity to better formulate their answers and, therefore, increases the depth of answers. It also lets students know the instructor will not be answering their own questions. Even when generating incorrect answers, deep learning is promoted.

- **Flat Affect:** In her book *Fourteen Talks by Age Fourteen: The Essential Conversations You Need to Have with Your Kids Before They Start High School*, author Michelle Icard (2021) shares that parents must show little to no affect when children react to situations. She uses the term *Botox Brow* to refer to the modest reaction parents should take when they interact with their children on a potentially emotional subject (for example, screen time or finishing homework). This approach is also helpful when students are answering questions in the classroom. The more teachers minimize their reaction to responses, the more students continue to think about their answers and those of others.

- **Rehearsal:** Providing students with opportunities to continually practice already mastered skills continues to support consolidation of such skills.

- **Quizzing:** Using brief, low-stakes quizzes keeps students actively engaged in their learning. Often, students will default to reviewing notes. Using brief practice tests will shift that habit from motion to action (Murphy, Little, & Bjork, 2023).

Space Things Out

Stop at key moments for students to summarize or demonstrate changes in their learning from feedback (for example, I Used to Think . . . Now I Think . . .) publicly (for example, everyone displaying answers on whiteboards).

- **Spaced Practice:** Have students rehearse or practice important skills during different sessions. Frank N. Dempster and Rebecca Farris (1990) and Nicholas J. Cepeda, Harold Pashler, Edward Vul, John T. Wixted, and Doug Rohrer (2006) found that when sessions were spaced further apart, students were more likely to retain material. Space learning sessions apart rather than mashing them together (Baddeley & Longman, 1978; Dempster & Farris, 1990).

- **Backward Fading:** This is a process by which a teacher slowly removes one step of a procedure and requires students to complete the missing step. Over time more steps are removed, and students complete more and more of the steps. This process often includes teachers asking questions for students to consider alternative procedures to address a problem.

- **Interleaving:** Interleaving is a process where students complete different types of questions across a variety of different topics. This approach to mixed review of problems is in contrast to blocked practice, which involves focusing specifically on one topic.

A core element of slowing down is to give students time to leverage Habits 1 and 2 (engage metacognition and navigate challenge) to think through their learning and determine the next steps to improve. Strategies that help in this effort during consolidation include the following.

- **Success Analysis Protocol:** This protocol centers students on evaluating their successes along the way in building new knowledge and skills.

- **What? So What? Now What?:** This protocol enables students to separate the facts of their performance, the stories or inferences they are drawing from their performance, and potential next steps.
- **I Used to Think . . . Now I Think . . . :** This protocol enables students to reflect on their previous performance and current performance. Sometimes, students need a bit of priming so you may ask additional question, including What would you like to remember that you found surprising? What is one thing I didn't ask you that you wanted to learn? What has been memorable, and why?
- **Critical Friends:** This collaborative protocol enables students to work together to determine strengths and potential questions to move forward in learning.
- **Take Away, Take Back, and Tension:** This reflective protocol supports students in identifying ideas they took from their learning, strategies they will begin to implement, and current challenges they are facing in moving forward.

Incorporate Small Changes in Routines

Consolidating our learning includes not only ensuring a high level of proficiency in one type of learning but being able to combine that understanding across surface, deep, and transfer learning (Hattie & Donoghue, 2016). One way to do this is for teachers to make slight adjustments to the task students are working on, the questions teachers ask, or the context of the problem students are working through.

While it sounds counterintuitive, one of the best ways to support consolidation is to introduce desirable difficulties into the learning process. Bjork and Bjork (2020) and McDaniel and Butler (in press) suggest that introducing certain difficulties into the learning process can greatly improve long-term retention of learned material.

For instance, a teacher may use a set of surface-level questions to reinforce student learning at the surface level but then begin to ask questions across the deep, and transfer levels (see table 3.11 and table 3.12, page 90). Or, imagine a student is learning about the transitional states of matter and is solving a problem about the evaporation of water and the teacher then tasks the student with looking at condensation of water or perhaps a new context like slime! These changes, known as curveballs as a metaphor for the slight adjustments to student work, include the following.

- **Change in the setting:** Change students' environment by having them go into the actual community or environment that they are studying.
- **Change in the context:** Provide students with a different contextual problem.
- **Change in the task:** Change the actual task students are presenting.

Table 3.11: Curveball Questions

Level of Learning	Verbs	Sample Questions
Surface	Name Tell Define Recall Recognize List examples Give examples and nonexamples	What information is given? Where does _____ happen? What are . . . ? What is . . . ? What part of the story illustrates . . . ? What events led to . . . ? What is the origin of the word . . . ? How did _____ solve the problem?
Deep	Analyze Argue Compare Contrast Synthesize Deconstruct Predict Assess	Would you have done the same thing? Why? How are _____ and _____ similar and different? What other ways could _____ be interpreted? What is the main idea of the story/article? What information supports your explanation? To what extent is that information valid and accurate? What is the author trying to prove? How do you back up your assertion? How does . . . contrast with . . . ? What is the point or "big idea" of . . . ? Where is . . . most/least . . . ? How do they work separately and together in different ways? What statements, insights, questions regarding symbolism, allegory, allusions, changes, and themes stand out? Why would the author _____? If _____ happened, then what occurred? What theme/thesis does the author create/change by _____? What are some of the limitations behind this claim?
Transfer	Formulate Generalize Produce and present Evaluate Critique Hypothesize Initiate Reflect Research	What would happen if _____? What would it be like to live . . . ? What parts of the story could have really happened? Where have you seen similar stories/patterns/themes in other texts or in the real world? What if the situation changed to _____? How would that impact the outcomes? To what extent should we . . . ? Of the various solutions, these . . . Where do we see alignment with our next steps . . . ? To what extent have others solved this problem? Where have we taken into account assumptions about the problem and our solution? Who is responsible for our next steps? Explain your reasoning and intent. I would like to check that assumption. You sound like you are confident in your answer/opinion. What questions do you have?

Table 3.12: Bridging Levels of Learning

Linking Levels of Learning	Sample Questions and Facilitative Moves
Surface to Deep	I think _____ and _____ are making two great points that may be related. I'd like to hear what _____ thinks about this point from the text. I feel like we might want to move to other topics; does anyone have something that they haven't had a chance to bring up yet? How can others build on the idea that was just shared? While I see we all have an understanding of this point, what about opposite points of view? For instance, take a look at page _____ where it says _____. Any thoughts? Was the hypothesis fully supported? Why?
Deep to Transfer	What might happen if you combined . . . and . . . in a different context? What evidence can you present for/against that extends to other contexts? To put that in context . . . To put that in perspective . . . What that means is . . . By comparison . . . Could you give me an example or an analogy to explain that . . . ?
Enhancing Conversations	What I hear you saying is . . . If I'm hearing you right . . . The author is saying . . . Where did you find a source to support . . . ? Who is being referred to/responsible for . . . ? Should the protagonist . . . ? I agree/disagree with . . . My rationale is . . . How do we find common ground? I predict the following will occur. Could you elaborate? Tell us more. Would you rephrase that?

Ensuring students experience a bit of confusion is critical as they consolidate learning. When a concept is difficult, allow students to experience and work their way through their frustration. When students are able to resolve their initial confusion themselves, deeper learning takes place (McNamara et al., 1996). Moreover, these types of subtle adjustments enable students to leverage metacognition, navigate challenges, and work well with others.

Incorporating Dispositional Habits Into a "We Do" Culture

Two important truths inevitably collide in our teaching: Change is difficult and painful, and our job is to cause change. As the new thing you are doing becomes a routine, you will gain *buy-in* from students. When you start, make sure that the work is small and doable. Pick a practice and stick to that for four to six weeks. You will gain buy-in through small and doable shifts.

People will not simply buy in to actual changes in behavior with the right blend of persuasion, research, and emotional appeal. They may buy in to the idea and may even plan and prepare for implementation. But the use of logos, ethos, and pathos doesn't move us to action. People must behave their way into buying in to an idea (Reeves, 2010). For instance, we may buy in to the idea of engaging metacognition, but for people to implement the idea, they need support, autonomy, and accountability (see table 3.13).

Table 3.13: Buy-In Factors

Buy In to Motion	Buy In to Action
Persuasion: Convincing others with logic	**Support:** Articulating out how people will be supported in trying something new
Research: Providing extensive rationale from credible sources	**Autonomy:** Clarifying where freedom of choice is in this work
Emotional Appeal: Convincing others with a compelling rationale	**Accountability:** Disagreeing and committing to trying something and exploring what we learn from the attempt

Conclusion

Developing dispositional habits is a process of building and refining the culture of a classroom as well as the heart, mind, and actions of each learner. Engaging in the routines in this chapter in small doable ways builds students' habits and a shared story of growth in the form of progress and renewal. Over time, as students develop familiarity with the dispositional habits, a new culture of learning of "we do" will begin to unfold in the classroom—a sense of shared power and responsibility over the progress of every learner. Moreover, these dispositional habits will begin infusing into the content-based habits related to surface, deep, and transfer learning. Over time, students will not only become expert learners but have expertise in what they are learning.

Reflection Questions

1. To what extent are your students engaging in Habits 1–4?

    a. To what degree are students engaging in these practices without prompting?

    b. To what degree do you have evidence of students engaging in these habits?

    c. To what degree are students requiring significant guidance from you and your colleagues?

2. To what extent are you finding trends and patterns with certain students in their development of habits 1–4?

3. How are you infusing Habits 1–4 into your practice?

    a. To what degree are you modeling routines that illustrate these habits?

    b. To what degree are you explicitly talking through these habits with students?

4. What are specific gaps in student practice and your own practice?

5. What are specific next steps in improving the development and sustainability of dispositional habits in your practice?

Next Steps

Go through the *Need It—See It—Start It—Show It* process. Work with colleagues to answer the following four questions.

1. **Need it: What is compelling to you and your team right now?** To address question 1, conduct a Learning Walk to observe the level of implementation and impact of these habits in your classroom. When observing, follow the What? So What? Now What? protocol (page 34).

    a. Write down only what was observed in class.

    b. Assign people to look at the interaction between two of the three elements of the instructional core.

        i. Teacher-student

        ii. Student-content

        iii. Teacher-content

    c. Debrief the observations by analyzing any patterns that emerge.

    d. Predict the kind of learning they might expect from the teaching they observed.

    e. Recommend the next level of work that could help the school better achieve their desired goal.

    Another option is to bring evidence of student work related to Habits 1–4 and discuss the findings using the What? So What? Now What? protocol.

2. **See it: How will you make what you want to improve observable in the next six weeks?** To address question 2, have staff complete an initial survey on the level of familiarity, employment, and inspection of teacher and student actions in the classroom as related to Habits 1–4. Debrief the survey data with department or grade-level groups using a What? So What? Now What? protocol. In addition, have staff identify small and doable practices within one of the four habits. Select the practice and identify what the practice would look like in the classroom in relation to the teacher, the student, and the task now, in three weeks, and in six weeks.

3. **Start it: How can you lower the threshold to move from evidence and ideas into action and from action into evidence and ideas?** To address question 3, lower the threshold of implementation by using the following strategies to make habits more doable.

    a. Small—make it manageable

    b. Stack—link it to your current practice

    c. Sustain—make it routine

    d. Shelter—protect this work by not adding other changes

    e. Sprint—start with a small group before you scale

    f. Share—measure your impact, discuss findings, and determine next steps

4. **Show it: How will you demonstrate your impact to others?** To address question 4, use the Consultancy Dilemma (page 204) or Critical Friends (page 88) protocols to discuss key learning of implementing the dispositional habits discussed in this chapter.

Making Surface Learning a Habit

*A child's appetite for discovery can be ruined by
an overly rigid pedagogical strategy.*

—*Stanislas Dehaene*

Surface learning is the development of readily accessible background knowledge and skills that may be accessed to solve problems (Hattie & Donoghue, 2016). This type of learning includes specific skills such as learning how to sound out a word or solving a quadratic equation and specific ideas within a subject area such as learning vocabulary in genetics or developing mnemonics to remember the order of dates in history. John Biggs (n.d.) shares in more colloquial terms that this phase is where we "first pick up only one or few aspects . . . then several aspects but they are unrelated."

The degree to which students learn at the surface level is related to the specific approaches teachers deploy in the classroom. Specifically, the most effective teachers teach new material in manageable amounts, provide substantial amounts of time in guiding practice, employ corrective feedback, and provide sufficient practice and review (Rosenshine, 2012; Mason & Otero, 2021). Interestingly, Barak Rosenshine (2012) finds that almost all teachers engage in the practices of effective instruction when building background knowledge, but the main difference is the degree of implementation. For example, in the article "Principles of Instruction," Rosenshine (2012) states, "The most successful teachers spent more time in guided practice, more time asking questions, more time checking for understanding, and more time correcting errors." In this way, the development of surface learning is an intricately interactive process between the teacher and the student. This chapter focuses on specific habits teachers should use routinely to build student knowledge and check and respond to current understanding with students to substantially enhance surface learning.

Mutual Learning

In Stanislas Dehaene's (2020) insightful book, *How We Learn: Why Brains Work Better Than Machines . . . For Now*, he argues that teachers can destroy a student's curiosity if there is lack of balance of interaction between students and teachers. Research concurs, illustrating that teacher-led instructional strategies have a devastating effect on students—an effect size of –0.26 on student learning (Hattie, 2023b). Given that a 0.4 effect size is the equivalent of approximately one year's growth in one year's time, lecture should be something that teachers stay clear from in their practices. However, student-driven methodologies are not a panacea either—for instance, discovery-based learning yields a modest 0.27 effect size (Hattie, 2023b).

Surprisingly, strategies such as explicit direct instruction and problem-solving teaching have effect sizes of 0.63 and 0.61, respectively, well above the one year's growth in one year's time threshold. The strongest case for the variance between these methodologies is the degree to which both teachers and students are engaging in action habits together. In chapter 2 (page 35), we discussed the variance between action and motion habits. Motion habits involve preparing or planning, and action habits are all about practicing (Clear, 2018). For instance, during a lecture, teachers are in action while students are in motion. Teachers are practicing their craft while students are observing teachers practicing. Students may participate in motion habits by taking notes and sketching out how they will practice later, but they are largely idle. As soon as teachers and students get into collective action by asking and answering questions, working through problems together, and acting on feedback, the effect size goes up significantly.

Discovery-based learning follows a similar pattern. In this inquiry-based methodology, teachers are largely in motion, observing students as they work through tasks in collaborative groups. As soon as the methodology adds teacher actions, problem-solving teaching emerges, and the impact on student learning doubles. When students and teachers are in action together, we begin to shed pendulum thinking of *either* students *or* teachers being in action and begin to see the pinwheel of mutual learning in the classroom (see figure 4.1, page 97). We develop what Ton de Jong and colleagues (2023) posit is an ideal combination of inquiry through questioning and direct instruction to ensure that students are not unassisted in learning and are rather in a synchronistic pattern together.

To support students in learning at the surface level, students and teachers work together to ensure students build background knowledge and continually check and respond to their understanding. This chapter illustrates two key habits for students to develop over time.

- **Habit 5:** *Build Knowledge Together*—develop an understanding of component parts of declarative and procedural knowledge
- **Habit 6:** *Check and Respond to Understanding Together*—refine and improve surface-level knowledge

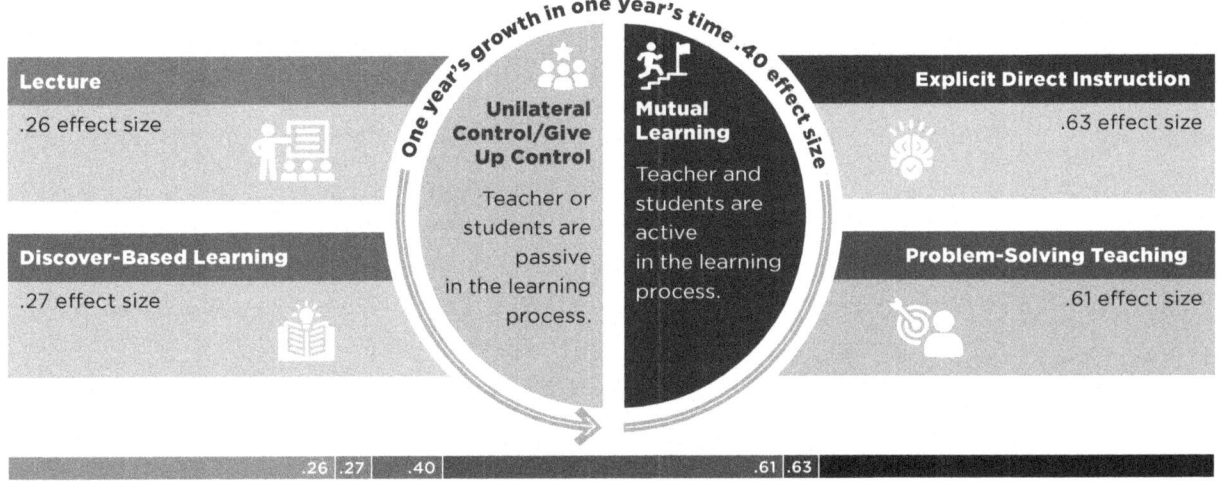

Figure 4.1: Growth flow chart.

Habit 5: Build Knowledge Together

As students engage in surface learning, they are developing new information that will link to concepts (deep learning) and contexts (transfer learning). Teachers must ensure students remain active in the learning by continually engaging with new material through two success criteria: (1) interact with new information, and (2) elaborate on and summarize new information.

Success Criterion 1: Interact With New Information

This success criterion stipulates that students actively engage with small bits of new information. When students are learning something new, teachers must offer lessons in which information is chunked in small, digestible bites that align to students' current understanding. For instance, if the aim is declarative knowledge, such as understanding the parts of a cell, then students need to be exposed to parts of the cell, not the entire set of organelles at once. If the aim is procedural, such as how to write the steps to follow a science lab, then students need each step broken down for them (Marzano, 2017). Strategies that are beneficial for building new knowledge adhere to the following criteria.

- **Chunking:** provides small amounts of new information that minimizes cognitive load
- **Repetition:** provides opportunities to experience chunked material repeatedly over time
- **Variation:** provides opportunities to experience chunked material in a variety of ways
- **Guided practice:** provides step-by-step support on meeting expectations of presented material

Each criterion in table 4.1 (page 98) maximizes students' mental effort on new information and reduces strain on working memory.

Table 4.1: Active Engagement Criteria With Surface-Level Knowledge

	Chunking	Repetition	Variation	Guided Practice
Example	When breaking down the process of photosynthesis into the key components and providing students with definitions of each component, the teacher spends time on each component and often breaks between components.	The teacher routinely shares the information in a variety of ways over time to ensure students learn photosynthesis.	The teacher provides the information using a variety of visual models to solidify understanding.	The teacher presents the components of photosynthesis and asks students to arrange them so they follow a logical process of converting carbon dioxide and water into glucose.

These criteria are essential for students to engage in surface learning. For example, guided practice should be considered a set of routines that occur throughout a surface-type lesson.

Guided Practice With New Knowledge

Teachers need guided practice routines to ensure students are active in the learning at the surface level. This involves spending less time on things like slides and oral rhetoric and more time on engaging with chunked material. Guided practice typically has the following characteristics.

- Students work toward completing a task and follow the steps just illustrated by the teacher.
- Students typically reference worked samples or have criteria out and visible.
- The teacher physically walks around the classroom and checks student understanding by asking questions and having students show their work and explain their reasoning.
- The teacher pauses the lesson and shares successes and challenges they are witnessing.
- The teacher continues to monitor the class for successes and challenges in meeting expectations. If 80 percent are proficient, they move toward extending practice. If less than 80 percent are proficient, they reteach the concept and extend practice.

The combination of guided practice with chunking, repetition, and variation ensures a higher probability of moving student learning forward. While certainly not exhaustive, the following strategies typically require only a few steps to implement, and they enable students to actively build background knowledge with teachers.

- **Direct Modeling:** This process involves a teacher demonstrating a specific concept or skill step-by-step, providing a clear and structured model for students.

- **Backward Fading:** In this process, teachers model success using worked examples and gradually omit specific steps or information to encourage students to solve problems and share new knowledge.
- **Zoom In, Zoom Out:** This strategy provides students with an understanding of specific ideas and the placement of those ideas within a larger idea.
- **Examples and Nonexamples:** This strategy requires students to discern examples from nonexamples.

DIRECT MODELING

Direct Modeling involves a teacher demonstrating a specific concept or skill step-by-step, providing a clear and structured model for students. For instance, teachers walk students through the specific steps of solving a Punnett square in genetics. This method is particularly effective in breaking down complex concepts into manageable components, facilitating comprehensive understanding. The process typically follows these steps.

1. Introduce the problem or topic and walk through what we know and need to know to address the problem.
2. Model each step or aspect of the content that you are covering in its entirety.
3. Demonstrate how you use the success criteria to check your understanding and to minimize error. Model the use of self-talk questions such as "How have I done?"
4. Repeat the same process but stop after each step and ask students to share what they notice about each step. Then show a second example and go through each step, stopping for students to discuss.

BACKWARD FADING

Backward Fading, where initial support is gradually reduced by slowly removing latter steps in the process of solving a problem, is a model for enabling students to develop problem-solving skills and grasp underlying ideas within a subject area. This process contrasts with forward fading where steps are omitted in the first few steps of a problem. Backward Fading is designed to enable students to independently work on the last few steps of a process or procedure as the cognitive demand of latter steps in a process are typically less demanding than the initial steps. Moreover, students have the opportunity to have the teacher show multiple examples of the more complicated steps. For instance, figure 4.2 (page 100) illustrates a Backward Fading example in mathematics in which the teacher is gradually removing specific steps from the procedure starting with the answer and moving back toward the questions. In this example, the teacher is using the same procedure while making slight adjustments to the task.

1. **The diagram shows three congruent rectangles A, B, and C.**

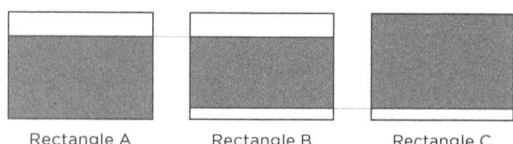

| Rectangle A | Rectangle B | Rectangle C |

$\frac{5}{8}$ of rectangle A is shaded.

$\frac{9}{11}$ of rectangle C is shaded.

Work out the fraction of rectangle B that is shaded.

How much of rectangle A is unshaded?	$1 - \frac{5}{8} = \frac{3}{8}$
How much of rectangle C is unshaded?	$1 - \frac{9}{11} = \frac{2}{11}$
How much of rectangle B is unshaded?	$\frac{3}{8} + \frac{2}{11}$ $\qquad$ $\frac{33}{88} + \frac{16}{88} = \frac{49}{88}$
How much of rectangle B is shaded?	$1 - \frac{49}{88} = \frac{39}{88}$

2. **The diagram shows three congruent rectangles A, B, and C.**

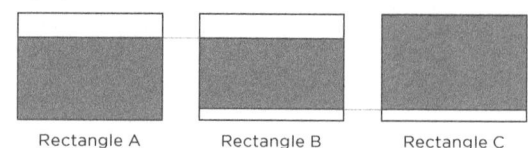

| Rectangle A | Rectangle B | Rectangle C |

$\frac{3}{4}$ of rectangle A is shaded.

$\frac{7}{10}$ of rectangle C is shaded.

Work out the fraction of rectangle B that is shaded.

How much of rectangle A is unshaded?	$1 - \frac{3}{4} = \frac{1}{4}$
How much of rectangle C is unshaded?	$1 - \frac{7}{10} = \frac{3}{10}$
How much of rectangle B is unshaded?	$\frac{1}{4} + \frac{3}{10}$
How much of rectangle B is shaded?	

3. **The diagram shows three congruent rectangles A, B, and C.**

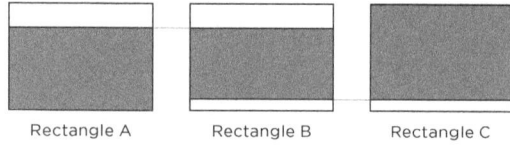

| Rectangle A | Rectangle B | Rectangle C |

$\frac{5}{6}$ of rectangle A is shaded.

$\frac{7}{9}$ of rectangle C is shaded.

Work out the fraction of rectangle B that is shaded.

How much of rectangle A is unshaded?	$1 - \frac{5}{6} = \frac{1}{6}$
How much of rectangle C is unshaded?	$1 - \frac{7}{9} = \frac{2}{9}$
How much of rectangle B is unshaded?	
How much of rectangle B is shaded?	

4. **The diagram shows three congruent rectangles A, B, and C.**

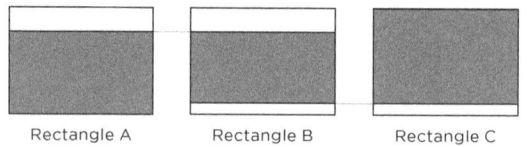

| Rectangle A | Rectangle B | Rectangle C |

$\frac{11}{15}$ of rectangle A is shaded.

$\frac{4}{5}$ of rectangle C is shaded.

Work out the fraction of rectangle B that is shaded.

How much of rectangle A is unshaded?	
How much of rectangle C is unshaded?	
How much of rectangle B is unshaded?	
How much of rectangle B is shaded?	

Figure 4.2: Backward Faded mathematics problem.

The following are steps for engaging in Backward Fading.

1. Introduce a learning intention or success criteria and model a successful example. Narrate your thinking. What have I done here? How does this reflect success?

2. Repeat step 1 with an additional example. Narrate your thinking. How is this example similar to and different from the last example?

3. Present a partially worked example omitting the last step and ask students to complete that step. Have students use the same meta-questions when completing the step (that is, What have I done here? How does this reflect success?). Repeat by removing additional worked steps or by providing different variations of the problem being shown or omitted.

4. Continue to fade the amount of information provided to students until they are completing tasks independent of scaffolds. Over time, the teacher removes all their worked steps, and they are replaced by students working through an entire problem.

ZOOM IN, ZOOM OUT

The Zoom In, Zoom Out process can be used to shift focus between specific details and broader contexts aiming to deepen understanding by shifting perspectives and scales of analysis. The teacher "zooms in" by focusing on specific details, examples, or data points to provide a deep understanding of a particular concept or phenomenon. This might involve analyzing a text passage, dissecting a scientific experiment, or examining a historical event in detail. The teacher then "zooms out" by stepping back to broaden the perspective, connecting the specific details back to larger themes, contexts, or historical trends. This helps students see the bigger picture and understand how the specific concept or event fits into a larger framework.

The following steps are recommended for using the Zoom In, Zoom Out strategy.

1. Introduce a broad overview of a learning intention using a visual (for example, a timeline of Reconstruction, a diagram of parts of a cell, or another concept map).

2. Introduce a specific aspect of the learning intention (for example, endoplasmic reticulum) and model as well as discuss the explicit link between the broader overview and the specific example.

3. Continue this process showing the link between the broader concept and specific example. Have students work in pairs to discuss and then share the explicit connections.

4. As students begin working on tasks, have them stop every few minutes and share with each other the links between the broader concepts and the specific examples.

EXAMPLES AND NONEXAMPLES

Students can greatly improve their learning when they are trained to routinely use tools such as rubrics and exemplars (Lipnevich et al., 2023). The examples and nonexamples strategy is based on the idea of teaching students how to identify different levels of success by reviewing exemplars with teachers and peers. The following steps are recommended for using the examples and nonexamples strategy.

1. Show students an example of success (worked mathematics problem, thesis statement, example of using appropriate citations).

2. Provide students with learning intentions and success criteria and walk step-by-step through each criterion in the successful example.

3. Provide students a nonexample and ask students to identify the first success criterion (for example, title as a question). Share with students how the nonexample is missing part of the criteria. Visibly display the nonexample and example and show the difference. Repeat for each success criterion.

4. Show another nonexample and ask students to review each criterion in pairs and decide whether it is correct, close, or completely off. Stop the class every 60 to 90 seconds and use probing and process questions.

With the advent of generative AI programs, teachers can have programs write work samples and ask students to evaluate the efficacy of that work and provide feedback. For instance, imagine a teacher providing students with an exemplar of an argumentative essay for a tenth-grade class. The teacher may have pulled the exemplar from a repository like Achieve the Core (www.achievethecore.org). The teacher could then walk through the success criteria and point out how the success criteria are shown in the exemplar. Next, the teacher may have an AI chatbot create an example and have students weigh the differences between the exemplar and the AI-generated work sample. This may also be an opportunity for students to give corrective feedback to the chatbot and see if the work samples improve.

Each of these strategies for guided practice supports students in breaking down new information into small, digestible bits of information. To ensure students learn the information, they need to interact with surface knowledge by making predictions, participating in building academic vocabulary, developing strategies for remembering processes, and engaging in surface-level tasks.

Interactive Activities With Surface Knowledge and Skill

As students are developing an understanding of success at a surface level through evaluating examples and explicit modeling, there are additional routines that ensure students are employing action habits.

- **Making Predictions:** This strategy requires students to actively make and evaluate their thinking during instruction to track and correct errors and strengthen correct knowledge.

- **Choral and Echo Reading:** This strategy requires students to verbally state (choral) with the teacher and peers or repeat (echo) academic vocabulary or portions of a section of reading.
- **Cloze Activities:** Cloze activities are surface-level tasks that require students to complete missing elements of a task.
- **Numberless Word Problems and Slow Reveal Graphs:** Numberless word problems is a strategy for understanding and solving problems involving by slowing revealing information and having students use guided questions to understand, generate, and solve problems.
- **Close Read:** This strategy is designed for understanding and solving problems involving literature.
- **Vocabulary Development:** This strategy is developed to enhance student academic development within the context that the vocabulary is used in reading, writing, and talking tasks.
- **Use Mnemonics:** A strategy for remembering bits of discrete information.
- **I Describe, You Draw:** This strategy promotes the use of academic vocabulary to develop an understanding of a concept.

MAKING PREDICTIONS

Making Predictions is a strategy that primes students to make predictions about what a specific term means, what they think the answer is to a question, and what may happen next in a set of steps to solve a problem. Students typically write down or share their predictions with others and then share as a class several predictions that may occur in the next sequence of instruction. Once the teacher reveals the answer, students discuss the similarities and differences between their answers and the one revealed by the teacher. This is a wonderful opportunity for students to evaluate the differences between prior knowledge and current thinking.

CHORAL AND ECHO READING

As students are building their vocabulary and constructing sentences, teachers should develop the habit of having students practice using academic language using echo and choral reading of material. *Echo reading* is a strategy where teachers share a term or read a passage and students simply repeat verbatim what the teacher states. This call-and-response strategy is commonly used when learning a second language, when people attend a sporting event, and when people attend a religious ceremony. Choral reading, in contrast, is a strategy in which students and teachers read information simultaneously. Incorporating such strategies in education builds student familiarity with core language in a discipline and a cultural expectation that everyone is expected to speak in the classroom.

From kindergarten to grade 12, students should have the opportunity to listen to core vocabulary words from teachers and state those terms in a low-stakes way. For example, the common terms in the field of genetics that students learn in elementary, middle, and high school include *allele, gene, dominant, recessive, homozygous, heterozygous, genotype, phenotype,* and *Mendelian inheritance.* Without practice, students will be unable to pronounce these terms and will feel less comfortable sharing their ideas. Practicing in public with everyone else builds confidence.

CLOZE ACTIVITIES

As stated, teachers should also provide all graphic organizers that are referenced during chunks of new content. However, we want students to actively engage with the material. One way to do this is through a cloze activity. In a *cloze activity*, either information is omitted, or additional information is required for students to complete, as in the following, for example.

Omitted Information

Omitted tasks range from filling in complete sentences (for example, The nucleus of a cell contains all of the cell's chr————mes, which encode the ge—tic material) to addressing short responses (for example, The role of the nucleus is to _____).

Additional information

Additional information tasks require students to improve or enhance information. For instance, students may be tasked with one of the following.

- After looking at a concept map, summarize the role of the nucleus in a eukaryotic cell.
- While this map includes the names of major cities and landmarks, articulate other features that would be useful to this resource.
- The following article provides a description of George Washington's childhood. What appositive could be included at the beginning of the paragraph to prepare the reader for the article?

NUMBERLESS WORD PROBLEMS AND SLOW REVEAL GRAPHS

The numberless word problems and slow reveal graphs area learning activities that can be used in a variety of subjects and contexts. The process involves reading a text (or a word problem) or evaluating a graph multiple times with different purposes each time. The initial reading is for a general understanding of the context of the problem, the second focuses on specific quantities that matter within the context, the third reading usually involves students generating questions that could arise from the problem situation, and finally, students are provided with the actual problem which they solve. Often, teachers will have students solve the problems they self-generated as a class before showing the actual problem.

For students who successfully complete the problem, either provide them with a new problem or have them use a different tool to solve the problem. For students who are struggling to complete the problem, walk through the problem together using the demonstrated approach. This process can also be utilized in reading. Students may start by reading for the general ideas within the text, then for the specific details and to answer comprehension questions, and end with a discussion on analyzing literary devices, themes, or the author's purpose. This process is typically referred to as a close read which is discussed below.

CLOSE READ

Close reading is a strategy for deeply analyzing and understanding a text, often used in literature and language arts but applicable to various academic disciplines. It involves moving between surface-level comprehension and delving into the complexities of the text to uncover its deeper meaning, structure, and authorial intent. The close reading process is not linear and rigid; it's an iterative and dynamic approach to reading that encourages students to revisit the text, refine their understanding, and engage with it on multiple levels. By actively engaging with the text through these steps, students can develop strong critical thinking skills, enhance their appreciation for language and literature, and gain deeper insights into the world around them. The close reading strategy typically has the following steps.

1. Ask students to read silently and note specific words or phrases that jump out at them because they are interesting, familiar, strange, confusing, funny, troubling, difficult, and so on. Share some of these words or phrases as a class. Questions to ask students at this stage of the reading are as follows.

    a. What can you already infer about the author of this text?

    b. How is the text structured?

    c. Does this structure make it easy or difficult to make meaning?

    d. Does this structure tell us anything about the author's style or purpose?

2. In small groups, have students read the text in chunks and answer a set of text-dependent questions. Text-dependent questions are those that can be answered based only on careful analysis of the text itself.

3. In small groups, have students create a visual image on paper that captures the essence of the text. You may also want students to include a three-word or one-sentence summary of each section of text. Groups can be assigned either the entire text or sections of text for this portion of the Close Read.

VOCABULARY DEVELOPMENT

Vocabulary development is an explicit strategy to build foundational knowledge of terms. The teacher provides direct definitions along with examples to explain the meaning of new words. Teach the students how to use context clues like synonyms, antonyms, and definitions within sentences to infer the meaning of new words. Then, support the learning by breaking down words into parts. During this time, teachers leverage strategies such as Choral and Echo Reading to develop familiarity with the words. Another powerful way to operationalize vocabulary development is through semantic mapping. This can simply be accomplished by having students discuss a word from a text, brainstorm related terms, group the terms, and then revise the grouping over time. Finally, provide multiple daily review tasks and low-stakes quizzes that require students to use the vocabulary.

USE MNEMONICS

Mnemonics are memory-enhancing techniques that can be incredibly useful in education to help students build knowledge together in several ways.

- **Facilitate recall and retention:** Mnemonics act as mental shortcuts, linking key information to familiar concepts, images, or rhymes.
- **Spark creativity and engagement:** Students can collaborate to come up with their own mnemonics, personalize them based on their interests, and share them with others.
- **Enhance understanding and application:** Effective mnemonics not only help with recall but also encourage deeper understanding by connecting information in meaningful ways to analyze relationships between concepts.
- **Promote collaboration and communication:** Students can learn from each other's mnemonics, refine their own understanding through feedback, and develop their communication skills.

Examples of mnemonic acronyms include the following.

- "Roy G. Biv" for the colors of the rainbow (red, orange, yellow, green, blue, indigo, violet)
- "HOMES" to remember the Great Lakes (Huron, Ontario, Michigan, Erie, Superior)
- "FANBOYS" for coordinating conjunctions (for, and, nor, but, or, yet, so)
- Stalactites hold on tight; stalagmites might reach the roof one day
- Dear Kate, Please Come Over For Great Spaghetti for the order of taxonomy in biology: Domain, Kingdom, Phylum, Class, Order, Family, Genus, Species

Other mnemonic examples include musical approach (such as "the ABC song" using the melody of "Twinkle Twinkle Little Star" to assist with alphabet memorization) and chunking digits (for example, 16425552489 to 1–642–555–2489).

I DESCRIBE/YOU DRAW

I Describe/You Draw is a collaborative activity that promotes communication and listening skills. The strategy requires students to work in pairs in which one student has a successful example and must describe the ideas clearly and precisely to another student who is required to draw or re-create that information simply from listening to the description. The describer needs to articulate their ideas clearly and precisely, while the drawer needs to actively listen and interpret the verbal information.

For example, let's imagine a pair of students (student A and student B) are working together in a mathematics class. The students face away from each other. Student A, the describer, has an image of a diamond with an inscribed circle. Student B takes a piece of paper and draws an image from student A's description. After they complete the drawing, students compare the drawing with the model drawing. The class then debriefs the following questions.

- What appeared to be the most challenging to describe or draw?
- To what extent did we use academic vocabulary in our description?
- What would we do differently next time?

The process is typically repeated.

The aforementioned strategies enable students to begin to formulate an understanding of new information. As they engage in this work, they need to elaborate and summarize this information.

Success Criterion 2: Elaborate On and Summarize New Information

As students engage with new content, they need to routinely elaborate on and summarize new information to solidify understanding. Teachers need to ensure that they form an active partnership with students in developing this understanding through a comprehensive grasp of surface knowledge. Akin to a swimming coach demonstrating the right way to swim the freestyle, the swimmer must then swim and receive further instruction. Both coach and swimmer are active. Table 4.2 displays strategies for elaborating and summarizing, which are detailed in the following sections.

Table 4.2: Strategies for Elaborating On and Summarizing New Information

Category	Strategy	Description
Elaborate	Full-Sentence and Academic Vocabulary Responses	This strategy promotes students' use of academic vocabulary.
	What Makes You Say That?	This strategy requires students to explain their rationale for responses to prompts.
	Clear and Muddy	This strategy asks students to compare their own answers to other students' answers, which may be different.
Summarize	Getting the Gist	This strategy requires students to synthesize key takeaways.
	Summarize the Story So Far	This strategy requires students to summarize key information from a predeveloped outline.
	Think-Pair-Share	This strategy requires students to summarize content on their own, pair up with another student to compare answers, and then share with the class.

Elaborate on New Information

The following strategies require students to elaborate on surface-level learning.

FULL-SENTENCE AND ACADEMIC VOCABULARY RESPONSES

To support students' academic language development, guide students to develop the habit of embedding vocabulary in full sentences when talking with peers and responding to teachers. In *Five Ways: A Series of Short Posts and One-Pagers Summarizing Some Everyday Classroom Practices,* Tom Sherrington and David Goodwin (n.d.) provide a number of excellent strategies that teachers may use in the classroom that ensure students are actively involved in developing declarative and procedural knowledge. Sherrington and Goodwin offer small, doable strategies that place students and teachers in an active mode of learning. For instance, Sherrington and Goodwin suggest that teachers require students to respond to questions using full sentences and incorporating academic vocabulary when they are explaining the information they are learning. Short and sharp strategies, such as this one, are powerful when done routinely. The power is in the relentless consistency of having students stretch their current habits of practice to using full sentences with vocabulary.

WHAT MAKES YOU SAY THAT?

When students are engaging in surface learning, this routine requires students to describe what they see or know about an idea or set of ideas to build explanations. It promotes evidential reasoning (evidence-based reasoning), and because it invites students to share their interpretations, it encourages students to understand potential misunderstandings and correct responses. Typically, students are presented with a question and asked to determine an answer and then respond to the prompt, "What makes you say that?" Students share their responses, and the teacher then provides the answer and the rationale. This process is repeated until students have developed a clear and accurate rationale for their answers.

CLEAR AND MUDDY

This strategy is a two-phase process students go through as they grapple with and solve problems. During the "clear" phase, students identify the task or problem and formulate an answer to the problem or task. Students work together to determine if their answers are similar to or different from others. Students then share their rationale for their answer. Students then move to the "muddy" phase, when there are differences between peer-to-peer answers and rationale. Students share out what they are clear on and what they are muddy on as a group. The teacher typically combines responses with additional questions such as "What makes you say that?"

Summarize New Information

The following strategies require students to summarize surface-level learning.

GETTING THE GIST

Getting the Gist is a routine that focuses students on synthesizing key takeaways, making meaningful connections from their prior knowledge, and preparing for further engagement with tasks. The routine typically begins with students skimming a text, a mathematics problem, or a question. Students then identify what is important to know within the text, problem, or question. They then summarize key ideas from what they have identified as important and share that learning with peers and the teacher.

SUMMARIZE THE STORY SO FAR

This routine provides students with an opportunity to analyze predeveloped information so that they may identify key points and summarize their own understanding. Initially, students are given a predeveloped outline or set of notes from a presentation. Students are then tasked with identifying the key points from the outline or notes and to create questions, identify additional examples, and write down other ideas that connect to the notes. After a few minutes, students are tasked with addressing the following prompts to summarize what they are learning.

- The key ideas so far include . . .
- The story so far is . . .

THINK-PAIR-SHARE

As students are observing teachers provide small chunks of new information, it is critical that students take an active role in the learning process by summarizing the learning up to a specific point in the lesson. Teachers should limit chunks of direct instruction to three before giving students time to elaborate and summarize key learning. Consider sharing information and then having students engage in a quick think-pair-share using the following instructions.

- **Think:** Take 60 seconds and summarize the new information.
- **Pair:** Share your summary with your partner using academic vocabulary and full sentences.
- **Share:** You will be randomly selected to share your or your partner's response.

Elaborating on and summarizing new learning are powerful ways to enhance student retention of new material. These approaches are buoyed by students and teachers working together to check and respond to current understanding of new knowledge. As with building new knowledge together, small, doable, and daily habits that are mutually engaged in by teachers and students make all the difference in the learning lives of children.

Habit 6: Check and Respond to Current Understanding Together

As students build their knowledge, teachers need to work with them to check the accuracy of learning and take further action to ensure proficiency. Teachers are working to develop the habit of stopping at key moments and demonstrating current thinking and acting from corrective feedback to improve learning. Two key success criteria include: (1) respond to surface-level questions, and (2) act on corrective feedback.

Success Criterion 1: Respond to Surface-Level Questions

As students process new material, teachers should use strategies that require students to respond on a nonvolunteer basis. The following illustrate examples of nonvolunteer strategies teachers could begin adding to their class strategies.

- **Popsicle Sticks:** Student names are placed on separate popsicle sticks, and teachers randomly select a popsicle stick with a name on it. Teachers call the name on the stick to answer a question.
- **Name Generator:** Student names are randomly generated on an online application or powerpoint.
- **Numbers on Chairs:** A different number is placed on the back of every seat in the classroom. The teacher draws a number, and the student in the chair that has the number called answers the question.

The shift in cultural expectations discussed in chapter 3 (page 63) is critical to develop the norm for nonvolunteer responses. To prepare students for this practice, teachers should provide wait time and show a flat affect when forming individual and collective opinions. When asking questions, teachers should use a series of probing and process questions (see table 4.3).

Table 4.3: Probing and Process Questions

Probing Questions	Process Questions
• What's the connection between A and B?	• What method did we use?
• Is there another example?	• Why did you put them in that order?
• What are the main reasons?	• That's not quite right—what were you assuming about factor B?
• What would be the most important factor?	• What made you think that?
• If we change variable C, what happens to variable D?	• Why do you think that would work?
• How does that idea explain this phenomenon?	• Where did that idea come from?
• What's the more formal/technical term for that idea?	• Can you suggest a different way of approaching this question?
• Does the graph just "go up," or is there a more technical term?	• How has your thinking changed since the last time we discussed this idea?
• Can you include a reason for the opinion to back it up? Remember we should be aiming for "I believe X is true because . . ."	
• OK, so if that's true, what about this?	
• Is there another way you can explain it?	
• What else could you add to explain the variation?	
• If A is true and B is false, what might we say about C?	
• In what ways is that similar to or different from the previous example?	
• What did you understand from _____'s response?	
• Do you agree with _____? Why?	
• Is that always true, or just in this case?	

Other approaches to questioning include anchoring inquiry to the four criteria of effective surface-level instruction. The questions in table 4.4 are simply suggestions and are designed to initiate a conversation with students. The power of the inquiry is the second question, or follow-up. There is often a need for teachers to have the right questions to ask students when they are learning new information. In professional learning workshops, the question of "How do I ask the right question to students?" is a frequent occurrence. I suggest that it's the second question that matters most. Use the first question to identify where students are in their learning, and then use the next question to adapt your instruction accordingly.

Table 4.4: Surface-Level Questions Linked to Active Engagement Strategies

Questions	Chunking	Repetition	Variation	Guided Practice
Questions before . . .	What prior knowledge do you bring to this idea? What prior knowledge are you confident about? Less confident about?	What do you think will be different this time you engage in this work?	How will a different perspective of this idea change your understanding?	Where are you unsure of completing the task?
Questions during . . .	What new information are you learning about? Can you provide an example of your new learning?	How are you improving your understanding?	What are you seeing differently in this idea or procedure right now?	Where are you stuck? Where are you moving forward successfully?
Questions after . . .	What do you know now that is different from before the lesson? What stayed the same?	How did the repeated practice or exposure support you?	How did the variation in explanation support your understanding?	How did guided practice support you? Where are you still stuck?

Teachers can also incorporate strategies that allow all students to respond, rather than calling on students randomly, such as the following.

- **True or False:** Students make a choice on whether a statement is true or false and then discuss why they selected their response with a partner or via a classroom discussion.

- **Agree or Disagree:** Students make a choice on whether they agree or disagree with a statement and then discuss why they selected their response with a partner or via a classroom discussion.

- **Four Corners:** Students are provided with a multiple-choice question and are tasked with making a choice and going to a corner of the classroom that is designated for that choice.

- **ABCD or 1234:** Students illustrate their choice to a series of questions using a small whiteboard.

True or False

Teachers provide students with a prompt that requires them to determine whether the statement is true or false. For example, a teacher may ask students, "True or false? Meiosis is the division of sex cells." Students write down their responses and then reflect on their responses during and after a lesson to see what changes they made. Student initial and future responses are often shown in public, and the teacher typically uses probing and prompting questions to better understand student thinking.

Agree or Disagree

Teachers provide students with a prompt that requires them to agree or disagree. For example, a teacher may ask students, "Do you agree that 3 is the odd one out of 2, 3, 4, and 8?" Students write down their responses and then reflect on their responses during and after a lesson to see what changes they made. Student initial and future responses are often shown in public, and the teacher typically uses probing and prompting questions to better understand student thinking.

Four Corners

The Four Corners strategy begins with giving students a prompt to address. For instance, a teacher may ask a class, "Which number is prime?" The teacher then designates that each corner of the classroom represents one of the multiple-choice answers. Students are then tasked to move to the corner of the room that represents the answer they picked. Students then talk to one another about their responses and are able to move about the room based on their response. The teacher then uses probing and prompting questions to discern student thinking. At the end of class students typically reflect on their initial answers and the actual answer.

ABCD or 1234

Teachers provide students with a multiple-choice prompt that requires them to select an answer. Students display their answers by writing them on an individual whiteboard and holding it up or holding up a preprovided cue card with either letters or numbers to demonstrate their choice. The teacher repeats this process multiple times throughout a lesson and shares changes they are noticing, as well as asking students to engage in self- or peer reflections (for example, I used to think . . . Now I think . . .).

Success Criterion 2: Act on Corrective Feedback

For feedback to have a substantial effect on student learning, students need to be in action when giving, receiving, and using feedback. Research supports this claim showing that students will likely make cursory adjustments unless the onus of feedback is shared between teachers and students (Hattie & Timperley, 2007). Strategies that support students acting on corrective feedback at the surface type of learning include the following.

- **Four-Quarter Marking:** A routine that provides a range of different specification levels of feedback, including direct corrective feedback, approximate feedback, feedback from peers, and self-assessment feedback.
- **Sticky Note Technique:** A peer-to-peer feedback process in which students give suggestions on posted work samples using sticky notes.
- **Quizzing and Correcting:** A routine in which students take low-stakes quizzes and then take specific actions to improve learning.
- **Deliberate Practice:** A routine where students pause from their current approach to completing a task and reflect on current process discussing strengths and weakness and developing a new strategy and commit to practice with feedback.

Four-Quarter Marking

Here, we are looking at how students can take a more active role in the feedback process. One strategy to ensure students and teachers are both in action is the Four-Quarter Marking approach. Developed by Dylan Wiliam (Hendrick & Macpherson, 2019), the approach combines both teacher and student involvement. The process includes these elements.

- The teacher marks 25 percent of what students do and then expects students to correct the work.
- The teacher skims another 25 percent to identify common patterns across the classroom.
- Students self-assess 25 percent with teachers monitoring the quality of that assessment.
- Students give and receive peer assessment for the remaining 25 percent.

Sticky Note Technique

The Sticky Note Technique is an approach where a teacher provides a group of students pieces of specific feedback on separate sticky notes or cards and asks students to determine which piece of feedback goes with each piece of work. Once students determine the specific feedback that is needed, they take immediate action and share it with the teacher.

Quizzing and Correcting

In "The Value of Using Tests in Education as Tools for Learning—Not Just for Assessment," authors Dillon H. Murphy and colleagues (2023) demonstrate that frequent and variable low-stakes quizzing can boost long-term retention of new knowledge and skill. Specifically, they state, "We suggest that instructors use frequent, low-stakes, cumulative exams and a variety of test formats and give students exams both prior to learning and following the presentation of the to-be-learned material." They illustrate two different visions of quizzing in which option B illustrates a high frequency of quizzing to better ascertain where students are in their learning so they can improve (figure 4.3, page 114).

HIGH-STAKES EXAMS (A)		FREQUENT TESTING (B)	
Lecture A	Lecture D	Lecture A	Lecture D
Review A	Review D	Quiz A	Quiz D + some A–C
Lecture B	Lecture E	Lecture B	Lecture E
Review B	Review E	Quiz A + some B	Quiz E + some A–D
Lecture C	Lecture F	Lecture C	Lecture F
Review C	Review F	Quiz C + some A–B	Quiz F + some A–E
Midterm A–C	Final D–F	Midterm A–C	Final A–F

Source: Murphy et al. (2023).
Figure 4.3: Example course schedule with high-stakes exams (A) and frequent testing (B).

Beyond frequency, variation is a critical aspect of quizzing. Using quizzes that include multiple-choice, short-answer, and fill-in-the blank, along with asking students to work in small groups to summarize the main points of a lecture or using closed-ended questions, can enhance learning. Once students identify their performance level, they should then take next steps to improve their learning.

Maree Karaka—Catholic Schools Office, Diocese of Maitland-Newcastle: Education Officer and Chairperson for Catholic Schools NSW High Potential and Gifted Education Network—Innovation Through Small Habits and Surface Learning

In a quaint cafe nestled within the heart of the diocese, the atmosphere buzzed and the aroma of freshly brewed coffee filled the air as I gathered the members of the gifted education team. Eager faces filled the room, each representing a unique perspective and expertise in the field. I had a mission—to cultivate a collective and surface-level understanding of high potential and gifted education research using Michael McDowell's *final word* protocol (derived from Harmony Education Center, National School Reform Faculty, 2014).

As we settled around a cozy table, I initiated the meeting by treating everyone to a cup of coffee. The gesture set a relaxed tone, fostering an environment conducive to open dialogue and collaboration. With warm beverages in hand, I handed out a selection of peer-reviewed research documents that delved into the intricacies of a systemic approach to gifted education.

The team, each equipped with a chosen document, sat in contemplative silence, absorbing the wealth of information before them. The weight of the topics—identification, assessment, twice- and thrice-exceptionality, underachievement, equity and inclusion, acceleration, and differentiation—hung in the air, creating a palpable sense of anticipation.

After the initial quiet reflection, members broke the silence by sharing a quote that resonated with them or offering insightful comments on the source material. As the words flowed around the table, a rich tapestry of perspectives emerged, weaving together a deeper understanding of the complex landscape of gifted education.

> The beauty of the final word protocol unfolded as each member responded to the insights shared. A dynamic exchange of ideas took place, enriching the conversation and deepening our collective comprehension. The protocol encouraged thoughtful reflection and considerate dialogue, fostering a sense of shared purpose and collaboration.
>
> Finally, the person who started the discussion had the "final word," summarising the key elements of the research document. This process was then repeated by all participants, creating a cascade of insights that further solidified our shared understanding.
>
> This ritual of collective exploration, guided by Michael's protocol, not only harnessed a shared understanding of our pedagogy but also laid the groundwork for informed decision-making. It brought clarity to our system priorities and allowed me to structure conversations that were meaningful and purposeful. This approach not only built the capacity of the team but also fuelled our collective drive for continuous improvement in the realm of gifted education.
>
> The power of small and doable habits is transformative when applied to the realms of surface, deep, and transfer learning. Michael's ideas, when viewed through a taxonomical lens rather than a rigid hierarchy, emphasize the interconnectedness of these learning processes. Engaging in small routines, I've witnessed the profound impact of consistent efforts on individual and collective understanding. Surface learning, often underestimated, plays a pivotal role as it serves as the foundation for deep and transfer learning. By incorporating manageable routines into our professional practices, such as the initial silence and absorption of foundational knowledge, we've cultivated a shared background. This shared foundation has proven crucial for meaningful discussions, informed decision-making, advocacy, and the continuous improvement of our approach to gifted education. Leading by example, I've encouraged the team to embrace these small habits, recognizing that it is the cumulative effect of these routines that propels us toward collective expertise and sustained innovation.

Conclusion

As with each type of learning, students gain understanding through the development of habits. Developing surface learning is a communal process requiring teachers and students to work together to ensure new ideas are formed. The formation of surface learning helps teachers to break information down and have students interact with the content, which includes engaging in tasks, elaborating on and summarizing information, and engaging in conversations through target inquiry and corrective feedback. As always, the emphasis should not be on swinging to focusing on surface learning but on finding small and doable, short and sharp practices that can be incorporated into your current practice and that of your students, so that you find balance. Be the pinwheel, not the pendulum.

Reflection Questions

1. What stood out or surprised you in this chapter?

2. After reviewing the results of the *Rigor Redefined* survey, which surface-level habits are students regularly engaging in? With which surface-level habits are students requiring significant guidance from you and your colleagues?

3. What specific routines are you already familiar with in enhancing student learning?

4. What specific routines stood out to you as a key area of potential inclusion in your practice?

Rigor Redefined © 2024 Solution Tree Press • SolutionTree.com
Visit **go.SolutionTree.com/instruction** to download this free reproducible.

Next Steps

Go through the *Need It—See It—Start It—Show It* process. Work with colleagues to answer the following four questions.

1. **Need it: What is compelling to you and your team right now?** To address question 1, conduct a Learning Walk to observe the level of implementation and impact of these habits in your classroom. When observing, follow the What? So What? Now What? protocol.

    a. Write down only what was observed in class.

    b. Assign people to look at the interaction between two of the three elements of the instructional core.

        i. Teacher-student

        ii. Student-content

        iii. Teacher-content

    c. Debrief the observations by analyzing any patterns that emerge.

    d. Predict the kind of learning they might expect from the teaching they observed.

    e. Recommend the next level of work that could help the school better achieve their desired goal.

    Another option is to bring evidence of student work related to Habits 5–6 and discuss the findings using the What? So What? Now What? protocol (page 34).

2. **See it: How will you make what you want to improve observable in the next six weeks?** To address question 2, have staff complete an initial survey on the level of familiarity, employment, and inspection of teacher and student actions in the classroom as related to Habits 5–6. Debrief the survey data with department or grade-level groups (see survey in chapter 1, page 33). In addition, have staff identify a small and doable practice within one of the four habits. Select the practice and identify what the practice would look like in the classroom in relation to the teacher, the student, and the task now, in three weeks, and in six weeks.

3. **Start it: How can you lower the threshold to move from evidence and ideas into action and from action into evidence and ideas?** To address question 3, lower the threshold of implementation by using the following strategies to make habits more doable.

    a. Small—make it manageable

    b. Stack—link it to your current practice

    c. Sustain—make it routine

    d. Shelter—protect this work by not adding other changes

    e. Sprint—start with a small group before you scale

    f. Share—measure your impact, discuss findings, and determine next steps

4. **Show it: How will you demonstrate your impact to others?** To address question 4, use the Consultancy Dilemma (page 204) or Critical Friends (page 88) protocols to discuss key learning of implementing the dispositional habits discussed in this chapter.

Developing the Habits of Deep Learning

A loud mind is greater than a loud mouth.
—*Matshona Dhliwayo*

Why does the body maintain a constant temperature? Why did Picasso paint *Guernica*? Why are themes of forgiveness repeated throughout novels? These are questions that require students to relate ideas, examine underlying principles, check evidence, make arguments, and examine the arguments of others (Hattie & Donoghue, 2016). For instance, to answer the first question, a student would need to relate the hypothalamus to internal temperature, share the underlying principle of homeostasis, provide evidence from their textbook or a research paper, and be prepared to answer questions or receive challenging feedback from others. In the later questions, students may link the themes from *For Whom the Bell Tolls* to the creation of *Guernica* and relate themes from books of atonement to make a case for the repeated themes of forgiveness. All these questions require students to integrate ideas into a whole.

Deep learning is the process of combining ideas to form a coherent whole. Students must develop the ability to make connections and identify patterns of knowledge and then apply that knowledge to solve problems with others that often have differing perspectives and ideas. To effectively develop and apply deep learning, students must engage in deliberate mental processing of information (McTighe, Silver, & Perini, 2020). Research shows that students need to engage in routines that promote organizing and elaborating ideas and evaluating and reflecting on those ideas through problem solving (Hattie & Donoghue, 2016). In addition, deep learning is socially constructed, requiring social interactions by seeking help from peers (effect size 0.83) and engaging in classroom discussion (0.75; Hattie & Donoghue, 2016). This chapter focuses on routines that promote the active development and application of deep learning.

Defining Deep Learning

Deep learning is the process of developing conceptual understandings within a discipline. Jay McTighe and Grant Wiggins (2013) state that understandings "are abstractions, not facts, they are not 'teachable' in the conventional sense" (p. 31). Specifically, enduring understandings are ideas that "reside at the heart of all disciplines" (McTighe & Wiggins, 2013):

> **[They are] timeless, cut across topics, and are embodied in *concepts* (for example, the modern "flat" world), *themes* (for example, love conquers all), *issues and debates* (for example, nature versus nurture), *paradox* (for example, poverty amidst plenty), *complex processes* (for example, scientific isolation and control of variables), *persistent problems and challenges* (for example, global warming), *influential theories* (for example, manifest destiny), *established policies* (for example, mandatory retirement age), *key assumptions* (for example, the markets are rational), or *differing perspectives* (for example, terrorists versus freedom fighter). (p. 30)**

Examples of how an enduring understanding might be communicated include the following.

- Great literature from various cultures explores enduring themes and reveals recurrent aspects of the human condition.
- Analysis and display often reveal patterns in data, enabling us to make predictions with degrees of confidence.
- Humans process both verbal and nonverbal messages simultaneously. Your communication becomes more effective when verbal and nonverbal messages are aligned.

For deep learning to occur, teachers must use strategies to support students in constructing meaning out of seemingly abstract notions and disconnected facts. Here again, McTighe and Wiggins (2013) share that "deep learning can be gained only through guided inferences whereby the learner is helped to make, recognize, or verify a conclusion" (p. 31). In this way, explicit direct instruction will likely only model a teacher's deep knowledge rather than enabling students to develop their own deep learning. As such, the typical explicit instructional strategies that have a substantial impact at surface-level learning have less impact and may even be counterproductive at this level of learning.

The process of finding patterns and structures among ideas that occurs when students search for understanding by exploring relationships between ideas combines synthesis, analysis, and evaluation. Synthesis, a process in which students formulate a new scheme for classifying and bringing ideas together, is the essence of deep learning. For instance, a student's ability to relate the internal similarities between eukaryotic and prokaryotic cells, see the relationships between rising and falling action in a story, form a theme when writing a paper, recognize the repeated themes within a text, or develop an understanding of the patterns of adding with tens are all ways to put parts of surface learning into a new whole.

Whereas synthesis brings new ideas together, analysis breaks ideas down into component parts to discriminate the uniqueness and similarity of each part. For example, eukaryotic cells and prokaryotic cells are both the building blocks of life, yet they also have distinct organelles for their specific functions. While all narratives carry rising and falling action, they are conveyed across various contexts and situations. There are multiple tools and representations of using the power of ten to add as well as to engage in other orders of operations. To develop analysis, students spend time showing the differences between the distinct organelles, the aspects of a narrative within a coherent whole, and the unique differences between tools.

Finally, evaluation is focused on assigning judgment to ideas, materials, and claims. These judgments are based on internal and external criteria. Internal criteria are often the elements that are required for the specific task. For instance, an effective argumentative essay requires a thesis statement and well-researched information to back an assertion. Moreover, an effective essay requires the consideration of other points of view. Internal criteria focus on consistency of the written material and the adequacy of claims in relation to evidence. In addition to internal criteria, judgments of an argumentative essay are going to be based on external criteria, which include the relevance, purpose, and audience of the paper. Does the paper create a level of relevance to the reader? A student's ability to evaluate the degree to which a claim is supported or refuted requires an understanding of relationships among ideas. In this example, students are developing deep learning by making links between claims, evidence, and reasoning.

Deep learning is the process of making meaning across multiple ideas or facts. Making meaning requires students to analyze, synthesize, and evaluate information. Surface routines such as direct instruction will not likely yield the results of deep learning at a desired rate of learning. Instead, students need to engage in deep thinking routines that require analysis, synthesis, and evaluation between ideas, and this, it turns out, is largely accomplished in social situations.

Developing Deep Learning Habits

"Those who do the talking do the learning" is a common adage in educational circles. While the research shows that classroom discussion has a high probability of being effective, the degree to which we see students relate ideas within a discussion is minimal

(Hattie, 2023b). The low percentages of students who spend time forming relationships across ideas and then using those relationships to make sound arguments are significant. Research shows that the use of high-quality classroom discussion occurs at the following rates (Hattie, 2023b).

- 60 percent of classes = 0 minutes of classroom discussion
- 15 percent of classes = 2 minutes or less per day
- 25 percent of classes = less than 15–30 seconds per day

As such, while classroom discussion bolsters student learning, the degree to which we actualize this strategy is rare at best. While students may spend time talking in class, the question is, What is the degree of complexity in their discussions? Therefore, the adage should change to "those who do the *quality* talking do the learning."

The frequency of quality writing in the classroom is akin to that of quality classroom discussion. In 2012, almost a decade before the COVID-19 pandemic, the Nation's Report Card found that three out of four twelfth-grade students were unable to write coherent argumentative essays (National Center for Education Statistics, 2011).

In terms of the frequency and quality of reading, the results are equally sobering. Between 2015 and 2019, proficiency of twelfth graders grew from 27 percent to 37 percent (Wang & Troia, 2023). To put this in perspective, the number of low-proficient readers graduating amounts to the total population of Idaho, Montana, and Rhode Island combined. Imagine if the entire population of these three states could not discern an opinion from a press release or a narrative from an argument.

Reading results are similar for younger students. Specifically, 33 percent of fourth graders performed at or above the National Assessment of Educational Progress proficient level, which was only 2 percentage points lower in 2022 compared to 2019. This is not a COVID-19 problem. This is a reading problem.

Obviously, students need to engage in high levels of reading, writing, and talking. Less obvious is that they need to engage in complex reading, writing, and talking. They must go beyond surface-level procedures and comprehension. Teachers must employ strategies that enable students to build habits for forming basic relationships between ideas, constructing and deconstructing arguments that are anchored to relationships across ideas, and consolidating deep learning through repetition and feedback.

Specifically, students must build the following habits.

- **Habit 7:** *Develop conceptual understanding*—develop relationships between ideas with others
- **Habit 8:** *Apply conceptual understanding*—answer and evaluate responses to questions that require relating ideas between and across ideas

The remainder of this chapter offers a number of routines that teachers can employ in the classroom to develop the habits of building and applying conceptual understanding.

Habit 7: Develop Conceptual Understanding

To develop students' conceptual understanding, teachers need to concentrate on small, doable deep learning habits that they engage in each day. The success criterion for this habit has teachers engage students in routines that involve comparing and contrasting concepts through reading, writing, and talking tasks.

Success Criterion: Compare and Contrast Concepts

To support students in developing habits recognizing relationships between ideas, they need to analyze, synthesize, and evaluate ideas and do so within social interactions with peers, as in the following approaches.

- **Gradually build complex dialogue:** Incrementally developing student complex thought between peers by starting with single sentences and moving toward complicated exchanges amongst peers
- **Infuse thinking routines:** Embedding short protocols that require students to analyze, synthesize, and evaluate information

Gradually Build Complex Dialogue

Given the rarity of high-quality dialogue in classrooms, students need to start with practicing techniques that serve as a building block for complex discussions (Hattie, 2023b). One place to start is developing the technique of sharing complex sentences between peers. In their book *The Writing Revolution*, Judith C. Hochman and Natalie Wexler (2017) share that the sentence is the basic building block of writing. A complex sentence is one in which two independent clauses are associated with one another using conjunctions (for example, *but, and, so*) or subordinating conjunction (for example, *because, although, while, if, since*). The recommendation here is to consider complex sentences in oral language as the building block for more complex sentences.

As such, we need to consider a spoken sentence as the building block of classroom dialogue. In writing, for students to produce a high-quality essay they need to write high-quality paragraphs, and prior to high-quality paragraphs they need to write high-quality sentences. Similarly, if we want high-quality classroom discussions in which students share multiple ideas and views, we need students to develop the routines of exchanging high-quality complex sentences in which students connect, contrast, and summarize the sentences of others. In order to achieve this, students need to get the sentence structure right. Reading follows suit. Students need to connect independent clauses to construct meaning, paragraphs for inferences, and essays, articles, and books for themes. As with all habits, we begin with frequently employing routines that are small and doable and then build from there. Table 5.1 (page 124) displays strategies at three levels of complexity that support students' growing ability to engage in complex dialogue.

Table 5.1: Strategies for Complex Dialogue

Layered Levels of Dialogue	Developing Conceptual Understanding	Applying Conceptual Understanding
LAYER LEVEL 1: Building complex ideas through complex sentences	Three- and Five-Interval Turn and Talks (Conjunctions, Subordinating Conjunctions, Appositives) Fronted Adverbial Drills Picture Worth 1,000 Words Backward Fading Sentence Development Revisiting Cloze Activities	Claim, Evidence, Reasoning Turn and Talks Claim, Support, Question Connect, Extend, and Challenge Imagine If . . . Think-Puzzle-Explore Kick the Tires
LAYER LEVEL 2: Comparing and contrasting multiple ideas across multiple sentences	Extended Think-Pair-Share Elaborative Interrogation Final Word In2out Wagon Wheel	Four As Elaborative Interrogation Friendly Controversy Perspective Analysis (with or without AI)
LAYER LEVEL 3: Expanding complex thinking across multiple ideas and sentences	Socratic Seminar Jigsaw Text-to-Text, Text-to-Self, Text-to-World World Café Open Space Technology (OST) Chalk Talk Chat Station	Town Hall Meetings Lincoln-Douglas Debates Chalk Talk Red Team

SCAFFOLD LEVEL 1: DEVELOPING THE COMPLEX SENTENCE STRUCTURE

Developing students' knowledge and skill in reading, writing, and talking at a complex level begins with routines that enable students to engage in complex sentences, as follows.

- Three-Interval Turn and Talk (conjunctions, subordinating conjunctions, appositives)
- Fronted Adverbial Drills
- Picture Worth 1,000 Words
- Backward Fading Sentence Development
- Cloze Activities

Three-Interval Turn and Talk

The Three-Interval Turn and Talk is an essential component of student discussion, an instructional strategy in which two students use content knowledge during a brief conversation with a peer. Students are provided with a short prompt to discuss content or a skill. Students turn to their predetermined partner and answer the prompt while their partner listens. To ensure that students engage in a high-quality Turn and Talk, students should answer the prompt with their partner in three stages.

1. Discuss the relationship between two or more ideas using one or more full sentences.

2. Discuss the relationship between two or more ideas and incorporate academic language using one or more full sentences.

3. Discuss the relationship between two or more ideas and incorporate academic language that includes conjunctions, subordinate conjunctions, or appositives.

Figure 5.1 provides an example of a high-quality Turn and Talk in elementary mathematics.

Step 1	Step 2	Step 3		
Comparison of Concepts	Academic Language	Conjunctions Because . . . But . . . So . . .	Subordinating Conjunctions While . . . If . . . Since . . . Although . . .	Appositives Fact, _____, related to fact
"Cubes are like squares because they are both objects we have touched in class."	"Cubes are 3-D shapes, and squares are 2-D shapes. We have touched both of these objects in class."	"Cubes are like squares because if you look at one face of a cube you have a square." "Squares are like cubes, but squares are 2-D and cubes are 3-D." "Squares are like cubes, so if you have six cubes you can make a square."	"While squares are like cubes, they both have different dimensions." "If squares are like cubes, then we should be able to build a cube with squares." "Since squares are like cubes, both have similar faces." "Although squares are like cubes, cubes have length, width, and height and squares only have length and width."	"The cube, a 3-D shape with 6 square faces, 12 edges, and 8 vertices, is related to the square in that all squares within a cube have the same side length."

Figure 5.1: Turn and Talk example.

In the preceding example, students are expected to engage in three brief conversations. These conversations build upon one another. In the first discussion, students are simply discussing relationships they know of that the concepts provided. Next, students are expected to incorporate academic language when they are discussing and relating academic terms. Often, students will not automatically apply academic language when they are speaking in class. By incorporating academic language in the second step, students will have already started their conversation, and this additional layer should reduce the amount of working memory required to engage in the learning.

In the third step, teachers should task students with either using conjunctions (for example, *but, so*), subordinating conjunctions (*because, although, while, if, since*), or appositives (noun phrases that describe a noun or pronoun) to both talk and write about the relationship between academic terms. While subordinating conjunctions and appositives are not often used in normal spoken language, they are common in nonfiction writing and expected in expository writing. Getting students familiar with these parts of writing within their discussions will provide them with familiarity when they get to their own writing and when they are reading complex material.

As students begin engaging in this process, teachers can begin differentiating the grouping of concepts and the academic vocabulary. For instance, a teacher may task separate groups of students in a mathematics class with comparing various shapes and using different academic language (see figure 5.2).

Step 1	Step 2	Step 3		
Comparison of Concepts	Academic Language	Conjunctions But . . . So . . . Because . . .	Subordinating Conjunctions While . . . If . . . Since . . . Although . . .	Appositives Fact, _____, related to fact
Cubes and squares	Length, width, and height	"Cubes have length, width, and height, but squares do not have height."	"If cubes have length, width, and height, then they have volume whereas squares have area."	"The cubes, a 3-D shape with six square faces, twelve edges, and eight vertices, is related to the square in that all squares within a cube have the same side length."
Circles and cones	2-D and 3-D	"Circles are 2-D shapes, and cones are 3-D shapes, so circles form the base of cones."	"Although circles form the base of cones, circles are 2-D shapes."	"The cones, a solid or hollow object that tapers from a base to a point, is a 3-D shape that has a circle that forms its base."
Triangular prism and triangles	Faces and rectangular sides	"Triangular prisms have five faces and three rectangular sides, but triangles have one face and zero rectangular sides."	"While triangular prisms have triangles at the base, triangles only have one face and prisms have five faces."	"The triangular prism, a 3-D polyhedron, has five faces, nine edges, and six vertices."

Figure 5.2: Turn and Talk example, including multiple concepts and academic vocabulary.

Other variations of this exercise are possible, including a teacher giving different students the same concepts but different vocabulary to use in the discussions.

Fronted Adverbial Drills

Beyond the use of conjunctions, subordinating conjunctions, and appositives, teachers should consider having students practice using fronted adverbials to further extend their use of complex sentences. A Fronted Adverbial occurs when the adverbial word or phrase is moved to the front of a sentence before the verb. The adverbial phrase describes the action in the sentence that follows. These sentences are beneficial in both figurative (*Like a cheetah*, Javier caught the player with the ball) and literal senses (*In the distance*, the bird snatched up the worm for dinner). These sentences can also be used for both fiction (*Mysteriously, the dragon fell from the clouds*) and nonfiction situations (*Quick as a flash*, the wolf tackled the baby elk). Like the Turn and Talks with conjunctions, subordinating conjunctions, and appositives, students can engage in taking turns using Fronted Adverbials. The following five activities or "drills" provide example Turn and Talk routines students can use in class.

Activity 1: Matching Fronted Adverbials With Sample Sentences

Provide students with several Fronted Adverbials and sentences (see figure 5.3). Next, task students with generating different sentences using the Fronted Adverbials. For instance, students might share the following: *Down by the cliffs, the girl found the glowing bracelet. Mysteriously, the girl found the golden bracelet. Barely alive, the girl found the glowing bracelet.* Next, teachers ask students to share what sentences they would write next in their story.

Fronted Adverbials	Sentence
Down by the cliffs, Somewhere near here,	The swallow used its beak to dig in the sand to look for food.
Far away, Mysteriously,	The girl found the glowing bracelet.
Barely alive, Suddenly, Three times,	The dragon fell from the sky.

Figure 5.3: Sample Fronted Adverbials and sentences.

Activity 2: Matching Fronted Adverbial Types With Sample Sentences

There are several different types of Fronted Adverbials (for example, time, frequency, place, and manner). If we want to add information in one of those categories (such as time), we have several Fronted Adverbial options (for example, *afterwards, already, immediately, in the morning*) to use. Like activity 1, students are tasked with completing sentences. This time the teacher prompts students with a specific type of Fronted Adverbial, and students then select a Fronted Adverbial and complete the sentence (see figure 5.4).

Type	Examples	Link Adverbial With Sentence
Time	Afterwards, Already, Immediately, In the morning,	. . . the dog ran out of the house looking for the boy. . . . the bird swooped down and picked up the worm from the ground. . . . the girl found the glowing bracelet.
Frequency	Often, Again, Sometimes, Once or twice,	. . . the dragon fell from the clouds.

Figure 5.4: Types of Fronted Adverbials with samples.

continued →

Place	Upstairs, In the distance, North of here, Under the ground,
Manner	Suddenly, Mysteriously, Carefully, Without a sound, Unfortunately,
Degree	Almost unbelievably, Hardly out of breath, Definitely confused, Obviously angry,

The fronted adverbial samples shown in figure 5.4 may be used across the various activities shown in this chapter.

Activity 3: Sentence Creation From Fronted Adverbials

As students develop a level of proficiency in using Fronted Adverbials with sample sentences, teachers may have students begin to develop their own sentences using a Fronted Adverbial. For instance, as students are learning about Martin Luther King Jr., a teacher may provide prompts such as *Courageously* or *Almost unbelievably*, and have students write a sentence that connects the Fronted Adverbial to an event in King's life (for example, *Courageously, Martin Luther King challenged the president of the United States to move faster in changing laws that ensured equitable rights for African Americans*).

Activity 4: Sequencing Fronted Adverbials

In this drill, teachers can begin to provide students with a variety of Fronted Adverbial types for students to consider using across the acts of a story and ask students to generate a sentence for each act of the story (see figure 5.5).

Phases of a Story	Types	Fronted Adverbial	Sentence
Act 1	Time	Once upon a time, Quick as a flash,	Once upon a time, a young girl lived in the forest above the village.
Act 2	Manner	Suddenly, Mysteriously, Carefully, Without a sound, Unfortunately,	Suddenly, a loud boom was heard above the alien.
Act 3	Degree	Almost unbelievably, Hardly out of breath, Definitely confused, Obviously angry,	Almost unbelievably, the water took the shape of the map she was holding in her hand.

Figure 5.5: Sample sequencing of Fronted Adverbials.

Within activity 4, teachers may consider tasking students with rearranging the various acts of a story and discussing if they would change the use of Fronted Adverbials. For instance, after students have created sample sentences that begin each act, teachers may ask students to hypothesize how they would change the sentences if the story began at a different act (for example, "How would you write this sentence if it began from act 2?") or from a different perspective (for example, "How would you write the sentence if the story was written from the antagonist's perspective?").

Activity 5: Changing AI-Generated Fronted Adverbials

In this drill, students review an AI-generated story that includes Fronted Adverbials across the three acts of a story (see figure 5.6). The students determine if the sentence structure is effective, if the arrangement of the story makes sense and is engaging to the reader, and how they, the students, would change the story. A teacher may simply ask students to do the following:

1. Identify the Fronted Adverbials in the sample.

2. Determine if the Fronted Adverbials are appropriate for the specific act of the story.

3. Determine how you might change the Fronted Adverbial and sentence to make it more effective for the reader.

Act 1: <u>With an otherworldly hum</u>, the alien spacecraft descended upon the iconic Golden Gate Bridge, casting an eerie glow over the city. In the heart of San Francisco, chaos ensued as people pointed skyward, capturing the historic moment on their smartphones. The extraterrestrial beings emerged, their shimmering forms both beautiful and intimidating. The city held its breath, caught in the grip of an unprecedented encounter.

Act 2: <u>Unbeknownst to the humans</u>, the aliens came in peace, seeking to understand Earth and its inhabitants. Their leader, a wise and empathetic being, chose to make contact with a renowned astrophysicist, Dr. Emma Rodriguez. Through a series of encoded messages, they arranged a clandestine meeting at the iconic Coit Tower. As Emma climbed the narrow stairs, she couldn't shake the feeling that this encounter would reshape humanity's destiny.

Act 3: <u>Armed with a translator device provided by the aliens</u>, Dr. Rodriguez engaged in a profound conversation. The extraterrestrials revealed their peaceful intentions and their desire to share knowledge that could benefit both worlds. Emma, torn between her duty to humanity and the potential for global harmony, faced an impossible decision. As dawn broke over the city, the fate of San Francisco hung in the balance.

Epilogue: <u>In the days that followed</u>, the people of San Francisco grappled with the revelation of extraterrestrial existence. The city became a hub for interstellar diplomacy, with leaders from around the globe converging to discuss the implications of this unprecedented encounter. As the world watched, the Golden Gate Bridge transformed into a symbol of unity, connecting not only two sides of a bay but also two worlds striving to coexist in harmony.

Write a story with fronted adverbials.

Source: ChatGPT.

Figure 5.6: Sample AI-generated story with Fronted Adverbials.

Picture Worth 1,000 Words

In this strategy, students are given multiple pictures and are asked to select one picture and write a series of complex sentences using a conjunction, subordinating conjunction, appositive, or Fronted Adverbial. For instance, a teacher may show a set of pictures of North American animals to students and say, "Finish a sentence that starts with 'Quick as a flash.'" Students then generate sentences such as "Quick as a flash, the wolves ran down the hill to hunt the injured elk." Or, a teacher may task the students with writing a sentence that includes a conjunction such as *because*; one student might create the sentence, "The flying squirrel leapt from the branch because the snake was slithering up the tree."

Backward Fading Sentence Structures

As students talk using complex sentences, teachers should expect students to write sentences as well. For instance, a teacher may task a student with the following: "Now that you have completed the Turn and Talk strategies, let's Backward Fade the development of a complex sentence in writing." (See chapter 4, page 99, for the complete description of Backward Fading.) The teacher illustrates step-by-step how to construct a sentence and then gradually removes one step at a time for students to complete in their own writing. For instance, in the example shown in figure 5.7, the teacher would show each step and then remove step 4, followed by 3, then 2, and then finally only show a fragment. The teacher should use multiple examples for students to use as they Backward Fade.

Steps	Example
Provide declarative fragments	Trunk, bark, branches, and leaves
Model creating a sentence	trees are living organisms that include a trunk, bark, branches, and leaves
Add capitalization and punctuation	Trees are living organisms that include a trunk, bark, branches, and leaves.
Add complexity (for example, conjunctions, subordinating conjunctions, appositives, fronted adverbials)	Trees are living organisms that include a trunk, bark, branches, and leaves because they need structure to capture sunlight and carbon dioxide.

Figure 5.7: Steps of structuring a complex sentence for Backward Fading.

Cloze Activities

As introduced in chapter 4 (page 104), a cloze activity is a routine in which designated words are omitted from a passage and students are required to complete the passage. For example, students may receive the following sentence with a subordinating conjunction and missing information that they need to complete.

Although viruses are often considered _____.

Although viruses are often considered living, they are not made of cells.

Providing students with a cloze activity for writing complex sentences is a useful scaffold to support students in writing at the deep learning level.

    Cubes are related to squares because _____.

    Cubes are related to squares but _____.

    Cubes are related to squares so _____.

    Cubes, _____, are related to squares because _____.

    While cubes are related to squares, _____.

    If squares are related to cubes, then _____.

The Three-Intervals Turn and Talk, Fronted Adverbial Drills, Picture Worth 1,000 Words, Backward Fading, and cloze activities are all routines that enable students to connect ideas. These strategies serve as a building block for more complex reading, writing, and talking.

SCAFFOLD LEVEL 2: EXPANDING COMPLEX SENTENCES TO PARAGRAPHS

Once students develop a level of familiarization and proficiency with reading, writing, and talking using complex sentences, teachers should begin extending this work through additional exchanges between students. Strategies that support drawing out deeper conversations include Five-Interval Turn and Talks and Structured Protocols.

Five-Interval Turn and Talks

Once students have developed a familiarity of using the Three-Interval Turn and Talk, teachers should add two additional steps to the conversation.

1. Add comparing and contrasting connectives to the statements made by another person (comparing connectives include *In the same way . . .*, *Likewise . . .*, and *In addition . . .*, and contrasting connectives include *On the other hand . . .*, *In contrast . . .*, and *However . . .*).

2. Conclude the discussion by summarizing the ideas shared during the conversation (summary statements include *In short . . .*, *On the whole . . .*, or *In general . . .*).

Steps 4 and 5 have students incorporate comparing and contrasting connectives along with summaries in their short discussion and through their writing. *Comparing and contrasting connectives* are words or phrases that act as links between sentences. Comparing connectives are conjunctions to illustrate how things are similar or the same. Examples of comparing connectives include *correspondingly, equally, for the same reason*, and *similarly*. Contrasting connectives are conjunctions that illustrate how things are dissimilar. Examples include *to the contrary, although, however, yet*, and *nevertheless*. *Summary statements* are used to pull ideas together. Summary statements include *in short, on the whole*, and *in general*.

When students incorporate all the components illustrated in figure 5.8, they have developed the habit of a full Turn and Talk. The five components are not only essential for elaborative discussions but also critical for developing the foundations of an essay.

Step 1	Step 2	Step 3			Step 4		Step 5
Comparison of Concepts	Academic Language	Conjunctions But . . . So . . . Because . . .	Subordinating Conjunctions While . . . If . . . Since . . . Although . . .	Appositives Fact, _____, related to fact	Comparing Connectives	Contrasting Connectives	Summary
Cubes and squares	Length, width, and height	"Cubes have length, width, and height, but squares do not have height."	"If cubes have length, width, and height, then they have volume whereas squares have area."	"The cubes, a 3-D shape with 6 square faces, 12 edges, and 8 vertices, is related to the square in that all squares within a cube have the same side length."	"In the same way, cubes are made up of squares."	"On the other hand, squares are 2-D, and cubes are 3-D."	On the whole, squares and cubes are both shapes but with different dimensions."

Figure 5.8: Five-Interval Turn and Talk example.

As students develop familiarity in the five-step process, teachers should begin supporting students in extending their discussions by incorporating questions between each of the five intervals (see figure 5.9). For example, as a student shares a sentence linking mean, median, and mode and using the academic language of central tendency, the teacher may ask the student whether they could create a different sentence then the one they created. By nudging students to generate a different sentence, the teacher is supporting students in thinking through the relationships between the ideas of mean, median, and mode. Moreover, the teacher is supporting students in spending more time talking through their ideas.

The infusion of questions to deepen student thinking between the five intervals is a strategy known as *elaborative interrogation*. Marzano (2017) argues that elaborative interrogation promotes deeper learning by extending student discussions and can assist students in improving their writing and re-evaluating their reading. Bringing questions into student discussions is a critical element to extending students' thinking time in deep learning (see figure 5.10).

Step 1	Comparison of Concepts	Mean, Median, and Mode
Step 2	Academic Language	Central tendency Skewness
	Infused Questions	*Can you say that in another way?*
Step 3	Conjunctions But . . . So . . . Because . . .	The median is the middle number of a given data set, but the mean is the average of all numbers in a data set.
	Subordinating Conjunctions While . . . If . . . Since . . . Although . . .	Although the mean is typically a tool to understand central tendency, the median is a more robust tool for skewed data. While the mean and median are typically the same value, when data are skewed these numbers differ.
	Appositives Fact, _____, related to fact	The mean, a number that is found by adding all numbers in the data set and then dividing by the number of values in the set, is related to the median when attempting to understand data sets.
	Infused Questions	*How do mean and median differ in use when we lack normally distributed data?*
Step 4	Comparing Connectives	Likewise, the median and the mode differ from the mean when data are skewed. In addition, when the data are positively skewed, the mode and the median are less than the mean.
	Contrasting Connectives	On the other hand, when the data are negatively skewed, the median and the mode are less than the mean. In contrast, the mode is greater than the median in negatively skewed distributions and less than the median in positively skewed distributions.
	Infused Questions	*Could you expand upon that?*
Step 5	Summary	In summary, all three numbers enable people to understand the distribution of numbers. In conclusion, mean, median, and mode are different measures of center in a numerical data set that enable people to summarize a data set with a single number to represent a "typical" data point from the data set. To put this work in context, let's look at scenarios where central tendency data are helpful, which include average rainfall and income levels.
	Infused Questions	*Could you put that in context? What is the big idea?*

Figure 5.9: Turn and Talk plus example with inquiry.

Questions After Step 2	Questions After Steps 3 and 4	Questions After Step 5
Could you put that another way?	How does . . . contrast with . . . ?	What is the point or big idea of . . . ?
How are _____ and _____ similar and different?	Where is . . . most or least . . . ?	What is an alternative summary?
Can you say that in another way?	What might someone who believed . . . think?	Could you put that in context?
Is this what you mean to say . . . ?	Can/did anyone see this another way?	Let me see if I understand you; do you mean . . . ?
What does this word or phrase mean?	Let me see if I understand you; do you mean . . . ?	What do you think is the main issue here?
	Could you expand on that?	

Figure 5.10: Sample questions to use in elaborative interrogation.

Structured Protocols

As students begin developing complexity within their language to discuss conceptual understanding, teachers should consider expanding the conversation across the classroom using structured protocols. *Structured protocols* are specific processes that provide specific logistical and outcome guidelines for discussions. The goal here is to enable students to engage in discussions that incorporate multiple relationships between concepts. Table 5.2 displays several protocols with examples and resources for learning more. As students are using these strategies, teachers should infuse Backward Fading and cloze activities to ensure students write their complex thinking.

Table 5.2: Structured Protocols for Scaffold Level 2

Protocols	Description	Example Elementary	Example Secondary	Resource
Final Word	Students form a group and read an article and select a quote that they think is important. Next, a student reads a quote without any elaboration. Students then respond to the quote with any and all reflections. Finally, the student who read the quote shares their rationale for selecting the quote. The group continues this process until every student has had a chance with the "final word."	Students read an excerpt from *The Giver* (Lowry, 1993). Students identify a quote that stands out to them in the passage and begin the protocol.	Students read an excerpt from *The Lord of the Flies* (Golding, 1959). Students identify a quote that stands out to them in the passage and begin the protocol.	www.schoolreforminitiative.org/download/the-final-word
In2out	This protocol emphasizes moving from personal understanding ("in") to broader perspectives with a peer ("2") and group discussion ("out").	Students read a passage from Jefferson's *Sons: A Founding Father's Secret Children* (Bradley, 2013) and are tasked with reflecting on the way in which Jefferson treated his children who were slaves at Monticello. Students then share in pairs and discuss their answers to the question, and finally the class discusses the question together.	Students read a passage from *Demon Copperhead* (Kingsolver, 2022) and are tasked with reflecting on the way in which Appalachia is reflected in American society in the book and in today's media. Students then share in pairs and discuss their answers to the question, and finally the class discusses the question together.	

Wagon Wheel	This protocol encourages students to explore different perspectives and consider multiple viewpoints on a topic. Students are provided a discussion prompt, and they have time for individual reflection, partner discussion, and then rotation with new students to explore new perspectives.	Students read *The Fun They Had* (Asimov, 1973) and then form into two circles (an inside circle and an outside circle). Students should face each other and address prompts from the teacher (for example, What perspectives are missing in this text? What assumptions does the author hold in this text? What does robot represent in this text?).	Students read *Examination Day* (Slesar, 1958) and then form into two circles (an inside circle and an outside circle). Students should face each other and address prompts from the teacher (for example, What perspectives are missing in this text? What assumptions does the author hold in this text? What does peppermint symbolize in this text?).	www.schoolreforminitiative.org/download/wagon-wheels-adapted-for-texts

These protocols enable teachers to structure the process so that they may focus on the actual content-level discussions of students. As shared with previous routines, the key is consistency. Over time, there is much less friction is conducting a protocol and students can quickly get started with the work and teachers can engage in the core learning.

SCAFFOLD 3: SUSTAINING COMPLEX THINKING ACROSS MULTIPLE IDEAS

As students move from effective sentence writing to effective paragraph writing, they begin preparing to write an effective essay. The same can be said for oral communication. As students progress from complex sentences to short-term discussion, they move toward longer sustained discussion. As students work toward sustaining complex thinking, they should begin to develop their convergent and divergent thinking. *Convergent thinking* is the process of using real-world limitations or constraints as filters and finding a single best solution or idea. *Divergent thinking* is the process of thinking without limitations or constraints while generating a wide variety of numerous and original ideas (Marzano & Heflebower, 2012). Both types of thinking are critical in deep and transfer learning. Routines that promote this type of thinking include the following.

- Chat Station
- Socratic Seminar
- Text-to-Text, Text-to-Self, Text-to-World
- Jigsaw
- Gallery Walk
- World Café
- Open Space Technology (OST)
- Chalk Talk

Chat Station

Chat Station is a structured protocol that has five specific steps to enable students to synthesize, analyze, and evaluate complex ideas. Teachers should do the following steps.

1. Place students in groups.
2. Engage students in a Five-Interval Turn and Talk about key concepts.
3. Write out specific questions and locate them around the room.
4. Mix students into new groups and record answers to the questions on the walls.
5. Engage in classroom discussion to summarize answers to each question.

The process begins with students working in small groups to discuss the relationship between key concepts related to enduring understandings of a subject area using the Five-Interval Turn and Talk. Next, teachers mix students to address several questions posed on the walls of the classroom. As students rotate around the room, they record answers to each question. After all the students have rotated around the room, the teacher then engages the entire class in a discussion about the questions.

For instance, imagine a high school class is tasked with developing an understanding of how the atrocities of World War II give contemporary governments insights into the importance of enacting safeguards against such atrocities in the future. The teacher places students into small groups to study the relationships between Nazi policies (for example, Law for the Restoration of the Professional Civil Service, Sterilization Law, Nuremberg Race Laws), propaganda (for example, establishment of the Ministry of Public Enlightenment and Propaganda), and forms of public humiliation and fear (for example, boycotting stores). Simultaneously, the teacher provides other groups the task of studying the external conditions that create an opening for the type of hatred, vitriol, and horrors of the Holocaust. The teacher has tasked these students with relating international policies (for example, Treaty of Versailles, U.S. sanctions on Japan's ability to trade) and leader rhetoric (for example, Adolf Hitler, Winston Churchill, Benito Mussolini, Franklin Roosevelt, Hirohito) with economic depression and social repression in Germany and Japan. As the students discuss within their groups, the teacher rotates and poses questions such as these.

- Why did the German people aid and abet the Nazi regime in the Holocaust?
- Why did the economic conditions of the 1920s and 1930s influence the rise of similar governmental approaches in Japan, Italy, and Germany?
- Why were leaders of both the Axis and Allied powers so successful with their people during World War II?
- How did the convergence of propaganda, policies, and policing catalyze mass genocide?
- Until seminal events occurred, why did countries like the United States take a quasi-neutral approach to World War II?
- Why was a new world order established after World War II?

At the primary level, imagine students are tasked with developing an understanding of how Indigenous communities within a local context (for example, Haudenosaunee [Iroquois] and Algonquian-speaking groups) interacted with the environment and developed unique cultures. As such, students are working on understanding the relationships between the strategies Native American tribes used for food, shelter, and clothing as well as relating the external environment to Native American cultures, customs, and government structure, beliefs, and values. Students are placed in small groups to focus on the comparisons between different aspects of the learning.

The teacher mixes up groups of students to enhance the level of integrated ideas between students. Before the teacher has students engage in step 3, they have students practice short Three- and Five-Interval Turn and Talks activities to enhance student learning. These critical building blocks will help students prepare and successfully execute larger classroom discussions. As the students are recording answers and rotating, the teacher infuses questions such as the following into their discussions.

- Why did the Haudenosaunee (Iroquois) and Algonquian-speaking groups structure their way of life the way they did?
- Why was the external environment a major reason for Native American ways of life?
- How did the ways of life for Native American groups differ across different landscapes?
- How did White settlers influence Native Americans' ways of life?
- Why were the cultures of Native Americans so different in a similar environment?
- How did beliefs and customs get passed down to future generations?

These questions will be used throughout step 4. Finally, students return to their seats, and the teacher asks the class to discuss the various questions discussed in smaller groups.

This protocol enables students to build complex dialogue gradually through the use of the Five-Interval Turn and Talk routine followed by addressing largely questions that require students to compare and contrast concepts that ultimately allow them to form general principles of a discipline.

Socratic Seminar

While the Chat Station is a powerful protocol to include in classroom discussions, there are many other structured processes that should be considered. For instance, the Socratic Seminar is a process for supporting students in understanding ideas, issues, and values reflected in a text or experience through a group discussion format (Facing History and Ourselves, 2020).

The Socratic Seminar is run by students, and as such, teachers need to work with students to use elaborative interrogation techniques with each other. To begin, a teacher should consider the five steps shown in table 5.3 (page 138).

Table 5.3: Steps to a Socratic Seminar

Steps	Primary Example	Secondary Example
STEP 1: Choose a text, question, statement, or experience to start the discussion.	Why are maps still important in our lives?	To what extent do parametric statistics give us useful information in making decisions in the world?
STEP 2: Provide students time to prepare.	Academic terminology to relate: • Contour • Grid • Latitude	Academic terminology to relate: • Normal distribution • Means and standard deviations • Variance
STEP 3: Give students questions.	Provide students with elaborative interrogation questions (see figure 5.10, page 133).	
STEP 4: Set up an inner circle and outer circle.	Separate the class into two groups. The first group will engage in the Socratic Seminar (inner circle). The second group will observe the first group and be prepared to discuss the quality of the deep learning conversation. The groups will rotate halfway through the discussion.	
STEP 5: Use questioning to enhance the discussion and the thinking.	Infuse elaborative interrogation questions to enhance conversation.	

Beyond the student-guided protocol, the power of the Socratic Seminar is that it builds endurance in deep learning discussions which cross multiple ideas and perspectives. This forms the basis of a socially-constructed oral essay with competing thesis, complex sentence structure, comparing and contrasting connectives, and the use of claims, evidence, and reasoning. While this protocol takes time to develop and implement, the results can be well worth the effort.

Text-to-Text, Text-to-Self, Text-to-World

The Text-to-Text, Text-to-Self, Text-to-World routine enables students to evaluate a text with others in three different ways. Initially, students make connections between the text they are reading and other texts they have read. If students are exploring the theme of identity, then they may connect to Tommy Orange's *Wandering Stars* to Kaveh Akbar's *Martyr* to James McBride's *The Color of Water* to Angie Thomas's *The Hate U Give* to H. G. Wells's *Invisible Man*.

Prompts that students address for the Text-to-Text portion of this protocol include the following.

- What I just read reminds me of . . . (story/book/movie/song) because . . .
- The ideas in this text are similar to the ideas in . . . because . . .
- The ideas in this text are different from the ideas in . . . because . . .

Next, students reflect on how specific texts connect to them and their own lives. For instance, imagine a class that is exploring the theme of forgiveness and redemption through reading Khaled Hosseini's *The Kite Runner* or Charles Dickens's *Great Expectations*.

Text-to-Self prompts the teacher may use for students to reflect on in writing or sharing with others include the following.

- What I just read reminds me of the time when I . . .
- I agree with/understand what I just read because in my own life . . .
- I don't agree with what I just read because in my own life . . .

Finally, students reflect on how specific texts reflect the world. For instance, imagine a class is reading Ernest Hemingway's *For Whom the Bell Tolls* and discussing the larger themes of mortality, warfare, and friendship. The teacher would prompt students to share or write a Text-to-World reflection using the following prompts.

- What I just read makes me think about . . . [event from the past] because . . .
- What I just read makes me think about . . . [event from today related to my own community, nation, or world] because . . .
- What I just read makes me wonder about the future because . . .

Jigsaw

Based on an analysis of thirty-seven studies, the Jigsaw method has an impressive effect size of 1.20 on student learning (Hattie, 2023b) The method is broken in down into multiple steps that include (1) forming expert groups to develop knowledge on a specific subtopic, (2) sharing expert knowledge with other groups, and then (3) summarizing key learning with the original expert group and the class. The specific steps are as follows.

1. Once groups have read their portion of the text, have them answer a set of probing questions to make sure they're ready to present the information. Select surface, deep, and transfer learning questions that they use in their presentation.

2. Regroup students so that each group has someone who is an "expert" for each portion of the text. Ask each person to share their learning and ask their questions to the group.

3. As each person is presenting, the rest of the group should work to answer the surface, deep, and transfer learning questions presented. This process is repeated for each group member.

Gallery Walk

The Gallery Walk is a deep learning strategy that prompts students to present their ideas on a poster or in some visible way so that other students can view their ideas and then to give and receive feedback on their work and the work of others. The steps for engaging in a Gallery Walk follow.

1. **Opening moves:** Display students' ideas around the classroom. Provide a set of questions for students to use to prompt their thinking for giving feedback to others. Prompts may include the following.

    ‣ I like how you have met the success criteria by _____.

- I wonder if you have considered _____.
- A next step might be _____.

2. **Conducting the gallery walk:** Conduct the Gallery Walk in a quiet room to ensure students share their own thoughts. Give students a set amount of time to provide written feedback on a sticky note to place on the poster.

3. **Reflections and next steps:** Have students gather the feedback on their poster and determine their next steps.

World Café

The World Café strategy seeks to replicate the informal atmosphere and open conversations that occur in cafés. The World Café strategy includes the following four steps.

1. Students are placed in small groups near a blank poster on the wall. One student is the scribe for the group. The teacher provides a prompt and an example for students to discuss. The scribe writes down the response (for example, list, analogy, concept map).

2. With the exception of the scribe, students move to a new poster (or "café"). Students should not go to a café with the same students. The scribe shares what the prior group discussed and hands the pen to a new scribe.

3. The teacher provides a new prompt, and students are tasked with integrating the new prompt with what has been previously discussed. Steps 2–3 are repeated two more times.

4. The teacher walks around the class and places one or two dots on each café and asks groups to determine if the dot means the work is accurate or if something needs to change.

For instance, imagine teachers working with students to develop a deep understanding that all organisms cause changes in the environment where they live and they, in turn, are affected by changes in their environment. Students have developed surface-level knowledge of habits, predator and prey relationships, survival techniques, means of reproduction, and pollution. Students are placed in groups and are tasked with writing everything they know about non-human-caused environmental changes. The students discuss their ideas, and the scribe writes lists, writes down ideas, and draws visuals to represent the group's ideas.

Next, the teacher prompts the students, with the exception of the scribe, to move to a different poster and to ensure they are not with the same people. Once they arrive, the scribe provides a detailed account of the last discussion, and then a new scribe is designated. The group now discusses a new prompt: animal survival and reproduction strategies. The process of writing, transitioning to a new group, switching the scribe, and addressing a new question occurs two more times. In this example, students might be prompted to discuss human-caused environmental changes and animal relationships in the last two rounds.

Finally, groups return to their original café and summarize the key learning across all four prompts as well as the ideas from classmates. As they reflect, the teacher places a small dot in a specific location of each café and asks groups to determine if the dot means the work is accurate or something needs to change (see Dots strategy, page 76). The group discusses and then shares out their thinking to another group or the rest of the class.

Open Space Technology

Open Space Technology (OST) is a divergent thinking protocol for discussions and learning experiences that allows participants to create and manage the agenda themselves. Participants propose topics they'd like to discuss, posting them on a board or setting up a space in the classroom (like a marketplace). Anyone can join any discussion based on their own interests and learning goals. During the "open space" portion, anyone can join any of the discussions, they can come and go as they please, and participants are encouraged to seek out sessions that engage and stimulate them. The steps of this protocol are as follows.

1. Share a topic with the class and ask students to write down a list of questions or issues that they have related to that topic. Students should place their names on the sticky notes.

2. Assign a small group of students to theme or group the sticky notes. Next, ask students to form into small groups to tackle one of the issues or topics.

3. In small groups, students work on their own to tackle the issue or topic together. The teacher should provide a list of probing or processing questions (see table 4.3, page 110) to assist the students in dialogue. Students are welcome to end the discussion at any moment and/or move to another group.

4. Bring the students back together to share key learnings and potential questions or other issues that have emerged.

Chalk Talk

A Chalk Talk is a versatile protocol that may be used for contemplating a question or for giving and receiving feedback with others. To promote deeper thinking, the strategy is conducted almost entirely in silence. The strategy can be broken down into the following steps.

1. Present a question for students to reflect on.

2. Ask students to form groups and stand near a large piece of paper. Students should each have a different-colored marker so that they may draw visuals, connecting lines to others, questions, comments, and so on. Students should not talk during this time.

3. Students should then begin drawing on the paper in response to the question they reflected on. Students should not talk during this time.

4. Students should then rotate to another group's paper and begin adding ideas and questions to the paper. Students should not talk during this time.

5. Next, students should return to their original paper and openly discuss any questions, comments, or understandings that emerged during the activity. These ideas are then shared as a class.

These strategies gradually develop students' abilities to develop conceptual knowledge. When these routines are frequently utilized and gradually built on through reading, writing, and talking, students will have deep-level knowledge and skills to engage in transfer learning more effectively as well as more efficiently access new surface-level knowledge.

Infuse Thinking Routines

In addition to complex dialogue strategies, the infusion of small and doable thinking routine protocols is recommended to enable students to analyze, synthesize, and evaluate new information. These routines can be used to reinforce and accelerate conceptual development in the classroom. Suggested routines to support students in developing conceptual understanding appear in table 5.4 and are detailed in the following sections.

Table 5.4: Strategies for Infusing Thinking Routines

Routine	Description
Frayer Model	This thinking routine requires students to address four different questions across a range of complexity levels.
2 Box Induction	This thinking routine involves analyzing similar and different examples or concepts within a larger topic.
Sentence Stems	This thinking routine prompts students to write and talk about conceptual understanding in a variety of ways.
+1 Routines	This thinking routine provides learners with a structure for identifying key ideas and committing them to memory by building upon their existing knowledge and understanding and sharing new learning.
Generate-Sort-Connect-Elaborate	A thinking routine designed to help students organize their understanding of a topic through concept mapping. The routine activates prior knowledge and generates ideas about a topic. It helps to facilitate making connections and encourages deeper exploration and elaboration of key concepts.
Parts, Purpose, and Complexity	This thinking tool is designed to help students develop close observation and critical thinking skills. The routine provides an opportunity to make students' thinking visible as they create lists, maps, and drawings of the parts, purposes, and complexities of various objects and systems.
Same Surface, Different Depth	This thinking routine requires students to solve problems that look similar but require different approaches to solve.
Graphic Organizers	This thinking routine tasks students with creating visual representations of a key idea or theme.

FRAYER MODEL

A Frayer Model is a graphic organizer that supports students in addressing tasks across surface, deep, and transfer learning. The model is helpful before, during, and after reading, writing, and talking. A template and an example of the Frayer Model are found in figure 5.11 (page 143). Students are tasked with writing a definition, sharing the characteristics of a concept, and then identifying both examples and nonexamples of the topic.

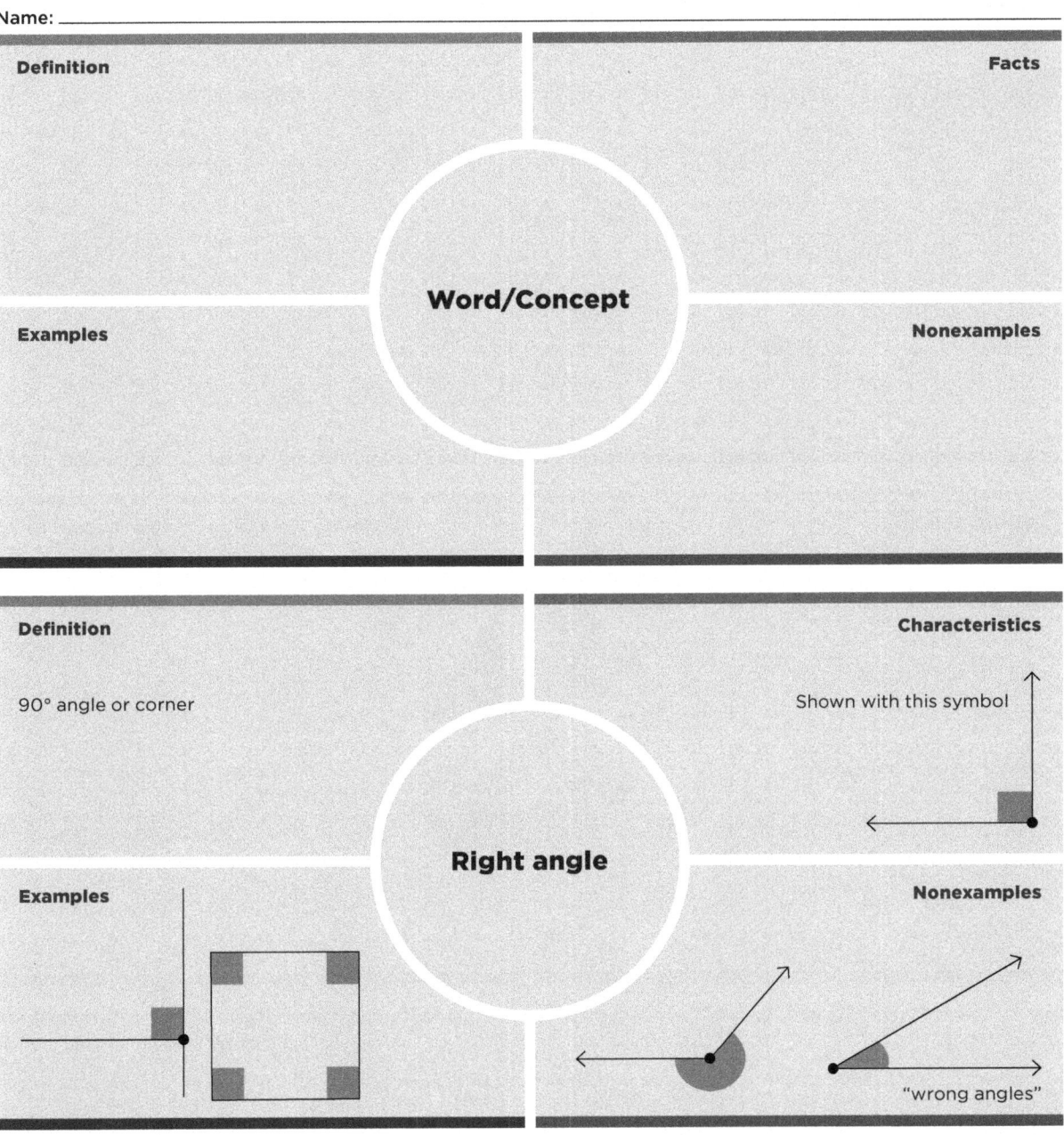

Figure 5.11: Frayer Model.

The tool may be augmented to ask questions that cut across surface, deep, and transfer learning (see figure 5.12, page 144, for a template and examples). This is a powerful strategy because it provides students with the use of reading, writing, and talking using complex sentences. A teacher could ask students to work together to complete the Frayer Model and then share out their responses.

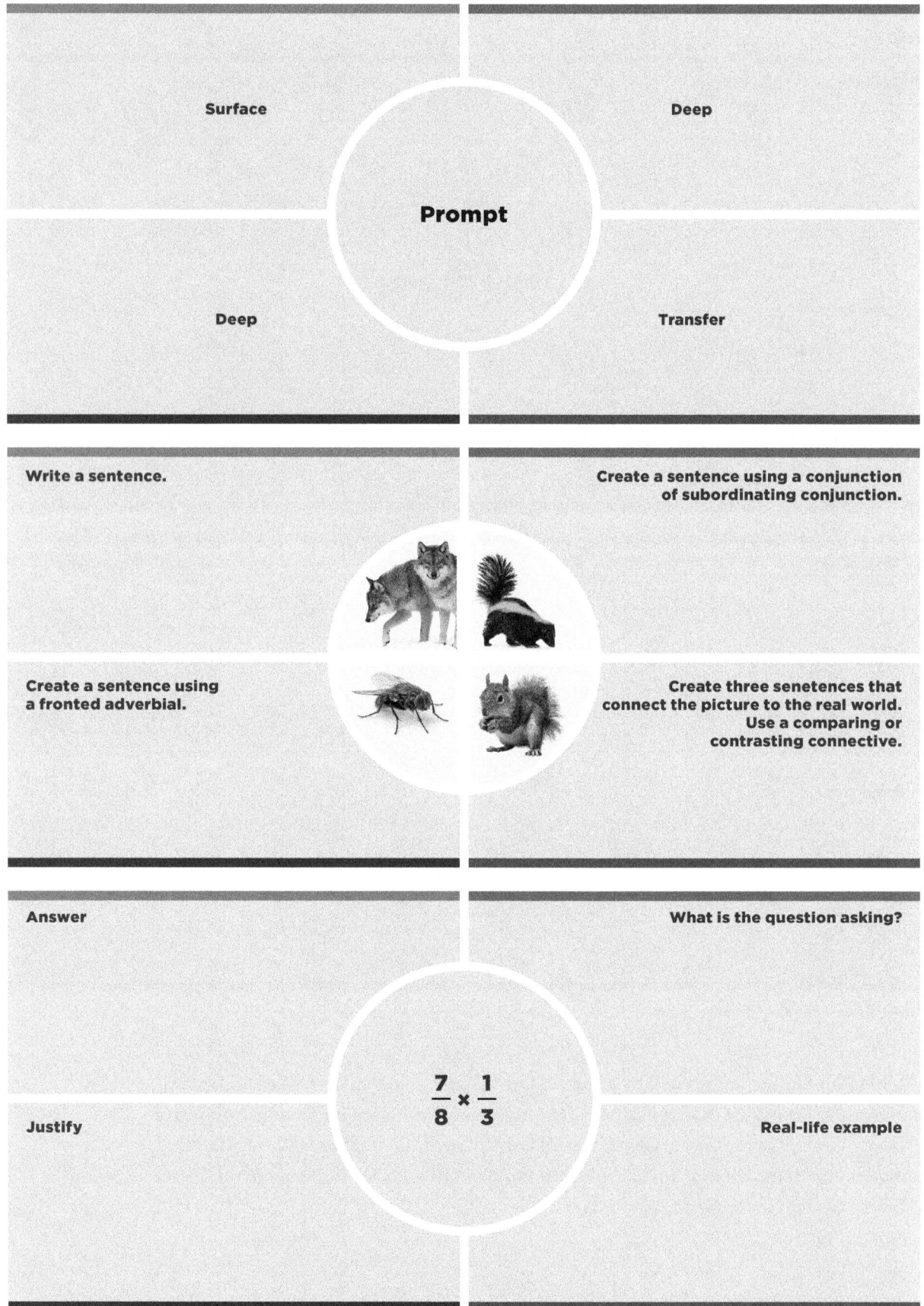

Figure 5.12: Modified Frayer Model for surface, deep, and transfer learning.

2 BOX INDUCTION

The 2 Box Induction strategy is designed to support students in comparing and contrasting different concepts. The strategy includes the following steps.

1. Present two boxes and share that students will need to make a rule for patterns found within each of the boxes.

2. Show students the first item in each box and have them share with peers what is similar and different across the boxes. Randomly check responses and write them down as "hunches" on the board. This is also a place for students to use the Three-Interval Turn and Talk strategy (page 124) to discuss similarities and differences.

3. Show the second strand of information. Repeat the discussion. Continue this process with at least four strands of information.

4. Ask students to share their rules for each box. Provide the actual rule and ask students to reflect on their accuracy.

Figure 5.13 displays an example of this protocol.

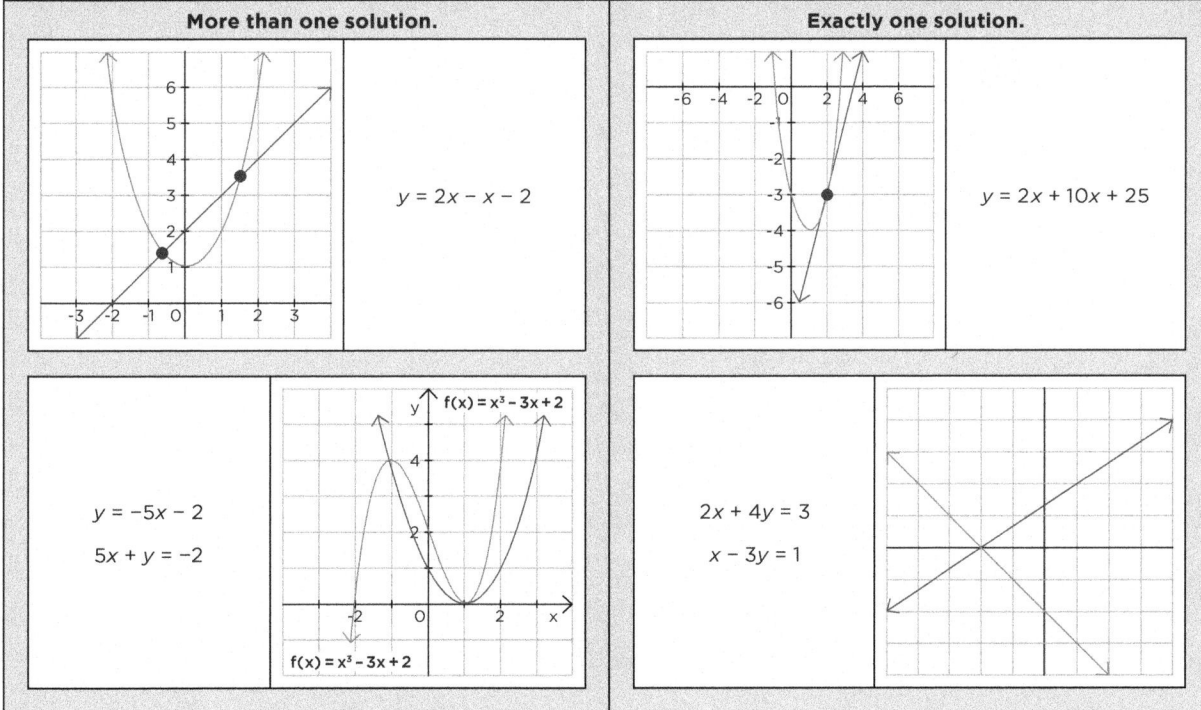

Figure 5.13: 2 Box Induction example.

SENTENCE STEMS

Another strategy that is helpful to build students' understanding of the relationship between ideas is using sentence stems. Sentence stems can be used in a variety of ways, including in beginning a statement, question, analogy, or metaphor or in scaffolding the order of ideas or processes. Table 5.5 lists a number of common types of stems.

Table 5.5: Sentence Stems

Strategy	Stems
Sentence Stem Comparisons	• X is similar to Y because/but/so _____. • Although/While/If/Since X is similar to Y, _____. • X, [define], is similar to Y in that _____.
Question Stem Comparisons	• How is _____ similar to and different from _____? • To what extent is _____ similar to and different from _____?
Analogies	• X is to _____ as Y is to _____.
Sequential	• First . . . • Second . . . • Third . . . • Last . . .

+1 ROUTINES

This routine, developed by Project Zero (Harvard Graduate School of Education, 2022), provides learners with a structure for identifying key ideas and committing them to memory by building upon their existing knowledge and understanding. The routine can be used at different stages of the lesson. Students are presented with new information, asked to share one thing they already know, and finally are asked to share one new thing they have learned from the new information, as follows.

1. After reading a text or watching a film or demonstration students should jot down three ideas that stood out. This should be from recall without notes.
2. Students should pass their paper to the right, and students should add one new idea or elaborate on an idea on the paper.
3. Students should then return papers and review their own paper for any and all additions.
4. Ask students to determine if the added information was novel, known, or nuanced. Have students share out in pairs.

GENERATE-SORT-CONNECT-ELABORATE

Another Project Zero (Harvard Graduate School of Education, 2022) thinking routine is designed to help students organize their understanding of a topic through concept mapping. The routine, known as Generate-Sort-Connect-Elaborate, activates prior knowledge and generates ideas about a topic. It helps to facilitate making connections and encourages deeper exploration and elaboration of key concepts, as follows.

1. Present students with a stimulus related to a particular topic or issue. Share that students will engage in four steps to explore the stimulus. Ask students in pairs or small groups to begin by generating a list of ideas and initial thoughts that come to mind when you think about this topic/issue.

2. Next, ask students to sort ideas according to how central or tangential they are. Place central ideas near the center and more tangential ideas toward the outside of the page.

3. Next, ask students to connect ideas by drawing connecting lines between ideas that have something in common. Provide students with a model of a concept map outside of the context they are exploring. Explain and write in a short sentence how the ideas are connected.

4. Next, prompt students to elaborate on any of the ideas/thoughts you have written so far by adding new ideas that expand, extend, or add to your initial ideas. Provide an example in a context outside of what you are modeling.

PARTS, PURPOSE, AND COMPLEXITY

Parts, Purpose, and Complexity is a thinking tool designed to help students develop close observation and critical thinking skills. The routine provides an opportunity to make students' thinking visible as they create lists, maps, and drawings of the parts, purposes, and complexities of various objects and systems (Harvard Graduate School of Education, 2022). The steps follow.

1. Present an idea and object to a group of students. Ask them to answer the following questions.
    a. What are its parts?
    b. What are its pieces or components?
2. Have students share their responses.
3. Repeat the same process with the following two questions.
    a. What are its purposes?
    b. What are the purposes of each of these parts?
4. Repeat the same process with the following two questions.
    a. What are its complexities?
    b. How is it complicated in its parts and purposes, in the relationship between the two?
5. Repeat the same process with the following question.
    a. What other systems or objects are similar within and across contexts?

SSDD PROBLEMS

SSDD problems, short for Same Surface, Different Depth problems, are designed to illustrate a similar surface-level challenge for students using different approaches. Designed by Craig Barton (n.d.) these problems may look the same at first glance but require different mathematical ideas to be solved. Examples designed by Barton appear in figure 5.14.

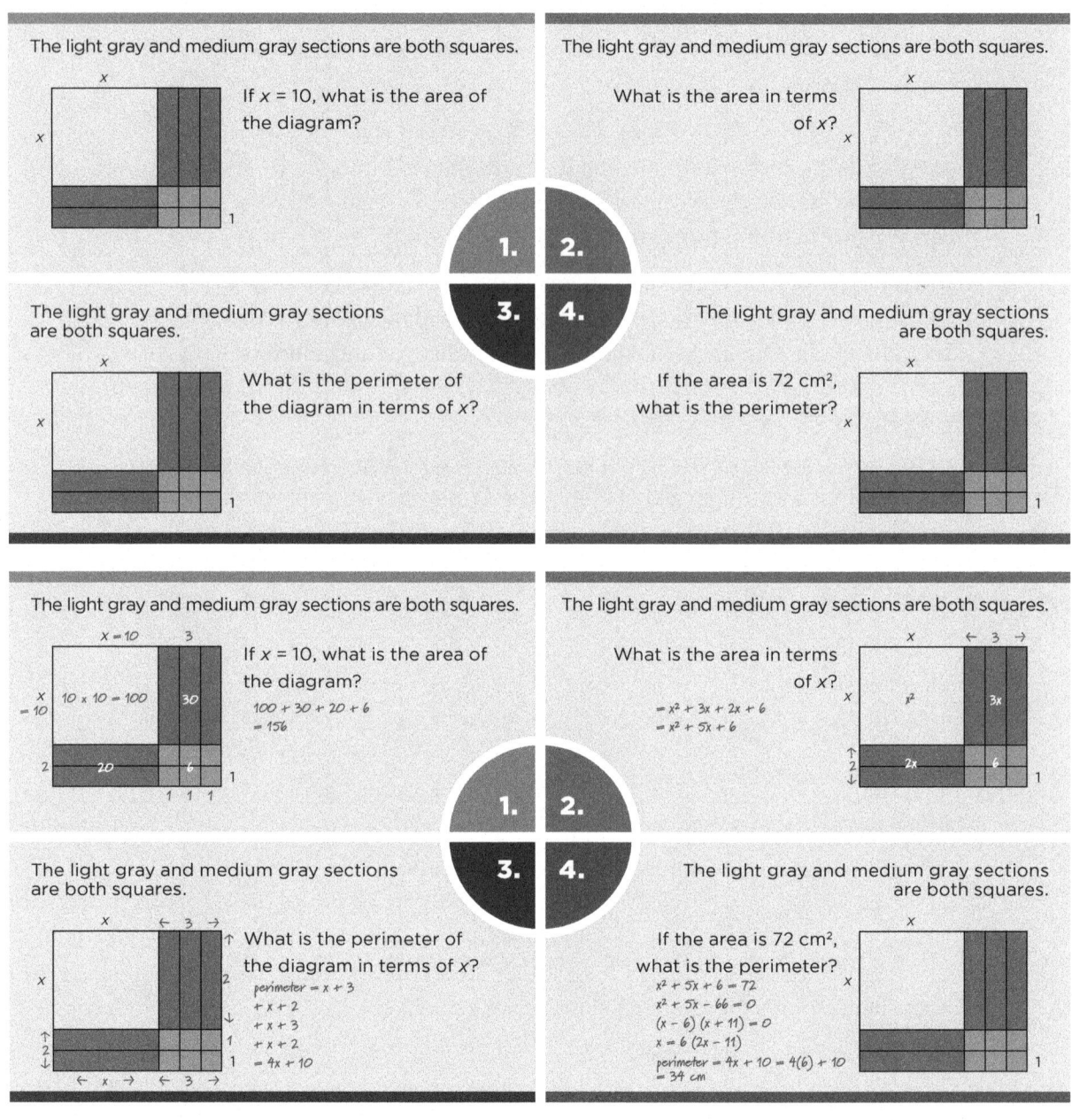

Developing the Habits of Deep Learning

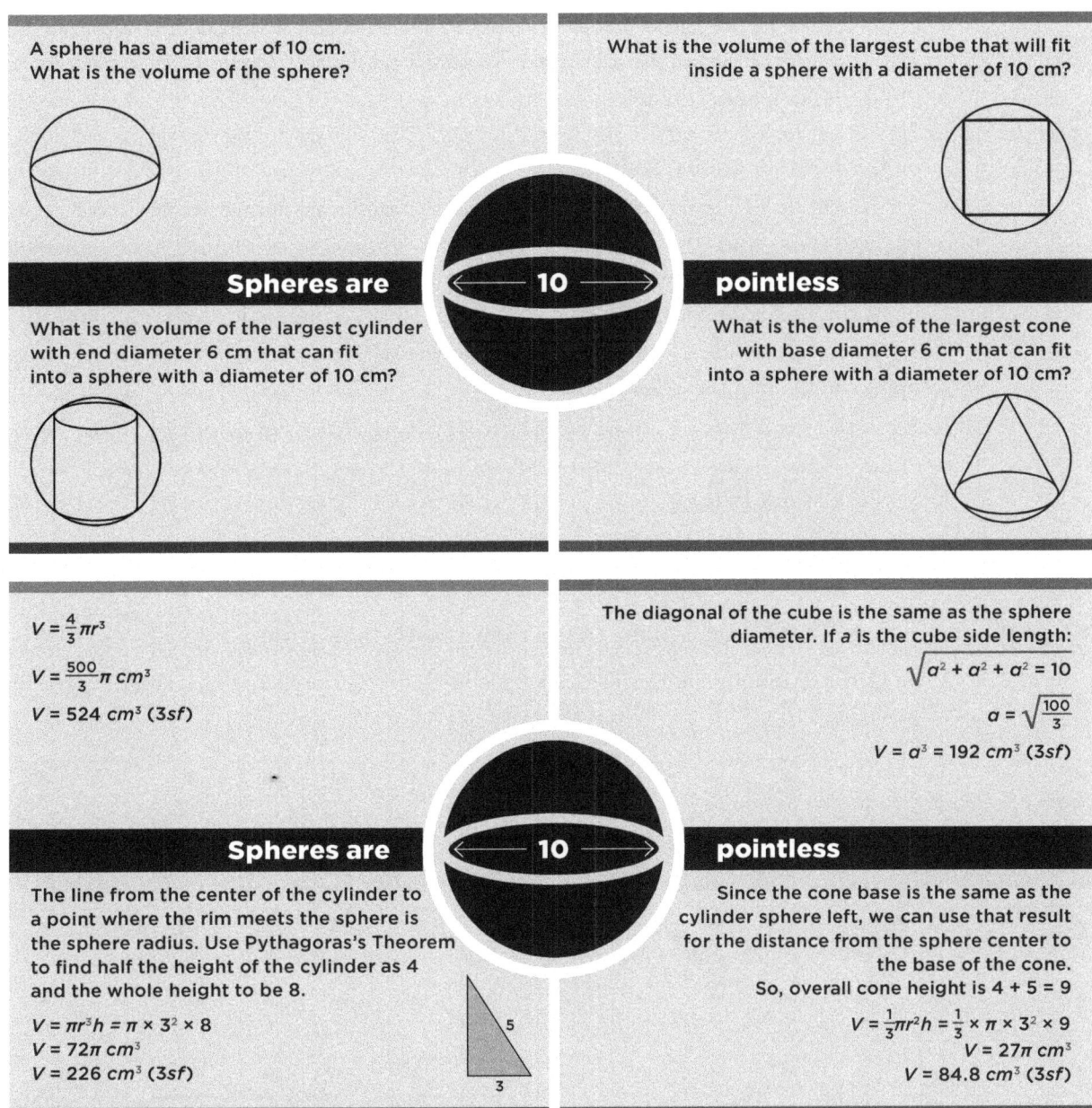

Figure 5.14: Example SSDD problems.

When engaging students in SSDD problems, the following steps are helpful.

1. Provide students with an SSDD problem.
2. Have students work in small groups to identify what surface features are the same.
3. Have students work in small groups to identify what deep-level features are different across the four tasks.

4. Using the Jigsaw method (see page 139), have different student groups solve one of the problems and then form new groups to share and check the accuracy of completion of the tasks.

GRAPHIC ORGANIZERS

In addition to linguistic tools, teachers should introduce nonlinguistic tools to support students in making connections between ideas. One form of nonlinguistic tools is a concept map that illustrates direct and indirect relationships between ideas. Concept maps are graphical tools that enable people to organize complex information in a way that furthers understanding and often enables people to produce new knowledge. Concept maps may contain the following.

- **Arcs:** Thsese are lines or arrows that connect ideas. These ideas are often denoted lines with labels to indicate direct and indirect relationships between ideas.

- **Boxes:** You can also organize concept maps in a more free-flowing structure, with a central idea that branches out into different ideas.

- **Nodes:** Each of the main ideas within the concept map is a node.

Other forms of graphic organizers include T-charts, Venn diagrams, and pictographs (see table 5.6).

Table 5.6: Graphic Organizer Examples

Graphic Organizer	Elementary	Secondary
Concept Map	*Diagram showing: roots find water; plant has roots; plant has leaves; leaves are green; plant has flowers; flowers need sunlight; sunlight can be yellow*	*Diagram showing Japanese Barberry with Foliar resources and Leaf-litter inputs connecting to Herbivore biomass, Herbivore richness, Detritivore biomass, Detritivore richness, leading to Predator biomass and Predator richness. Direct effect and Indirect effect arrows shown.*
T-Chart	Direct vs. Representative Democracy	

Pictographs	Day | Cupcakes Monday | 🧁🧁🧁🧁🧁 Tuesday | 🧁🧁▎ Wednesday | 🧁🧁🧁 Thursday | 🧁🧁▎ Friday | 🧁🧁🧁🧁🧁🧁 Saturday | 🧁🧁🧁🧁🧁🧁🧁🧁 Sunday | 🧁🧁🧁🧁🧁🧁🧁🧁▎ 🧁 = 6 cupcakes	**Profits Earned by a Company** Year | Profit 2018 | 💰💰💰💰💰▎ 2019 | 💰💰💰💰💰💰💰 2020 | 💰💰 2021 | 💰💰💰💰💰 💰 = 100,000.00
Venn Diagrams	**Fractions**: They have a numerator; They have a denominator; Cannot go on forever; Can be simplified; Example: ⅗ — **Both**: Parts of Numbers; Can be connected — **Decimals**: Can be irrational; Can go on forever; Has a decimal; Cannot be simplified; Example: .316	**Ratios**: Comparison of 2 or more of the same units; Example: apples to oranges — **Comparison of both** — **Rates**: Comparison of 2 or more different units; Example: miles per hour

The consistent use of these routines enables students to relate two or more ideas within a subject area. The strategies incorporate a significant number of reading, writing, and talking strategies that, over time, build student conceptual understanding. However, developing conceptual knowledge is not an exercise in and of itself but rather should be used to answer questions, work with others to solve problems, and give and receive feedback to further advance understanding and the application of that understanding within the heart of a discipline.

Habit 8: Apply Conceptual Understanding

As students are developing their understanding of the relationships between different ideas, patterns, and procedures, they also need to apply that understanding to different situations, different perspectives, and different tasks. Whereas developing conceptual understanding is static, focusing on developing knowledge about relationships, applying conceptual understanding is dynamic, testing developed knowledge about relationships between ideas, patterns, and procedures. The two success criteria for this habit are: (1) create and inspect claims, evidence, and reasoning; and (2) develop, discuss, and challenge ideas with others.

Success Criterion 1: Create and Inspect Claims, Evidence, and Reasoning

As students begin building the habit of using more complex language in their conversations, in their reading, and in their writing, teachers need to transition students from describing relationships to applying those relationships to actions that include explaining a rationale for a decision, expressing opinions with evidence, producing a piece of informative or narrative writing, or making an argument. Routines that build students' active engagement with conceptual understanding include the following.

- **Claim, Evidence, Reasoning (CER) Turn and Talks:** This routine is designed for students to build claims, evidence, and reasoning using short-duration conversations that are akin to the Three-Interval Turn and Talk.
- **Claim, Support, Question:** This routine is designed for students to engage critically with information and develop their reasoning skills.
- **Connect, Extend, and Challenge:** This routine is designed for students to think through the efficacy of different claims, evidence, and reasoning.
- **Imagine If . . . :** This routine is designed for students to understand the claims, evidence, and reasoning across multiple perspectives.
- **Think-Puzzle-Explore:** This routine is designed for students to evaluate the strength of their evidence and reasoning.
- **Kick the Tires:** This routine is designed for students to determine the strength of their claims, evidence, and reasoning.

CER Turn and Talks

To initiate students' development of applying conceptual understanding, students should use an abbreviated version of the Turn and Talk routine to ensure a strong link between a claim, evidence to back up that claim, and a rationale for the claim. Whereas the Turn and Talk process in Habit 7 (page 124) was concerned with relationships between concepts (animals and plants, for example), the CER process is concerned with ensuring accuracy between an assertion, the available body of facts, and inferences drawn from facts (see figure 5.15, page 153). The two-phase process is as follows.

1. In pairs, students share a claim, evidence, and their reasoning. Students then check to determine if both sets of CER meet criteria.
    a. Make a claim—offer a new idea or assertion.
    b. Connect to evidence—verify reliability and credibility of the information.
    c. Check your reasoning—provide a rationale for the claim that links to the evidence.
2. In pairs, one student shares their claim, evidence, and reasoning again, but the other student asks a question between claims and evidence and after reasoning.
    a. Make a claim—offer a new idea or assertion.

b. Students ask questions about the evidence that backs up the claim.

c. Connect to evidence—verify reliability and credibility of the information.

d. Students ask questions about the relationship between the evidence and the claim.

e. Check your reasoning—provide a rationale for the claim that links to the evidence.

f. Students ask questions about the credibility of the rationale for the claim and evidence.

Claim Type	Priming Claim	Step 1	Step 2	Step 3
	Topic	Claim I/We claim . . . I/We argue . . .	Connect to Evidence . . . because _____	Check Your Reasoning In conclusion . . .
Problem Statement	Weather prediction is a perfect science.	I would argue that weather prediction is not a perfect science.	Weather prediction is not a perfect science due to reports from the National Weather Service that there are too many variables to accurately predict the weather and we simply lack the tools needed to capture all the data.	In conclusion, the current technology does not meet the complexities of weather patterns around the world.
Concepts to Claims	Extinction is increasing.	I would argue that extinction is growing more now than in the past.	Because scientists have established a natural baseline extinction rate, we are able to measure the exponential growth of extinction. Scientists from organizations at the Smithsonian and Stanford University have identified that extinction is increasing at an alarming rate.	In conclusion, using scientific standards for measuring extinction, there is a clear increase in the decline of living organisms on Earth. This is in large part due to global warming.
Essential Question	Is fair always equal?	Fair is not always equal.	Because of the vast difference in income inequality in the world, not all people come from equal backgrounds or equal opportunities in life. Between 2015 and 2021, the total amount of income distinction in New Zealand did not change, resulting in more access to services and quality of life for the wealthy.	Due to factors such as income inequality, fairness and equality are not the same thing. Governments must focus their efforts on incorporating fairness into their policies.

Figure 5.15: Turn and Talks for CER examples.

When students evaluate the type of claim they are making, they should consider whether they are making problem statements, forming claims from concepts, and asking essential questions (see table 5.7).

Table 5.7: Claim Types and Examples

Claim Types	Examples
PROBLEM STATEMENT: A claim to a problem	- Russia started the Cold War. - PEMDAS (parenthesis, exponents, multiplication, division, addition, subtraction) always works. - Aspartame causes cancer. - *Hamilton*, the musical, is historically accurate.
CONCEPTS TO CLAIMS: A conceptual understanding that is transformed into a claim	- Dinosaurs evolved from birds, not reptiles. - Global temperatures are directly caused by humans. - Medical insurance is a human right, not a personal responsibility. - The role of the United States in global affairs is best described as a form of imperialism.
ESSENTIAL QUESTION: A question that focuses on the essence of a topic or subject	- Can we predict the future? - Why does the human body have a relatively consistent temperature? - Why did Picasso paint *Guernica*? - Do we all "have a code" that we live by?

To build students' abilities to make, evaluate, and discuss arguments, they again need small doable habits from which to build. The suggestion here is to start back at the sentence level and move to expanded forms of argument. As students begin forming claims, building in evidence, and including reasoning to back their claims, they will need to form the skill of evaluating their thinking and that of others. One way to do this is to infuse a set of questions after each step in the Claim-Evidence-Reasoning Turn and Talk process. Those questions can be grouped into three general categories.

- General CER questions
- Perspective and scenario questions
- Logical error questions

GENERAL CER QUESTIONS

As students begin engaging in CER discussions or reading, teachers should infuse a series of questions across each step to build on and enhance students' CER responses (see table 5.8).

Table 5.8: Questions to Infuse in CER

Questions After Making a Claim	Questions After Connecting a Claim With Evidence	Questions After Checking Your Reasoning
• What makes you think that? • How did you formulate your claim? • What assumptions are you basing your claim off of?	• Where did you get this idea? • Do your friends or family feel the same way? • Has the media influenced you? • Have you always felt this way? • What caused you to feel this way? • Did you originate this idea or get it from someone else? • What evidence do you have for that conclusion? • What would be an example? • How do you know? • Why do you think that is true? • Do you have any evidence for that? • But is that good evidence to believe that? • Is there a reason to doubt that evidence? • Who is in a position to know if that is so? • What other information do we need? • How does that apply to this case?	• Can someone else give evidence to support that response? • By what reasoning did you come to that conclusion? • How could we find out whether that is true? • Would that necessarily happen or only probably happen? • What is the probability of this result? • Are these reasons adequate? • Do you see any difficulties with their reasoning here? • Can you explain how you logically got here? • What would you say to someone who said _____? • Could you explain your reason to use _____? • What would change your mind?

Table 5.9 provides an example of the process of infusing questions into the claims-evidence-reasoning process.

Table 5.9: Example of CER With Infused Questions

Question	STEP 1: Claim	Claim Check	STEP 2: Connect to Evidence	Evidence Check	STEP 3: Check Your Reasoning	Rationale Check
What is an ideal weight?	A person's ideal weight should be based on their exact body mass index (BMI).	Question: How did you formulate your claim?	Using research from the American Medical Association	Question: How do you know that this is a credible resource?	The following research has been gathered from a number of reputable resources and has a higher robustness level because it consistently shows that BMI is a critical factor in managing body weight.	Question: What would change your mind?

PERSPECTIVE AND SCENARIO QUESTIONS

As students become familiar with the CER process, teachers should begin adding scenario planning questions that prime students to evaluate their claims and begin considering possible challenges to their current ideas. Following are several suggested questions that prime student thinking.

- Based on what you've said, what would be an *if-then* statement that is true?
- You've said that is true. What else must be true then?
- If X happened, what else would have to happen?
- What is another conclusion that may be feasible?
- Where might you be wrong? How would you test this idea?
- What assumptions are you operating under to make this claim?
- What perspectives are you omitting?
- What effect would that have?
- What is an alternative?
- If this and this are the case, then what else must also be true?
- If we say that this is unethical, how about that?
- What are you implying by that?
- When you say X, are you implying Y?
- But if that happened, what else would happen as a result? Why?

LOGICAL ERROR QUESTIONS

As students are engaging in the CER Turn and Talk process, teachers should begin using questions related to potential errors in student arguments after each step.

1. Faulty logic occurs when a person committing an error is not using sound reasons to form a conclusion. Examples of faulty logic include contradiction, arguing from ignorance, and begging the question. Contradiction occurs when someone presents conflicting information. Arguing from ignorance occurs when someone makes a claim that something is true because it has not been proven untrue. Begging the question occurs when someone defends a claim by only restating it.

2. Attacks involve a person defending their errors by focusing on related but irrelevant information. Examples of attacks include ad hominem attacks and the straw man fallacy. An ad hominem attack occurs when someone makes a personal attack on an opponent rather than addressing the topic of debate directly. This doesn't work because the attack isn't about the topic at hand. The straw man fallacy involves misrepresenting or exaggerating your opponent's argument, making it easier to attack. This makes it easy for your opponent to point out that your argument is just an exaggeration.

3. Weak references mean untrustworthy or unreliable sources are used. Errors include appealing to authority, using sources that reflect bias, and sources that lack credibility.
4. Misinformation means incorrect information is used to defend a claim. Often, people will confuse facts or misapply a concept or generalization.

Teachers should stop at certain points of students' conversations and have students and peers use a series of questions that prevent errors through the CER process (see table 5.10).

Table 5.10: Potential Error Questions

Potential Error Questions After Step 1	Potential Error Questions After Step 2	Potential Error Questions After Step 3
Check your claim: • Do you see any potential faulty logic errors? • Do you see any potential attacks? • Do you see any issues of misinformation?	*Check your connections to evidence:* • Do you see any potential faulty logic errors? • Do you see any potential attacks? • Do you see any weak references? • Do you see any issues of misinformation?	*Check your summarization:* • Do you see any potential faulty logic errors? • Do you see any potential attacks? • Do you see any weak references? • Do you see any issues of misinformation?

Claim, Support, Question

Claim, Support, Question is a thinking routine that helps students engage critically with information and develop their reasoning skills (Harvard Graduate School of Education, 2022).

1. **Form a claim:** Students make an interpretation or assertion based on the information presented. This could be a summary of the main idea, a conclusion drawn from evidence, or an opinion supported by facts.
2. **Provide support:** Students back up their claim with relevant and credible evidence. This could include factual information, data, examples, or quotes from the text. The evidence should directly connect to and strengthen the claim.
3. **Pose a question:** Students go beyond simply stating their claim and supporting it. They generate a question that challenges, extends, or deepens their understanding of the topic. This question can be open-ended, prompting further inquiry and discussion.

Connect, Extend, and Challenge

The Connect, Extend, and Challenge thinking routine is designed to help students engage deeply with new information and build meaningful connections. This adapted routine from Project Zero (Harvard Graduate School of Education, 2022) involves three key steps.

1. **Connect:** Students make connections between the new information and their prior knowledge, experiences, or understanding of similar concepts.
2. **Extend:** Students push their understanding of the new information by exploring its implications, applications, and potential consequences. They might ask questions like "What if . . . ?" or "How does this relate to . . . ?"
3. **Challenge:** Students identify any uncertainties, ambiguities, or potential limitations in their understanding. They might question assumptions, consider alternative perspectives, or identify areas for further investigation.

Imagine If . . .

The Imagine If . . . thinking routine asks students to imagine new ways to improve an object or system by looking at the possible space around an object or system through four different lenses. Specifically, it asks, "In what ways can an object or system be made to be more effective, efficient, ethical, or beautiful?"

1. Present students with a stimulus (for example, object, picture, system). Ask students to discuss in pairs to identify the various parts, purposes, and people who interact with the stimulus. Have students share their ideas with the class.
2. Ask students to discuss the following question: "In what ways could it be made to be more effective?" After three minutes, ask pairs to share their thoughts. Each pair should share how their idea builds upon or contrasts with others in terms of purposes and who is involved in using the object or engaging with a system.
3. Repeat the process with the following questions.
    - In what ways could it be made more efficient?
    - In what ways could it be made more ethical?
    - In what ways could it be made more beautiful?
4. To enhance transfer, repeat with a new stimulus that is connected to the same content.

Think-Puzzle-Explore

The Think-Puzzle-Explore process is a versatile thinking routine used to spark curiosity, deepen understanding, and guide inquiry (Harvard Graduate School of Education, 2022). This activity encourages students to activate their prior knowledge and recall what they already know about the topic at hand. This could involve brainstorming ideas, identifying relevant experiences, or making connections to similar concepts (that is, think). Second, the activity requires students to turn their attention to uncertainties, gaps in their knowledge, or questions that arise from the initial thinking phase. This might involve identifying confusing aspects, noticing inconsistencies, or formulating open-ended questions (that is, puzzle). Finally, the activity engages students in activities that address the puzzles they identified. This could involve research, experimentation, listening to experts, or exploring different perspectives (that is, explore). The process can be broken into the following four steps.

1. Present a stimulus (idea, prompt, picture) and ask students to jot down what they noticed (for example, "I noticed that . . . ").

2. Next, ask students to determine the rationale for what they noticed (for example, "Why is it that way?" or "Why did it happen that way?"). Have students share their thoughts with the class.

3. Ask the class to debrief what they notice are patterns from the class sharing information.

4. Repeat with a new stimulus.

Kick the Tires

Kick the Tires is a routine that focuses students on determining the strengths and weaknesses of an idea. The process walks students through the four key steps that focus on developing an idea, determining the strengths and weaknesses of a claim based on evidence and reasoning, deviating by creating suggested changes to the claim, evidence, and reasoning, and then sharing changes with others.

1. **Develop:** Create a claim or evaluate a claim from others.
2. **Determine:** Consider the strengths and weaknesses of the claim.
3. **Deviate:** Create suggested modifications.
4. **Discuss:** Share your changes with others.

One of the most powerful practices we can infuse in the classroom is to integrate thinking routines and conversational routines related to CER.

Success Criterion 2: Develop, Discuss, and Challenge Ideas With Others

As students make claims and read and listen to the claims of others, they need to ensure they are critiquing the accuracy and consistency of those claims with others. This is done by incorporating student discussion and debate through structured protocols.

As students begin to engage in discussions that move toward debates, teachers should consider using structured protocols to prepare them for challenging ideas, conducting debates, and checking the quality of arguments.

Preparing for Challenging Ideas

The following protocols prepare students to engage with challenging ideas.

FOUR As

The Four As routine is used for analyzing and discussing texts. The routine has students focus on four key aspects.

- **Assumptions:** Students identify the underlying assumptions and biases presented in the text. This includes examining the author's perspective, cultural context, and potential hidden agendas.

- **Agreements:** Students discuss and identify the points of agreement they find in the text. This helps them build consensus and focus on shared understanding.

- **Arguments:** Students analyze the arguments presented in the text, identifying evidence, reasoning, and potential fallacies. This encourages critical thinking and evaluation of ideas.

- **Aspirations:** Students consider the text's implications and potential impact. They discuss how the text relates to their own values, goals, and aspirations for the future.

ELABORATIVE INTERROGATION

The Elaborative Interrogation routine is designed to use inquiry strategically in students' tasks to deepen their understanding. The focus areas are as follows.

- Generating explanations
- Drawing inferences and implications
- Formulating questions
- Discussing and refining explanations

Conducting Debates

The following protocols relate to conducting classroom debates.

FRIENDLY CONTROVERSY

The Friendly Controversy routine is designed to support students in explaining and defending their positions on topics about which they disagree. The teacher asks students to follow specific guidelines when engaging in friendly controversy. Guidelines should be designed to ensure that students feel free to disagree with others but do so respectfully and allow for everyone to express their opinions.

TOWN HALL MEETINGS

The Town Hall Meeting routine is designed for students to engage in open discussions and exchange of ideas. The format often involves a moderator who guides the discussion, facilitates Q&A sessions, and ensures everyone has a chance to contribute.

LINCOLN-DOUGLAS DEBATES

Modeled after the historical debates between Abraham Lincoln and Stephen Douglas, this format encourages students to research and debate complex issues from opposing viewpoints. Debates focus on intricate issues with multiple perspectives and nuances. Students use evidence-based arguments, and debaters must rely on credible sources and logical reasoning to support their claims. The process also encourages civil discourse with an emphasis on respectful dialogue and open-mindedness while presenting opposing views.

Checking the Quality of the Argument

The protocols in this section guide students to analyze the quality of arguments.

RED TEAM

Students are divided into two groups and one group shares their current solution to a problem. The opposite group, or "Red Team," presents weaknesses and vulnerabilities to the presenting group. The Red Team provides diverse perspectives to challenge assumptions, explore worst-case scenarios, and identify potential risks associated with implementing the solution.

ISSAQUAH

The Issaquah routine centers on an individual sharing a dilemma to a group and receiving feedback. The group asks open-ended questions to gain a deeper understanding of the situation and identify key challenges. The group brainstorms potential solutions and approaches to the dilemma. The group analyzes and evaluates the proposed solutions, considering their feasibility, potential consequences, and alignment with the presenter's goals and values. The group collaborates on developing a concrete action plan to address the dilemma.

Infusing these structured protocols strengthens the CER process and enhances students' ability to engage with one another through extending CER understanding, debating ideas, and checking the quality of arguments.

Making Deep Learning Feedback Social

There is a myth that brilliant discoveries and understandings of the world are moments where everything comes together for a person. The idea is so pervasive in our culture that words like *Eureka moment* and *light bulb moment* pass through TED Talks, popular books, and school hallways without even a hint of skepticism. Interestingly, deep learning challenges this idea. Deep learning is the place where ideas linger in the background of a student's thinking. Deep learning is more a "slow hunch" or anti–light bulb moment than a Eureka moment. And such learning is formed through high-quality interactions with ideas and people (Johnson, 2011).

Where deep learning is a slow process for both teachers and students, surface learning is explicit, and often learning occurs in the same time and space as teaching. In other words, during surface learning, light bulbs are turning on in the same time and space as teaching. While surface learning is reinforced through strategies like Spaced Practice, initial uptake of enduring understanding takes time and effort to form and ultimately solidify.

To solidify the habits of deep learning, students need to develop the understanding that the results of their deep learning work will take time. Developing the ability to analyze, synthesize, and evaluate core academic content and discern the feasibility of arguments within disciplines occurs through the routine effort of reading, writing, and talking about core academics.

How do teachers support students in navigating the slow-burn process of deep learning? How do teachers support students in ensuring they maintain the habits of high-quality reading, writing, and talking? The answer is feedback and reflection together with peers. Hattie (2023b) argues that feedback and reflective processes are critical leading indicators for consolidating the habit of deep learning. Here, students need to reflect on their use of strategies to grow in their own learning, use a series of strategies to ensure they were clear on expectations as well as their progress over time, and consider how they gave and received support to and from their friends. Table 5.11 lists feedback protocols.

Table 5.11: Approximate Feedback Protocol Examples

Protocol	Description
Harkness Protocol (Discussion Mapping)	The Harkness protocol is a student-led discussion strategy designed to develop student self-awareness of the quality of meaningful discourse in the classroom. It encourages students to actively engage with course content by sitting in an oval formation, fostering open communication. This approach supports students in monitoring the efficacy of their discourse, as they take responsibility for the direction and quality of the discussion, promoting collaborative learning and critical thinking skills.
Consultancy Dilemma	The Consultancy Dilemma protocol is structured process used to help students identify, analyze, and address challenges they are facing on a piece of work, project, or class. It is a collaborative learning tool that encourages students to share their experiences and perspectives with their peers, thereby gaining new insights and developing potential solutions to challenging situations.
What? So What? Now What?	The What? So What? Now What? process can be used in various contexts within education. It guides individuals or groups through a three-step process of analyzing information and generating insights. (1) It promotes active engagement and critical thinking, encouraging participants to deeply analyze information and form their own interpretations. (2) It develops communication and collaboration skills, facilitating discussion, exchange of ideas, and collaborative problem solving. The "What?" phase focuses on clearly identifying and understanding the information presented. This could involve reading a text, observing a situation, analyzing data, or listening to a presentation. The "So What?" phase moves beyond mere comprehension and explores the significance and implications of the information. The "Now What?" phase focuses on action and applying the insights gained.

As students begin to engage in the protocols discussed in this chapter, teachers should begin to assess the quality of the conversation and give the data back to students to evaluate the quality of their conversation. In figure 5.16 (page 163), a teacher has mapped out two different conversations. In the first column, the teacher is focused primarily on equality

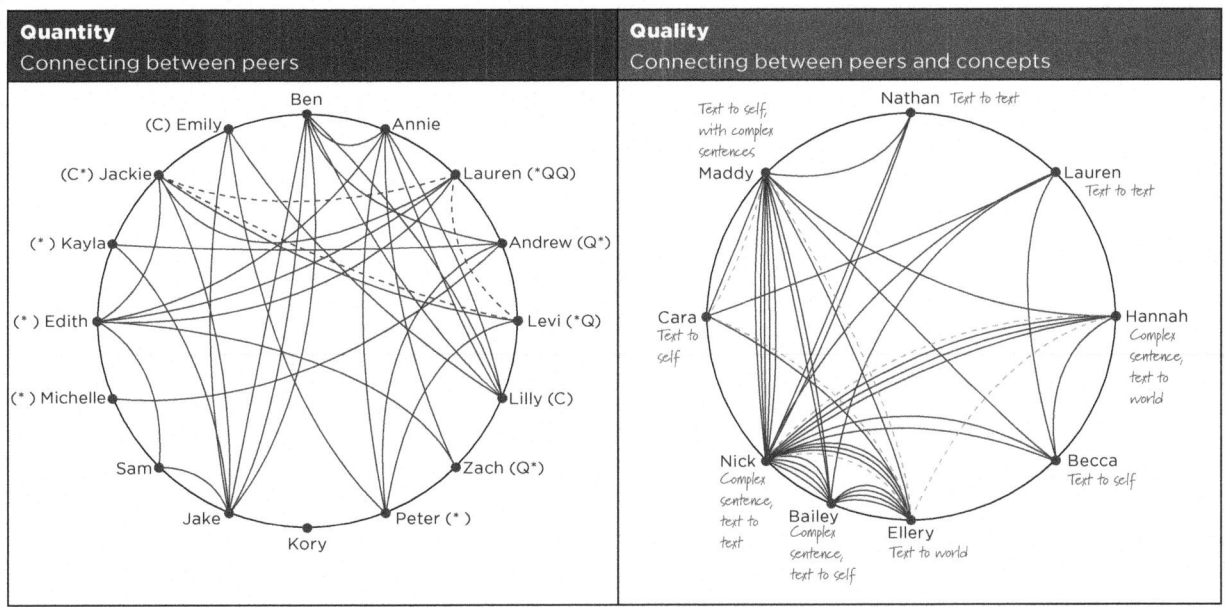

Figure 5.16: Harkness protocol examples.

within the discussion. Each direct line illustrates an exchange between two students in which one of the students recognized the other student's comments. For instance, a student may say, "I agree with Jamal's claim that government policies may be abused by some people; however . . ." A dotted line illustrates an exchange between two students in which no one is recognized by another student. The second column illustrates a teacher's focus on the complexity of the conversation between students. Here a teacher uses highlighters to mark where students use strategies to illustrate relationships between ideas (for example, conjunctions) and support claims with high-quality evidence (for example, claims with grounds, backing, and qualifiers).

As teachers use the Harkness protocol, they should consider having students evaluate the data without their initial commentary. One protocol that is helpful here is What? So What? Now What? (see figure 5.17, page 164). This protocol is designed to separate what we can observe from our inferences and suggestions. For instance, if we observed two dotted lines between Jackie and Lauren and Levi, then we may assume that Jackie is struggling with listening to and connecting to what other people are saying. Or, in the case of column 2 in figure 5.17, we may assume that Lauren is struggling with engaging in the discussion using conjunctions or connecting claims with evidence. However, before we jump to our conclusions, we should slow down the process and write down what we observed, followed by a potential solution.

Another process that teachers can use with students to evaluate the efficacy of their deep learning is through *Talk Detectives*. Talk Detectives is a process in which two students are selected each day to track the quality of dialogue. The Talk Detectives process has three key steps shown in table 5.12 (page 164).

Table 5.13 (page 164) includes sample discussion guidelines for the Talk Detectives process.

Agenda Items	Steps
Presentation	The presenter provides a set of data for a group to understand and develop next steps. The presenter answers clarifying questions during this time.
What?	The group identifies only key details that are specifically found within the data or resources shared. One member writes down this information and shares it with all group members. The presenter is *silent*.
So What?	The group identifies only key inferences that are drawn from the key details presented earlier. One member writes down this information and shares it with all group members. The presenter is *silent*.
Now What?	The group identifies only next steps that are drawn from the key inferences presented earlier. One member writes down this information and shares it with all group members. The presenter is *silent*.
Priority	The presenter shares the specific next steps they will take, when they will take those next steps, and when they will share their results with the team.

Figure 5.17: What? So What? Now What? protocol.

Table 5.12: Talk Detectives Process

STEP 1. Pick Detectives and Hand Out Guidelines	STEP 2. Observe discussions and take notes	STEP 3. Report and reflect
The teacher picks a few students to be Talk Detectives and reviews the suggested Talk Detectives guidelines for deep learning (see examples in table 5.13).	The Talk Detectives observe discussions and take notes of their observations.	The entire class debriefs the results and determines next steps.

Table 5.13: Talk Detectives Discussion Guidelines

Discussion Guidelines	Person or Group Name
Compares and contrasts concepts related to learning intentions and success criteria	
Uses comparing and contrasting connectives when responding to a student or a question	
Summarizes a group member's ideas or a group's ideas	
Links claims with evidence	
Uses questions to: • Clarify understanding from each person • Link claims with evidence • Ensure everyone has a solid reason for their opinions	

One of the most powerful tools for supporting students in their learning is to give them an opportunity to reflect on their learning and receive feedback from peers. One way to support this learning is through the use of a Consultancy Dilemma (see table 5.14).

Table 5.14: Consultancy Dilemma Protocol

Agenda Items	Steps
Dilemma Overview	The presenter gives an overview of the dilemma.
Clarifying Questions	This is an opportunity for participants to ask clarifying questions to the presenter.
Dilemma Discussion	What did we hear? What didn't we hear that might be relevant? • What assumptions seem to be operating? • What questions have been raised for us? • What meaning are we making about the dilemma and what we heard? • What haven't we considered/thought about?
Reflections	The presenter shares reflections.

Making Deep Learning Feedback Routine

As students engage in deep learning feedback, there are several daily feedback strategies that can support this learning (see table 5.15).

Table 5.15: Sample Approximate Feedback Strategies

Strategy	Feedback
Sort it Out Protocol	Students use sticky notes and place Feedback on a cards or sticky notes for a group of students and asks students to determine which piece of feedback goes to each paper.
Dots Strategy	The teacher places a dot on a student's work and shares that the dot denotes a place in the work that is particularly strong or that needs to be corrected. The student then determines what next step they need to take.
Questions Before Comments	When giving feedback, the teacher provides questions rather than comments. The teacher provides guidance on a potential change a student needs to make in the form of a question. The teacher typically provides probing and processing questions. The teacher checks back in several minutes to discuss the changes that were made and need to be made.
Out of Many	The teacher provides students the exact number of errors and students attempt to identify them and fit them. Students then determine the difference between their perception of what needs to change and what actually needs to change in regard to a piece of work. Students then determine next steps and take action.

> **Pricilla Ruiz de Vergara—Altmira International School: School Director—A Movement to Deeper Learning**
>
> As an innovative director and leader, my focus in recent years has been immersed in educational research. The goal is to lead an exceptionally effective school that actively fosters student learning, better preparing them for success in college, careers, and beyond.
>
> In close collaboration with my leadership team, our overarching objective has been to champion innovative approaches that cultivate a culture of rigorous learning in every classroom. Two years ago, we enthusiastically embraced project-based learning to

elevate academic achievement by employing a methodology that nurtures critical thinking, creativity, and a lasting passion for learning in our students. However, during the implementation of project-based learning, we recognized that effective project design necessitated thorough planning to ensure relevance, meaning, and a focus on addressing real-world problems or scenarios. Our teachers invested considerable time and effort in crafting these meaningful projects, translating inspiring ideas into tangible plans. As we progressed, we observed increased enthusiasm among ourselves and our students, leading to greater engagement and happiness.

Yet, during our instructional rounds and formal classroom observations, our leadership team noted a dearth of direct instruction and a lack of high-impact teaching strategies that could demonstrate deep, rigorous learning taking place. Consequently, students' retention of learning was found to be fleeting after major assessments, leaving teachers feeling drained despite their significant efforts in planning what appeared to be enriching learning experiences. The primary emphasis seemed to be on showcasing the final project exhibition to parents, peers, and community partners.

Red flags were raised as we discerned that students' comprehension of content remained superficial, acquiring ideas or skills without progressing to the deeper processes of relating and applying them across various contexts.

At this juncture, I discovered Michael McDowell's work on rigorous project-based learning. Michael collaborated closely with our staff, offering small, manageable shifts aligned with his recent book, *The Project Habit* (McDowell & Miller, 2022). This book equips educators with accessible habits transitioning from *motion* habits, such as those involving extensive planning and learning activities outside of direct implementation, to *action* habits that actively engage students through explicit instruction that moves students through understanding foundational knowledge and skills, gaining clarity over learning intentions and success criteria to creating transfer-level learning experiences. Through the routine use of these action habits, learning becomes truly ingrained.

Our staff is now deeply engaged in acquiring these habits to meticulously structure projects, guiding students' basic understanding to profound and applicable learning experiences. By actively staying in action, we are making a meaningful impact on student learning. As a school leader, my aim is for *observable impact*, validating the work of our students and educators with outcomes that can readily be observed at the classroom level, which truly matter the most. I am learning to avoid the leadership drift, resisting the temptation to adopt every new trend, and instead, focusing on empowering my faculty in the extensive exploration of fostering deeper, more rigorous learning experiences.

Conclusion

Developing and applying deep learning is cultivated through a series of daily and weekly routines. A core focus of deep learning is gradually building students' ability to compare concepts and create an enduring understanding of core content knowledge through reading, writing, and talking. Developing and applying deep learning is all part of balance for the pinwheel, a process for creating an equal intensity of surface, deep, and transfer learning. The goal is not to overly focus on one aspect over the other but to search for an equilibrium. This only occurs if we stack new routines into our current habits. In the next chapter, we shift from comparing content to comparing context.

Reflection Questions

1. What deep learning process habits (habits 7–8) are students regularly engaging in?

2. With what deep learning process habits (habits 7–8) are students requiring significant guidance from you and your colleagues?

3. To what extent are you finding trends and patterns with certain students in their development of habits 7–8?

4. How are you infusing the dispositional habits (habits 1–4) into your practice?

5. To what degree, are you using high-impact deep-level teaching strategies?

6. To what degree are students engaging in deep-level declarative and procedural knowledge?

Next Steps

Go through the *Need It—See It—Start It—Show It* process. Work with colleagues to answer the following four questions.

1. **Need it: What is compelling to you and your team right now?** To address question 1, conduct a Learning Walk to observe the level of implementation and impact of these habits in your classroom. When observing, follow the What? So What? Now What? protocol (page 34).

    a. Write down only what was observed in class.

    b. Assign people to look at the interaction between two of the three elements of the instructional core.

     i. Teacher-student

     ii. Student-content

     iii. Teacher-content

    c. Debrief the observations by analyzing any patterns that emerge.

    d. Predict the kind of learning they might expect from the teaching they observed.

    e. Recommend the next level of work that could help the school better achieve their desired goal.

    Another option is to bring evidence of student work related to Habits 7–8 and discuss the findings using the What? So What? Now What? protocol (see page 34).

2. **See it: How will you make what you want to improve observable in the next six weeks?** To address question 2, have staff complete an initial survey on the level of familiarity, employment, and inspection of teacher and student actions in the classroom as related to habits 7–8. Debrief the survey data with department or grade-level groups (see survey in chapter 1). In addition, have staff identify a small and doable practice within one of the two habits. Select the practice and identify what the practice would look like in the classroom in relation to the teacher, the student, and the task now, in three weeks, and in six weeks.

3. **Start it: How can you lower the threshold to move from evidence and ideas into action and from action into evidence and ideas?** To address question 3, lower the threshold of implementation by using the following strategies to make habits more doable.

    a. Small—make it manageable

    b. Stack—link it to your current practice

    c. Sustain—make it routine

    d. Shelter—protect this work by not adding other changes

    e. Sprint—start with a small group before you scale

    f. Share—measure your impact, discuss findings, and determine next steps

4. **Show it: How will you demonstrate your impact to others?** To address question 4, use the Consultancy Dilemma (page 204) or Critical Friends (page 88) protocols to discuss key learning of implementing the dispositional habits discussed in this chapter.

Developing Transfer Learning Habits

*Life is not about accumulation,
it is about contribution.*
—**Stephen Covey**

Transfer learning is related to applying knowledge and skills from one situation to a new situation (Hattie & Donoghue, 2016). Such learning requires students to develop strategies to detect similarities and differences across situations and to apply knowledge across situations in a complex problem-solving situation (Mayer, 2008).

Prior to engaging in complex problem solving, students need practice learning how to detect differences between various contexts. As Hattie and Donoghue (2016) state, "transfer is a major outcome of learning and is more likely to occur if students are taught how to detect similarities and differences between one situation and a new situation before they try to transfer their learning to the new situation."

In this way, transfer is related to two specific habits of practice. First, students need to learn the skill of stopping before addressing a problem and understanding the similarities and differences between one problem and another problem (effect size = 1.32; Hattie & Donoghue, 2016). Students must analyze patterns across situations and determine the core connections across contexts. Habit 9 focuses on developing contextual understanding by ensuring students employ strategies related to comparing contexts. Second, students need to learn strategies to solve problems in new situations. Identifying patterns in new situations (effect size = 1.14) and using *far transfer* to apply knowledge and skills to new situations (effect size = 0.80; Hattie & Donoghue, 2016) are the centerpiece for Habit 10.

Learning to Transfer

Whereas surface and deep learning necessitate a sharp and narrow focus on core academic knowledge, transfer learning is focused on applying knowledge across different situations, using that knowledge to solve in-depth problems, and refining the solutions to those problems over time. To support students in understanding the relationships between different contexts, students need to leverage similar skills as those needed for deep learning. Habits 7 and 9 are related because they both focus on comparisons. Deep learning is focused on comparing content, and transfer learning is focused on comparing contexts. For example, suppose in deep learning students are focused on the similarities and differences between the transitional states of matter whereas at the transfer level students are evaluating the similarities and differences between situations such as creating slime or freezing water. Or, students may be learning about the conflicts within the American colonies and the relationship between the patriots and loyalists in the late 1700s. At the deep level of learning students are comparing these groups of people while at the transfer level, they may be evaluating other situations that follow a similar pattern of internal conflict (for example, the American Civil War, the Arab Spring, Taiwan and China).

Developing students' skills to transfer is not conducted as a means in and of itself. As Guy Claxton (2021) shares, our brains have evolved to contribute. Students need to contribute, and this is most effectively accomplished when they solve real-world problems. To the greatest extent possible, students need to engage in authentic problems that combine the skills and knowledge across surface, deep, and transfer learning. For instance, in lieu of students comparing water and slime as may occur when developing habit 9, students should evaluate, for example, problems associated with oil spills and issues of global warming. We transition from theoretical questions such as *In what ways does the Constitution limit abuse of government powers?* or *Why do people move?* or *How does an organism's structure enable it to survive in its environment?* to questions that put students into a problem-based context such as *To what extent should the Constitution be reformed to limit abuse of government powers?* or *Should we create greater restrictions on preventing migration in our country?* or *Should we modify certain insects to enable them to kill invasive species in our local community?*

How do we build the habits of transfer-level teaching and learning? The following two habits of transfer will support teachers in developing students' abilities to transfer across a variety of situations.

- **Habit 9:** *Build Contextual Understanding*—find similarities and differences across multiple contexts
- **Habit 10:** *Solve Complex Problems*—solve wicked problems with others

Habit 9: Build Contextual Understanding

Habit 9 is critical to the cycle of surface, deep, and transfer learning because it allows students to scan multiple problems and identify patterns between situations and across multiple contexts. For instance, students read various articles from major news outlets on inflation around the world. Students read about gas prices, grocery stores, mortgage prices, rental markets, and so on. The teacher asks students to form groups and compare and contrast these real-world situations and determine the key underlying patterns that connect these situations.

In another classroom, teachers might give students a mathematics word problem and ask them to create an analogous problem. Students form into pairs and generate as many scenarios as possible and then compare those problems with others. The teacher then asks students to share the similarities and differences between the problems. Imagine students are trying to understand the implications of reintroducing a species into its native environment. As they study this situation, the teacher asks the students to identify any patterns with reintroducing a species, removing an invasive species, or preventing the reduction of current species in an environment.

In both scenarios, students are comparing and contrasting the contextual differences and underlying patterns of the economic and mathematics problems. Teaching students how to think laterally or across problems rather than only thinking through a particular problem is critical for innovation.

Stephen Johnson (2011) calls this thinking "adjacent possible." He states that the:

> **adjacent possible is a kind of shadow future, hovering on the edges of the present state of things, a map of all the ways in which the present can reinvent itself. Each moment in our history unlocks new doors of adjacent possibilities. The trick is to figure out what they are exactly, and whether they're leading us to beneficial places. (p. 30)**

He goes further by stating how innovation is limited to the amount of change that can occur in a system. He uses the metaphor of a chessboard to explain: "Think of the pieces of a chessboard halfway through a game of chess: there are a finite set of moves that are possible at that moment of the game, given the rules of chess, and a much larger set that can't be made. The set of moves that you can make define the adjacent possible at that moment in the game" (Johnson, 2011, p. 30).

Biological or cultural systems can only change so much. If you think of it in terms of technology, there's simply no way to invent a microwave oven in 1650, however smart you might be. But somehow, in the middle of the 20th century, the idea of a microwave oven became imaginable, or part of the adjacent possible. In this way, innovation comes through noticing small differences in situations. Getting students to begin noticing these differences between situations and ideas is a critical step in innovation and can be encouraged with the following two success criteria: (1) compare contexts and (2) make predictions.

Success Criterion 1: Compare Contexts

The first success criterion for this habit is that students develop the ability to engage in the adjacent possible by scanning multiple contexts. Six strategies that are helpful include the following.

1. Co-construction (for example, Matrix, Assessment Scramble)
2. Graphic organizers (for example, Venn diagrams, T-charts, visual thinking maps, classification charts)
3. Semantic analysis
4. Generating analogies and metaphors (via sentence stems)
5. Leveraging deep learning strategies such as Turn and Talks and Turn and Talk Plus
6. Leveraging CER Turn and Talk to create and test hypotheses (across contexts).

Co-Construction

By introducing students to a myriad of contexts early in the unit, teachers can use strategies that enable students to separate different contexts and the content they are learning. In this process, known as co-construction, students and teachers work together to develop shared attention on expectations of learning.

Dehaene (2020) argues that "a teacher's greatest talent consists of constantly channeling and capturing children's attention in order to properly guide them" (p. 150). Co-construction can be a useful strategy for orienting students' attention to the patterns across multiple contexts and the unique differences that may reveal nuanced problems and potentially new solutions. For example, let's say we gave students four mathematics problems, inflation problems, or animal problems at the beginning of a unit and asked them to determine the learning intentions of the unit as well as potential questions that need to be solved across all problems.

Other co-construction strategies are shown in table 6.1.

Table 6.1: Co-Construction Strategies That Promote Transfer Learning

Name	Description	Example
Matrix	Students are provided with multiple scenarios to review. They work together to find the pattern that connects each of the scenarios.	Using the Jigsaw method, students are broken into four large groups and tasked with exploring one of four newspaper articles. Each article is related to the limits of power across the judicial, executive, and legislative branches of the U.S. government. New groups are formed that encompass one person from each of the original groups. New groups attempt to identify the key patterns across the four articles.

Assessment Scramble	Students are given questions from an assessment on separate sheets of paper. Students are tasked with arranging the questions into categories (surface, deep, and transfer). Students are then tasked with generating new transfer-level questions.	Students are given an assessment that has questions related to central tendency (mean, median, and mode). Students place questions related to defining the terms and calculating mean, median, and mode at the surface level of learning. Students place questions related to comparing and contrasting mean, median, and mode and articulating why central tendency data are important at the deep level of learning. Students then generate hypothetical questions that could be asked at the transfer level (for example, "To what extent would the normal distribution curve change . . . ?").

While co-construction is a powerful way to start a unit, students need routine check-ins in daily lessons to ensure they continually separate the context and the content. One technique a teacher should embed as a daily routine is to have students quickly share the content and context. Known as "To and Through," teachers can stop a class at any time and ask students, "What are we learning *to*?" and "What are we learning it *through*?"

Starting units with co-construction provides students with the opportunity to immediately separate the content from the context. When students concentrate on the content as opposed to the context, they will be more likely to assess their own progress and transfer their learning across contexts.

Graphic Organizers

In addition to linguistic tools, teachers should use nonlinguistic tools to support students in making connections between ideas at the transfer level. In chapter 5 (page 119), we discussed the use of graphic organizers such as concept maps, T-charts, Venn diagrams, and pictographs to compare content. In this chapter, these same tools are used to compare contexts. Table 6.2 highlights the differences between the use of the tools at deep and transfer levels. Teachers can leverage familiar tools such as T-charts and Venn diagrams to move between deep learning (comparing content) and comparing contexts (comparing contexts).

Table 6.2: Graphic Organizer Comparisons Across Deep and Transfer Learning

Organizer	Deep Learning Example	Transfer Learning Example
T-Chart	Comparison between Indigenous and colonial people	Comparison of the impact of Indigenous and invasive interactions on human communities to the impact on plant and animal communities
Venn Diagram	Comparing plants and animals	Comparing a Venus flytrap to a slug

Semantic Analysis

To develop a bridge between linguistic and nonlinguistic representations, teachers should use semantic analysis. Semantic analysis is a process of drawing meaning from texts through visual representations of the links between words. While this process is used in both deep and transfer learning, the process is shown here to illustrate comparisons across contextual knowledge in transfer learning. Semantic analysis infuses linguistic and nonlinguistic strategies to enable students to form relationships between ideas. For instance, as students begin to read, observe, or talk about core academic content, they can denote the relationships by using the symbols in table 6.3.

Table 6.3: Symbol Relationships

Relationship	Symbol
Addition	=
Contrast	≠
Time	→
Cause	•••

For instance, imagine a student is watching a short film or reading an article on aquatic animals. A teacher may prompt them to write down addition, contrasting, time, and causal relationships. For instance, they may ask them to do the following.

- Whales are like sharks = both spend their entire lives in the water
- Whales are mammals and sharks are fish ≠ they differ in how they acquire oxygen
- Whales move similar to how land mammals move when running → evolving from terrestrial animals
- Whales live in pods ••• the majority of sharks pursue other prey for their meals because of the defensive structure of the whales

Secondary students may go further in forming relationships between ideas. For example, students may use the signal words in table 6.4 to denote relationships in a research abstract.

Table 6.4: Subtypes and Signal Words for Basic Relationships

Relationship	Signal Words
Addition Equality Restatement Example Summation	And, moreover, equally, too, besides Actually, in fact, namely, that is to say For example, next, then Altogether, overall, therefore
Contrast Antithesis Alternative Comparison Concession	But, yet, or rather, what is better Alternatively, either, neither In comparison, in contrast, like However, anyhow, besides, else

Cause	By, due to, owing to, through
Direct cause	Consequently, hence, now, so, therefore
Result	Because of, since, so on account of
Reason	Else, otherwise, in that case, then
Inference	Now that, providing that, if, then, where
Condition	
Time	Afterward, in the end, subsequently
Subsequent action	After, earlier, initially, in the beginning
Prior action	Simultaneously, while, meanwhile
Concurrent action	

Source: Adapted from Marzano and Heflebower (2011).

The following vignette illustrates how relationship diagramming can be used with secondary students.

> Blue whales are often characterized as highly stable, open-ocean swimmers who sacrifice maneuverability for long-distance cruising performance (INFERENCE). However, recent studies have revealed that blue whales actually exhibit surprisingly complex underwater behaviors, yet little is known about the performance and control of these maneuvers (ANTITHESIS). Here, we use multisensor biologgers equipped with cameras to quantify the locomotor dynamics and the movement of the control surfaces used by foraging blue whales (REASON). Our results revealed that simple maneuvers (rolls, turns, and pitch changes) are performed using distinct combinations of control and power provided by the flippers, the flukes, and bending of the body, while complex trajectories are structured by combining sequences of simple maneuvers (DIRECT CAUSE). Furthermore, blue whales improve their turning performance by using complex banked turns to take advantage of their substantial dorsoventral flexibility (DIRECT CAUSE). These results illustrate the important role body flexibility plays in enhancing control and performance of maneuvers, even in the largest of animals (RESULT). The use of the body to supplement the performance of the hydrodynamically active surfaces may represent a new mechanism in the control of aquatic locomotion (INFERENCE).

Source: Segre and colleagues (2019).

Turn and Talks

Students will employ deep learning strategies in transfer learning scenarios to discuss contextual similarities and differences and patterns across contexts. Many of the strategies we use in deep learning are relevant at the transfer level. Whereas deep learning is focused on connections across concepts, transfer learning is connected across contexts. Teachers should consider using the Turn and Talk, Turn and Talk Plus, and CER Turn and Talk processes with students. Figure 6.1 (page 176) illustrates examples of the Turn and Talk Plus process at the transfer level.

	Step 1	Step 2	Step 3			Step 4		Step 5
	Comparison of Contexts	Academic Language	Conjunctions But... So... Because...	Subordinating Conjunctions While... If... Since... Although...	Appositives Fact, → related to fact	Comparing Connectives	Contrasting Connectives	Summary
Comparison of contextual knowledge	Whales and sharks	Keystone	Whales are related to sharks because they are both keystone species.	Although whales are like sharks, whales show more complexity in body movement.	Blue whales, the largest animal on Earth, are related to sharks in that they both serve as keystone species.	In addition, blue whales and sharks both augment the ecosystem in which they coexist.	On the other hand, whales and sharks have adapted to the ways in which they hunt and defend themselves in dramatically different ways.	In conclusion, both sharks and whales are keystone species that indirectly and directly influence the aquatic ecosystems they live in.
Comparison across contexts in a discipline	Wolf reintroduction and removal of the lantern bug	Endemic and invasive	Wolf reintroduction and lantern bug removal are related because they both influence how an ecosystem interacts.	While wolf reintroduction and lantern bug removal are related because reintroducing a species is likely beneficial to an ecosystem.	Wolf reintroduction, the intentional relocation of a native species into its original habitat, is like lantern bug removal because both processes involve humans.	In addition, ecosystems will largely benefit from both types of human intervention.	On the other hand, ecosystems will largely be directly influenced by humans in indirect ways that we may not fully understand.	In conclusion, human involvement in the alternations of ecosystems is a complicate endeavor.

| Comparison across contexts in different disciplines | Electric cars and supply and demand | Economy Cobalt extraction | The supply of electric cars and the extraction of cobalt are directly related because of the demand of customers and incentives from companies and governments. | If government incentives increase the demand for electric cars, then organizations need to find a way to curb such incentives. | Supply and demand, a directly related influence in market economies, is dramatically influenced by government incentive and new products. | In addition, as cobalt becomes cheaper to extract, car prices will reduce, which will make electric cars more attractive. | However, cobalt extraction has a negative impact on local communities and the environment, largely affecting the economy in the long term. | As a result, the invention of electric cars is not a panacea and should be evaluated from multiple perspectives, including economics and environmental science. |

Figure 6.1: Five-Interval transfer-level examples.

As students are engaging in Five-Interval Turn and Talks, teachers can infuse perspective and scenario and logical error questions. For instance, as students are discussing relationships between different contexts such as the ways in which colonialism impacted Aboriginal communities and Native Americans, teachers may pose additional questions related to CER. A teacher may ask, "What assumptions are you operating under to make this claim? What perspectives might you be missing? What is an alternative thesis?" In addition, a teacher may use logical error questions such as "Do you see any potential faulty logic errors? Do you see any weak references? Do you see any issues of misinformation?"

Analogies and Metaphors

How is government oversight on TikTok similar and different when it comes to public school book banning? To what extent are space exploration and deep-sea expeditions related? What metaphors can you generate when wealthy people use their money to aid communities and initiatives that have fewer resources? Deep learning strategies such as analogies and metaphors are powerful at the transfer level of learning because they require students to think of different situations that have the same underlying patterns. Here these tools are used for contextual comparisons and support students in developing their ability to think laterally and develop the ability to find the adjacent possible.

Whip-Around

The Whip-Around protocol is designed to enable students to generate multiple responses to a prompt. Students typically write down responses to a prompt, and then the teacher calls on students around the classroom at a quick pace. When students are called on, they should not repeat a response but rather add something new. When students are engaging in transfer-level learning, teachers may prompt students to generate new analogies to a specific problem, share out their responses to the Three- or Five-Interval Turn and Talk process, or provide a relationship that they made in the semantic analysis protocol. As students share, teachers encourage students to create new ideas.

Success Criterion 2: Make Predictions

As students are developing an understanding of the similarities and differences across contexts, teachers can begin to support them in predicting what might happen within those contexts over time. There are several strategies that support students in developing routine prediction thinking, including the following.

- **Generate hypotheses:** Drawing upon their reasoning and existing knowledge, students make predictions that evolve into clear statements outlining the expected outcomes.

- **Predict and verify:** Involves predicting outcomes or concepts based on prior knowledge, and then verifying those predictions through research, experimentation, or analysis to revise understanding accordingly.

- **SCCG:** Students analyze the sequence, causes, and consequences of an event, then generate alternative scenarios by creatively applying their analysis to consider potential changes or solutions.
- **Scenario planning:** Students practice divergent thinking by collaboratively adjusting plans or solutions in response to hypothetical "What if…?" scenarios presented to them.

Generate Hypotheses

Generating hypotheses is a powerful learning strategy that has a high probability of making a substantial impact on student learning (Marzano, 2017). Faced with a question or observation, students brainstorm possibilities—their hypotheses. Students make predictions based on their hypotheses, which morph into clear statements about expected outcomes based on reasoning and knowledge. Students then partake in experiments, and designs emerge to test the hypotheses; experiments, simulations, or data analysis become the tools. Observations and measurements are collected, analyzed, and compared to predicted outcomes. Hypotheses are confirmed, revised, or rejected based on evidence, leading to deeper learning and new questions.

The strategy boils down to a few simple steps.

1. Provide students with a situation (for example, the Supreme Court passes or overturns a law) and ask them to describe the situation.
2. Have students share what they think may occur next. Have them create an *if-then* statement.
3. Have students generate potential strategies for testing their hypothesis.
4. Have students give and receive feedback to each other on their hypotheses.

Predict and Verify

An alternative version to generating hypotheses is the Predict and Verify routine. It encourages active learning, critical thinking, and deeper understanding. In the Predict stage, students make educated guesses about what will happen, how something works, or what information they will find based on existing knowledge, observations, clues, or hints. In the Verify stage, students test their predictions by gathering information, conducting experiments, or analyzing data. This might involve reading, researching, observing, experimenting, or engaging in discussions. The goal is to evaluate the accuracy of their predictions, gather evidence to support or refute them, and revise their understanding based on new information.

This routine requires the following procedure.

1. Have students review predictions others outside of class have about a particular topic or issue.
2. Have students check and challenge the various predictions using class textbooks, primary resources, and their notes.

3. Have students generate their own predictions and discuss how their predictions are similar to or different from those they originally discussed.
4. Have students reflect on the changes in their thinking from reviewing predictions and using evidence to challenge and support predictions.

SCCG

The framework has students examine the *sequence* (order of events), *cause* (reasons and motivation behind the events), and *consequences* (outcomes and implications of the events) of an event and then *generate* an alternative (creative thinking and application by prompting students to consider new questions based on the analysis). This strategy may be used for students to review solutions people take to solve problems and determine if changes can and should be made. The strategy includes the following four steps.

1. **Sequence:** Review the typical sequence of a process or procedure and determine if it can be changed. For example, review the typical sequence of a narrative and determine if the sequence can and should be changed to influence more interest from readers and a greater appreciation of perspective from other characters in the story. Let's imagine *The Book Thief* (Zusak, 2007) started in Act II as opposed to Act I, or that the story was told not from the perspective of Death but by another character. How would that have shaped the book?

2. **Cause:** Discuss the importance of each step of a sequence and the feasibility of changing the steps. For instance, students may explore potential changes to a story if the acts were rearranged and the perspectives of the story were changed.

3. **Consequences:** Generate a list of "What if . . . ?" questions about what would happen if the process or procedural steps were changed or omitted. For instance, students begin creating different sequences of a story and sharing different perspectives. In this example, students could have an AI chatbot generate a story and then evaluate the story from different perspectives and arrangements of the story.

4. **Generate:** Generate a new process or procedure or a case for maintaining the current process or procedure. For instance, students create a new story and discuss the strengths and limitations of a new approach.

3 Cs

The following routine tasks students with engaging in critical thinking, criticality, and contribution in a routine that moves students from deep to transfer in one lesson. The students start with analytical thinking followed by criticality. The difference between these terms is best summed up by Gholdy Muhammad who shares that criticality is focused on power, equity and anti-oppression while critically thinking is associated with deep and analytical thinking (Ferlazzo, 2020). Students combine these tools to then contribute to a real-world problem.

1. **Critical:** Present an AI-generated summary on a topic, an opinion piece, or an argumentative essay. Have students work in pairs to determine the accuracy of the document based on credible source material discussed in class.
2. **Criticality:** Provide students with a set of questions to explore missing perspectives, voices, or approaches to information presented.
3. **Contribution:** Based on the previous discussions, students draft a question to solve a real-world problem.

Plan Scenarios

Scenario planning is a powerful strategy for enabling students to develop divergent thinking, which is focused on generating ideas and determining possibilities. Students are prompted with a variety of different scenarios formed in the "What if . . . ?" structure. In a collaborative group, students need to adjust the plan or solution based on the new "What if . . . ?" scenario.

The routine includes the following four steps.

1. Each group receives five "What if . . . ?" scenarios, such as: What if funding is cut? What if the client doesn't agree with your proposed solution? and What if a new issue arises within the context?
2. Each group brainstorms solutions to their "What if . . . ?" scenarios. They display their solutions to one of the scenarios publicly.
3. The teacher walks around the classroom and places a dot on each paper and shares that teams need to determine if the dot represents a strength or a potential weakness in relationship to meeting the success criteria or meeting the contextual problem.
4. Each group discusses the rationale for the dot and then presents their ideas to another group. The alternative group listens and then presents clarifying questions, "I liked" statements, and potential "I wonder" questions. This process is repeated with groups switching roles.

The power of prediction is that it requires humans to determine possible outcomes to situations and potential rearrangements in how we think about problems and solutions. The development of prediction thinking is that it gives students the ability to begin planning and moving toward problem solving.

Habit 10: Solve Complex Problems

The core focus of Habit 10 is developing the knowledge and skills to solve complex problems in unique contexts. To do this, students need to learn how to employ routines to solve problems in wicked environments, engage with authentic audiences, and handle setbacks. Such interesting questions are accessible not only to adults with a doctorate but to the average moviegoer and to students as well. For instance, students at PS 45, an elementary school in New York City, are deciding whether Staten Island residents should lobby the

U.S. Congress to build a statue that recognizes the Indigenous people that originally lived on the island. Students have learned that a statue was promised to the Indigenous people of the land by President Taft in 1913 but was thwarted due to the costs of World War I. A few miles away at PS 68 second-grade students are tasked with determining what steps they would take to reduce the growth of invasive species like Japanese stilt grass, lantern bugs, and zebra mussels in and around their local community. In both of these situations, students are solving real-world problems.

In both schools, students are going beyond one context and answering important questions that test enduring understandings across real-world situations. For instance, as students exploring the Native American communities within their local communities, they are evaluating systems of oppression by evaluating agreements between governments and Indigenous people of the United States. To ensure transfer, teachers are tasking students with exploring multiple contexts by exploring connections between the Aboriginal communities and the Australian government, the Black communities in apartheid South Africa, and the Osage Nation and the U.S. government. Similarly, students in science are going beyond their local context and looking at the reintroduction or removal of multiple species within their local community as well as global contexts that may involve terrestrial and aquatic life in faraway places for their learners.

Such work is happening around the world. One high school is tasking students with transferring the idea that war is a form of chaos and stability to the question of whether President Biden should send armaments to the Ukraine government. They are exploring other contexts, including conflicts related to Kashmir and Pakistan, as well as India and China. A middle school is challenging students with presenting a solution to figuring out a solution to rising energy consumption and the reduction of nonrenewable energy sources. Schools have taken up the challenge of putting students into a problem-centric position. They have employed strategies to build the habits necessary for students to contribute their ideas, connect their conceptual understanding, handle setbacks, and analyze contexts to solve real-world problems.

Of course, not all units of study will have all these elements of transfer learning. Sometimes, we simply don't have the options to engage in real-world contexts and work with authentic audiences; however, we can always give students the opportunity to build transfer habits. The important point for students is that transfer becomes a habit and not treated as an event. We need to think less of the papier-mâché volcanoes, or the big project after testing, and think more about small doable habits that link to relevant questions that drive students' transfer-level thinking.

The habit of solving complex problems has three distinct success criteria related to problem solving, working with others, and navigating change. These are: (1) employ problem-solving processes, (2) engage with authentic audiences, and (3) address setbacks and changes.

Success Criterion 1: Employ Problem-Solving Processes

While there are multiple ways to frame problem solving, the OECD's (2021) description of the three phases of adaptable problem solving is a clear and easily transferable process for K–12 classrooms. The three stages include the following.

1. Define the problem.
2. Search for information.
3. Apply a solution.

OECD states that students switch between the different stages or might even employ them simultaneously when solving problems. To solve authentic problems, students should learn to use a number of routines that will enable them to move across all three steps. Each routine should support students in divergent and convergent thinking.

Divergent thinking focuses on generating multiple ideas from the driving question. This is a place for generating a multitude of solutions to a problem and being disciplined to not add too many constraints so that creative thinking can occur. Convergent thinking, on the other hand, is about taking ideas such as constraints, solution criteria, and the realities of the problem and then determining what solutions will likely work in the situation. Both types of thinking, which are illustrated in figure 6.2, are critical, and ensuring they become habitual occurs through the routine use of structured protocols.

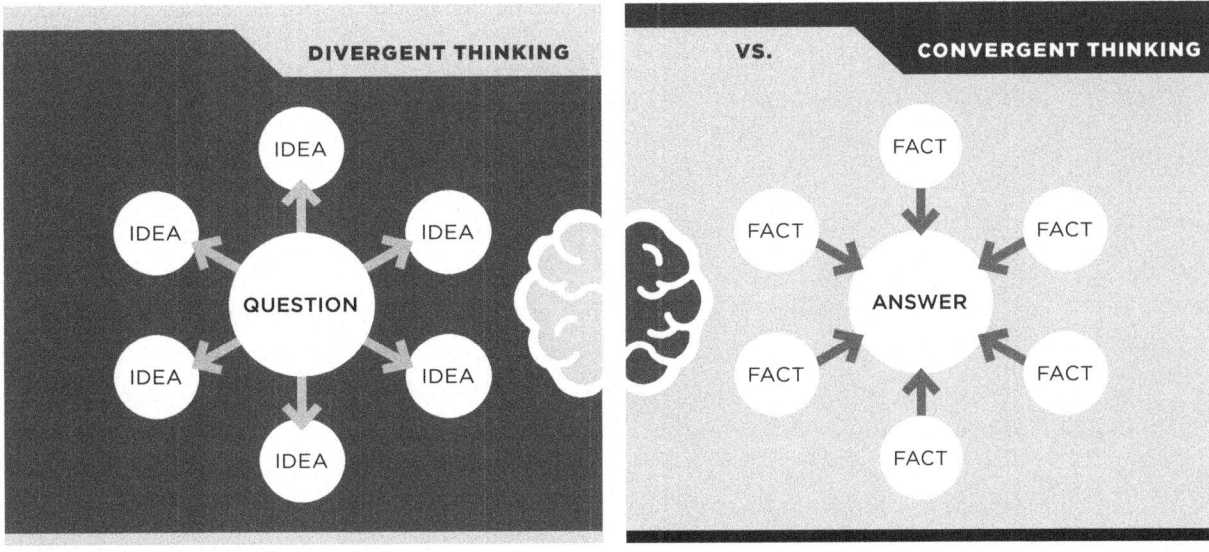

Figure 6.2: Divergent versus convergent thinking.

Another way to think of divergent and convergent thinking is using the term *insideout process* for divergent thinking and problem solving and *outside in* for convergent processes in which we take multiple perspectives and options and weigh them against solution criteria.

- **Inside-out process:** This is a divergent process in which we start with a question or set of criteria and then expand toward greater possibilities. We begin to explore multiple options.
- **Outside-in process:** This is a convergent process in which we take our understanding of multiple perspectives and options and begin converging those ideas to create criteria for decision making.

Both inside-out and outside-in processes can and should be considered complementary and necessary.

While there are many protocols students can utilize when solving transfer problems, table 6.5 shows strategies that are helpful in engaging in divergent and convergent thinking across the three problem-solving stages. We explore these protocols in the following sections.

Table 6.5: Sample Divergent and Convergent Protocols for the Three Stages of Problem Solving

Protocols	Defining the Problem	Searching for Information	Applying a Solution
Divergent Thinking Inside-Out Protocols	Open Space Technology (OST) Skunkworks Socractic Seminar Chalk Talk Step In, Step Out, Step Back	SWOT Option Explosion Revise Carousel Brainstorm Orchard Cove Scenario Planning SCCG Creative Comparisons	Gallery Walk
Convergent Thinking Outside-In Protocols	Fishbone Five Whys Realm of Concern Portable Surprises Gap Analysis Circles of Action	Affinity Mapping Friendly Controversy Nominal Group Technique Town Hall Meeting SCCG	What? So What? Now What? Critical Friends Charette

There are a number of divergent and convergent protocols and processes that can be referenced through the National School Reform Faculty and many others. The protocols shown here are provided to give you an idea of how to engage in these protocols with students.

Stage 1: Define the Problem

During the initial stage of the problem-solving process, students work to understand the contextual nature of the problem or problems and how those problems relate to core success criteria. To support students in building habits for understanding how to understand a problem, teachers should consider engaging in both divergent and convergent problem-solving processes.

As students engage in defining the problem, they should engage in routines that enable them to understand the root cause of a problem and determine the specific criteria for solving the problem. Routines that support students in developing and understanding of the root causes of a problem include the following.

- **Five Whys:** Determining the root cause of a problem by addressing multiple questions that require them to analyze the rationale for the answers to prior questions.
- **Realm of Concern:** Determining the various levels of influence that are related to the problem they are solving.
- **Fishbone:** Identifying the root cause of a problem by following a set of questions that are aligned to a flow chart.
- **Skunkworks:** Exploring an array of different problems.
- **Portable Surprises:** Finding patterns in a topic and similar patterns in very different situations.
- **Circles of Action:** Organizing one's understanding of a topic through concept mapping. It invites students to distinguish personal, local, and global spheres and make local-global connections. It also prepares them for an intentional deliberation about potential courses of action and their consequences.
- **Socratic Seminar:** Exploring a text, video, or other resource that expresses highly opinionated perspectives about a key issue or topic related to the curriculum content. Groups contain three to five members with specific roles, such as moderator, recorder, timekeeper, synthesizer, and group representative. After discussion in small groups, the whole class joins together to discuss. All groups might explore the same resource, or each group might investigate a different perspective on the same topic.
- **Gap Analysis:** Identifying an ideal and current state and identifying the discrepancy between both states.
- **Open Space Technology (OST):** Collaboratively generating potential problems to solve through self-forming agendas and discussions.

Routines that support students in understanding the criteria for any solution include the following.

- **Chalk Talk:** Involves groups working together to understand problems by writing ideas through linguistic and nonlinguistic representations and then building off of other ideas. This is a largely silent process.
- **Step In, Step Out, Step Back:** Focuses students on understanding perspectives and determining what potential next steps they should take.

When students engage in mixing these routines to promote divergent and convergent thinking, better problem solving emerges (Marzano, 2011). Example divergent and convergent routines for defining a problem are illustrated in the following sections.

DIVERGENT THINKING WHEN DEFINING THE PROBLEM

Stephen Johnson (2011) states that "the trick to having good ideas is not to sit around in glorious isolation and try to think big thoughts. The trick is to get more parts on the table."

To engage in divergent thinking and build good ideas, people need to get lots of ideas out and discuss them, challenge them, and explore them with others.

One of the most powerful protocols is called Open Space Technology (OST). OST is a methodology of co-creating an agenda and facilitating a meeting around a central topic or issue. The guidelines of an OST include the following (Corrigan, n.d.).

- Whoever comes is the right people.
- Whatever happens is the only thing that could have.
- When it starts is the right time.
- When it's over it's over.

Imagine students come together to discuss solutions to online child and youth safety. The United Nations has noted the online environment as an accelerator for children's access to education and community and, at the same time, a critical vector for potential sexual abuse and cyberbullying. Moreover, the U.S. Surgeon General (2023) has submitted an advisory arguing that a preponderance of research has shown that social media can also have a profound risk of harm to the mental health and well-being of children and adolescents. There are an abundant number of combinations of social studies, ELA standards, and mathematics standards that are transferable to this situation. By having students explore a multitude of different perspectives, interests, and ideas, students are expanding their thinking, which enables them to form more inclusive and interesting questions to solve. That is the power of OST and other divergent strategies.

CONVERGENT THINKING WHEN DEFINING THE PROBLEM

While divergent thinking promotes expanding our thinking, convergent thinking requires people to narrow their thinking and work to find the root cause of a problem. The Fishbone, illustrated in figure 6.3, is a great strategy for enabling convergent thinking.

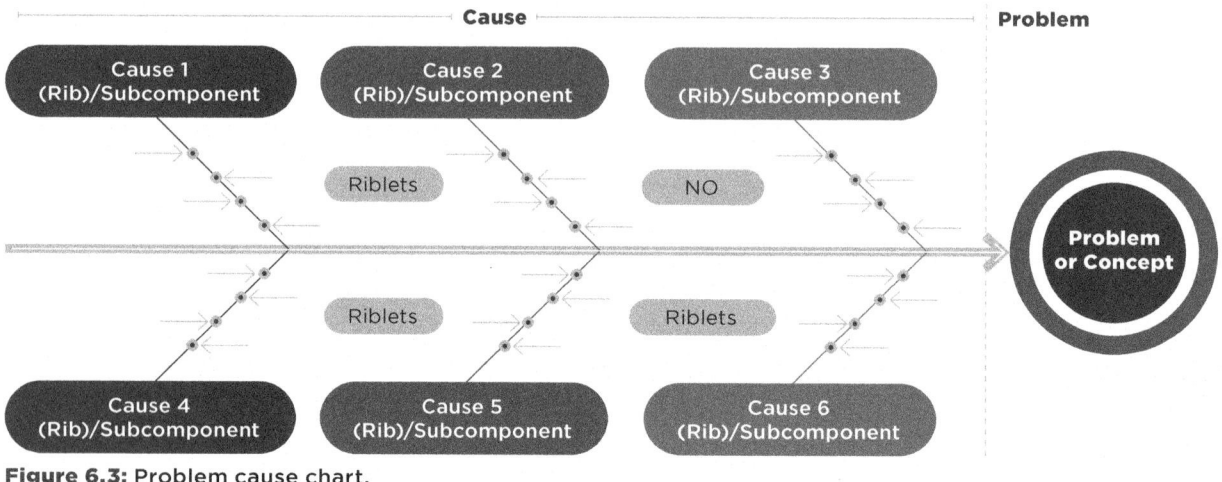

Figure 6.3: Problem cause chart.

Norms (California Department of Education, 2017):

- Avoid solutionitis. The goal is to understand the issue, not solve it (yet).
- "Yes, and . . . ." The goal is to generate lots of ideas, and not fixate on one.
- Embrace "definitely incomplete; possibly incorrect." You can (and should) revisit and revise.
- Share the air . . . . Step up, step back, and invite others in.

1. Generating our problem statement (5–7 minutes)
   a. *Individual*: What is the problem we need to solve? Express the problem in one sentence.
   b. *Share around*: Share problem statements.
   c. Choose one or create a new one (without getting hung up on the perfect wording). Write your group's problem statement at the "head" of your fishbone diagram.

2. Initial brainstorm of causes (5 minutes)
   a. Based on your work digging into the problem (empathy interviews, expert convenings, relevant data, research, and so on) and your own ideas/experiences, *individually brainstorm* as many causes as you can that might contribute to the problem/issue. Write each cause on a different sticky note.

3. Share and categorize (15–20 minutes)
   a. *Share around:* Each person shares one cause contributing to the problem. If others have a similar cause, you can start to group those sticky notes together on your poster.
   b. *Continue to share* your initial brainstorm, building on each other's ideas and adding new causes that may contribute to the problem.
   c. *Cluster on your poster:* Group related causes together, and give each category a title. (The stuff on the sticky notes is the details/bones on the fishbone).

4. Post and reflect (5 minutes)
   a. Post your poster on the wall. Does your diagram capture the root causes you think are important? Is anything missing? Then *each person* gets to vote with *one heart* and *one star*.
   b. *High leverage*: Put a heart by the factor that, if addressed, you think would have a significant impact on the problem.
   c. *Practical*: Put a star by the factor that your team could address with little effort.

5. Debrief (5 minutes): How did we do upholding the norms? How might we adjust this protocol in the future? What perspectives might we be missing?

When students begin using convergent and divergent thinking routines, they begin to learn how to effectively understand problems and are on the path to solving those problems.

Stage 2: Search for Information

During stage 2, students work together to identify and select potential solutions to a problem. This is done by engaging students in problem-solving protocols. Students should learn to use both divergent and convergent problem-solving protocols when identifying and selecting solutions to a problem. Divergent thinking focuses on generating multiple ideas from the driving question. This is a place for generating a multitude of solutions to a problem and being disciplined to not add too many constraints so that creative thinking can occur. Convergent thinking, on the other hand, is about taking ideas such as constraints, solution criteria, and the realities of the problem and then determining what solutions will likely work in the situation. Both types of thinking are critical, and to ensure this type of thinking becomes habitual occurs through the routine use of structured protocols.

As students engage in searching for information, they should engage in routines that enable them to understand possible solutions to the problem as well as identifying a solution that they will implement. Routines that support students in developing understanding possible solutions include the following.

- **Option Explosion Revise:** Students can use this routine for personal decision making, or teachers and students can use it for classroom decision making. Also, you can use it with students as a way of exploring and understanding important decisions in the news or history or literature or science policy or medical policy, etc. You can ask students to make the decision personal by role playing, imagining that they were in the situation.

- **Carousel Brainstorm:** A Carousel Brainstorm is an active, student-centered method to generate data about a group's collective prior knowledge or beliefs on a variety of issues associated with a single topic. Flip-chart-sized papers containing statements or issues for student consideration are posted at strategic locations around the classroom. Groups of students brainstorm at one station and then rotate to the next position where they add additional comments. The carousel "stops" when the original teams reach their starting locations. Each team prepares a summary of the chart at their stopping place and presents it.

- **Orchard Cove:** This collaborative learning strategy is designed to facilitate in-depth discussions and analysis of complex topics in a relatively short time frame. It is particularly useful for addressing issues that require a variety of perspectives and expertise.

- **Scenario Planning:** Students are prompted with a variety of different scenarios formed in the "What if . . . ?" structure. In a collaborative group, students need to adjust the plan or solution based on the new "What if . . . ?" scenario.

- **SCCG:** This critical thinking framework is designed to help individuals analyze information and develop deeper understanding of complex topics. The framework has students examine the sequence (order of events), cause (reasons and motivation behind the events), and consequences (outcomes and implications of the events) and generate an alternative (creative thinking and application by prompting students to consider new questions based on the analysis).
- **SWOT:** This is a process for analyzing strengths, weaknesses, opportunities, and threats within a situation or potential solution.
- **Creative Comparisons:** This is a routine for metaphorical thinking that enables students to frame potential solutions.
- **Friendly Controversy:** Students explain and defend their positions on topics about which they disagree. The teacher asks students to follow specific guidelines when engaging in Friendly Controversy. Guidelines should be designed to ensure that students feel free to disagree with others but do so respectfully and allow for everyone to express their opinions.

Routines that support students in making a choice to solve a problem include the following.

- **Nominal Group Techniques:** This is a structured group discussion method for generating and prioritizing ideas or solutions to a problem. It encourages equal participation, minimizes dominance, and facilitates consensus decision making. The nominal group technique also promotes equal participation and creativity (everyone has a chance to contribute without being overshadowed), encourages divergent thinking and brainstorming (a wide range of ideas are generated without filtering), and facilitates effective decision making (priorities are established through discussion and consensus).
- **Red Team:** Students are divided into two groups and share their current solution. The opposite group presents a series of "I wonder" statements and variable changes that the team reflects upon to improve their solution. They also identify weaknesses and vulnerabilities and present them to the group. They provide diverse perspectives to challenge assumptions, explore worst-case scenarios, and identify potential risks associated with implementing the solution.
- **Town Hall Meeting:** This is a forum for open discussion and exchange of ideas. Like traditional town halls, it provides a platform for students, teachers, administrators, and community members to discuss relevant educational issues openly and directly. Topics might include school policies, curriculum changes, budget allocations, challenges faced by the school community, or broader educational issues like equity and access. The format often involves a moderator who guides the discussion, facilitates question-and-answer sessions, and ensures everyone has a chance to contribute.

- **Affinity Mapping:** This protocol is designed to form key themes to understand and make choices across a range of options.

Example divergent and convergent routines for searching for implementation are shown in the following sections.

DIVERGENT THINKING—SWOT

SWOT stands for strengths, weaknesses, opportunities, and threats. A SWOT analysis, as illustrated in figure 6.4, is a simple protocol for students to list all the strengths, weaknesses, opportunities, and threats of potential solutions.

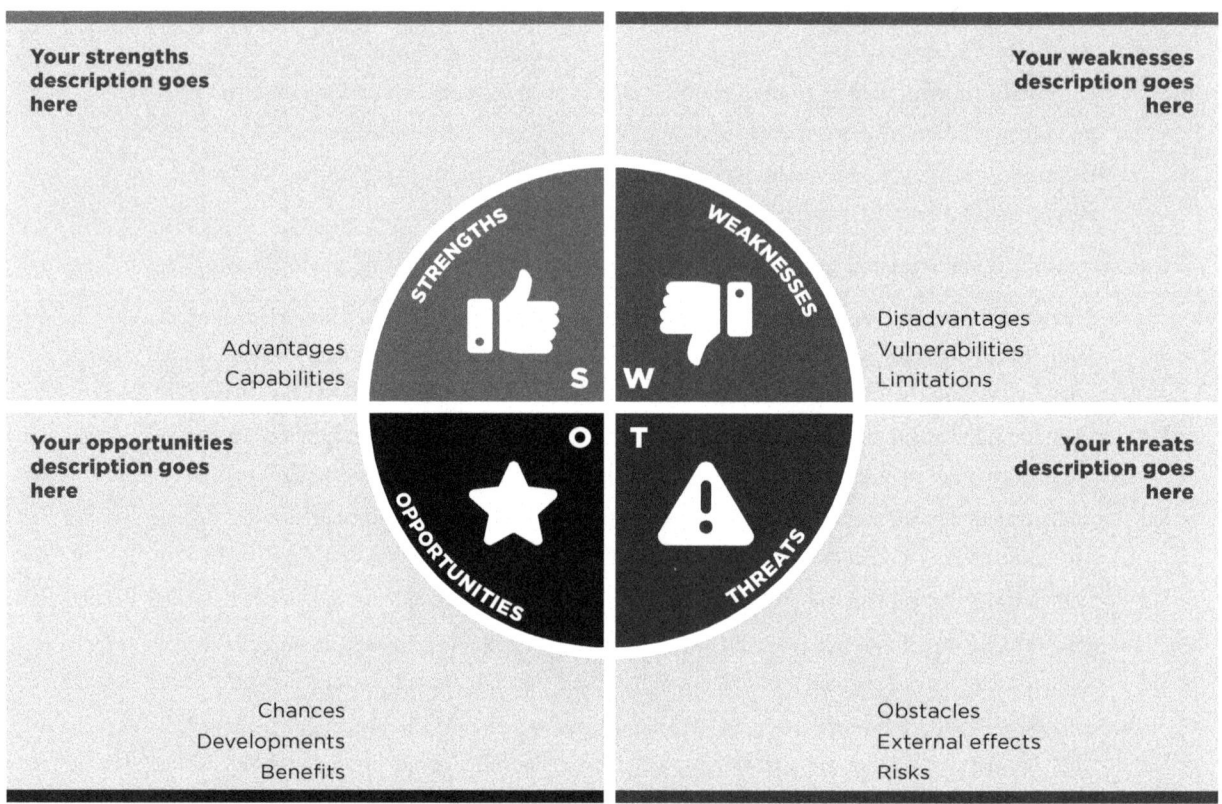

Figure 6.4: SWOT analysis.

As an example, imagine students are tasked with infusing standards related to the formation of NATO or the Cold War into addressing multilateral disarmament and arms limitation in the United States and other countries around the world. The teacher uses the SWOT analysis to have students identify the internal strengths and weaknesses in making policy changes as well as external opportunities and threats. The SWOT protocol integrates both convergent and divergent possibilities and is a great way to support students in analyzing situations and possible solutions.

CONVERGENT THINKING—AFFINITY MAPPING

Affinity Mapping is putting a bunch of sticky notes with ideas on them on a wall and then grouping them based on their similarities (affinities). These groupings can help you extract insights and themes to help you build effectively toward next steps. See the appendix (page 205) for more details on Affinity Mapping.

By having students engage in a multitude of routines of divergent and convergent thinking, students will have a better chance of understanding possible solutions and solution choices.

Stage 3: Apply a Solution

Once a solution has been selected, teams need to figure out how to implement and inspect implementation over time. The key is for students to receive feedback quickly as they share out and implement their plans. Several protocols have been shared throughout the book that can be helpful here, including Gallery Walk (page 139), Critical Friends (page 88), Tuning Protocol (page 204), What? So What? Now What? (page 34), and the Consultancy Dilemma (page 204). One additional strategy that is helpful is the use of the Charette protocol. A Charette protocol is designed to resolve conflicts and map out solutions in a short duration of time. The protocol has the following four steps.

1. The team receiving feedback shares out their current implementation challenge or update on progress.
2. The team providing feedback asks clarifying questions.
3. The team providing feedback shares out strengths and weaknesses of the implementation of the solutions. Typically, teams frame this feedback using "I like" and "I wonder" statements. The team receiving feedback doesn't speak during this time.
4. The team receiving feedback shares out specific next steps they will take.

The Charette protocol along with the other routines mentioned earlier are great routines for students to receive feedback on the solution.

Success Criterion 2: Engage With Authentic Audiences

Learning to transfer is not a purely academic exercise, but rather it is a type of learning that is critical for students to successfully navigate life. Students will face a number of problems in their lives that will require them to retrieve prior knowledge, see patterns in new situations, and work with others to solve wicked problems. Accordingly, teachers should infuse the idea of working *with* authentic audiences in all transfer-level problems. An authentic audience includes community members, nonprofit organizations, and for-profit organizations who are engaging in the problem context. Students who work with authentic audiences should consider themselves "knowledgeable others" who are present to learn from the community, engage with, and offer ideas that may be helpful to integrate with the authentic audience.

A critical aspect of working with authentic audiences is the practice of empathy. Sherry Turkle (2021), author of *The Empathy Diaries*, argues that there are four key practices for building an understanding and respect for others. Those practices include:

- **Embrace not knowing:** You can't put yourself into someone else's situation if you have preconceptions about its contours. This isn't easy. We're trained to relate to others by expressing what we think we share with them: "Oh, you lost your job. I know how tough that is; I lost mine as well!" It's the opposite—the strategy of not knowing—that leaves you open to the truth of things.

- **Embrace radical differences:** Empathy doesn't start with a reassuring "I'm like you." On the contrary, empathy accepts friction. Colleagues may have profound disagreements, just like family members, neighbors, and friends. Empathy is not about being conflict-averse—it's noisy because people are. To be empathetic, we must be willing to get in there, own the conflict, and learn how to fight fair. It's about full engagement, even when it is uncomfortable.

- **Embrace commitment:** Empathy implies that you will do the work necessary to comprehend not just the place the person is coming from but their problem. It's a discipline of basic respect, both personal and civic. You have a stake in helping your neighbor make things better. You can't get bored or turn away.

- **Embrace community:** Empathy isn't altruistic. It enlarges those who offer it and binds them to others. It fights anomie. If you've been heard, and the rules you've been asked to follow take your situation into account, you feel part of something larger than yourself.

Using empathy as a driver for understanding and respecting others is essential for working with peers and external audiences. The Collaborative for Academic, Social, and Emotional Learning (CASEL) is a nonprofit organization that is helping make evidence-based social and emotional learning an integral part of education from preschool through high school. They offer a number of different tools and resources to assist schools in building and implementing empathy-based practices (see https://learningforward.org/wp-content/uploads/2020/10/tool-empathy-interviews.pdf). One specific tool that is particularly powerful to support students is the Empathy Interview protocol from High Tech High (see https://schoolguide.casel.org/resource/empathy-interview-protocol).

When using empathy interviews, note that the California Department of Education (2017) created a number of protocols that center on understanding, respecting, and sharing the thoughts and feelings of others. The goal of the Empathy Interview exercise is to gain a deeper understanding of a user's experience of the issue you are working on. The Empathy Interview protocol has four key components.

1. Set up norms that include the following: (1) seek to understand, not confirm, (2) ask once, clearly, (3) ask questions that elicit stories and feelings, (4) probe. Make comments and ask questions such as, "Tell me more . . . " and "What was that like for you?"

2. Prepare for the interview by selecting four to six questions. Questions may include: Tell me about a time when you felt successful in X; what happened? What made this a success? (What did you do? What did others do?) Tell me about a time when X was hard; What happened? How did that feel?
Why was that hard? How did you react? What do you wish would have happened? What would have helped?

3. Conduct the interview.

4. Reflect on content (What did we hear? What are we learning about the causes that contribute to the problem?) and process.

Along with the Empathy Interview, other protocols to assist with engaging with authentic audiences are listed in table 6.6.

Table 6.6: Protocols for Engaging With Authentic Audiences

Strategy	Description
Empathy Interviews	The goal for the Empathy Interview exercise is to gain a deeper understanding of a user's experience of the issue you are working on.
True for Whom?	This routine (Harvard Graduate School of Education, 2022) is designed to help students consider the roles of context and perspective in shaping what people believe. The protocol focuses on understanding the situation about which a claim is made, who made it, and what were their interests. Students list the different points of view and choose a viewpoint to dramatize (My viewpoint is . . . I think this claim is true/false/uncertain because . . .). Then, they step outside the circle of viewpoints and take everything into account and ask new questions.
Three Stories	This routine (Ganz, 2009) is designed explore ideas, concepts, and experiences from multiple perspectives: a "personal story," which involves reflecting on your own experiences and understanding of the topic at hand; a "disciplinary story," which delves into the established knowledge and expertise within a specific discipline related to the topic; and a "cultural story," which broadens the scope to examine the topic within a broader cultural context. By considering different narratives, individuals develop a more nuanced and multifaceted understanding of the topic.
Thinking Hats	You and your team members can learn how to separate thinking into six clear functions and roles. Each thinking role is identified with a colored symbolic "Thinking Hat." By mentally wearing and switching "Hats," you can easily focus or redirect thoughts, the conversation, or the meeting (De Bono Group, 2023).
Think, Feel, Care	This thinking routine (Harvard Graduate School of Education, 2022) is used to encourage empathy and perspective-taking among students. It helps them develop a deeper understanding of different viewpoints and consider the emotions and perspectives of others. Students are presented with a situation or scenario to consider. They are asked to "think" about the situation from a different perspective, "feel" about the situation from their perspective and another perspective, then "care" and consider why it matters to them.

Success Criterion 3: Address Setbacks and Changes

The OECD created a report in 2021 about the critical need for students to be adaptive problem solvers. Adaptive problem solvers are prepared to adjust to problems where changes occur in the problem situation. In one study, researchers gave adults a problem in which they had to buy and sell stocks. As in real life, the stock market changes during the problem where some companies begin to outperform or underperform earlier performance levels. The problem is adaptive and much more realistic than static problems whereby the problem does not change based on the choices of the student or the external environment (Greiff et al., 2017). These problems are critical for students who will be facing nonroutine positions that largely require quick and flexible adaptation to new circumstances (Pellegrino & Hilton, 2012).

Classroom teachers need to plan and place challenges along the way for students to navigate when they are solving a problem. One way to engage in this work includes curveballs. Curveballs are slight shifts in students' work that begins to create a more adaptive situation for students and simulates the wicked environments of the real world. There are many types of curveball strategies which are illustrated in table 6.7.

Table 6.7: Curveball Strategies

Adaptive Qualities	Description
Dynamic Presentations	This routine focuses on engaging students in addressing questions that involve clarifying information and handing potential curveballs to the task, context, and perspective.
Open the Success Criteria	This routine focuses on engaging students in slight changes in the success criteria.
Situation Room Type 1	This routine focuses on engaging students in a new task format. For instance, in lieu of a student writing a paper, they may be required to present a skit, podcast, or presentation.
Situation Room Type 2	This routine focuses on engaging students in a new task format. For instance, in lieu of a student working on antitrust issues with a transit system, they now must evaluate a power company.
Situation Room Type 3	This routine focuses on engaging students in a new task format. For instance, in lieu of a student writing a story about one hero, they are tasked with writing a story from the antagonist's point of view.
Sequels	This routine focuses on engaging students in analyzing a brand-new situation after a unit has been completed. For instance, a student may receive an alternative problem and then analyze the connections regarding the problem and solution to the problem they just solved.
Skunkworks	This routine focuses on ensuring more than one context is evaluated in the class at one time. The routine provides one context and problem to the class, and then other specific students in the class are given an entirely separate problem to solve that connects to the same content.

Recall the discussion of kind and wicked environments from the introduction (page 1). For example, in kind environments, presenters are not interrupted or directly questioned before, during, or after the presentation. Wicked environments are ones in which the presenter is challenged and directly questioned before, during, or after the presentation. Being able to practice handling being challenged on ideas or knowledge will give students the experience to handle them in real time. This will also provide you and them with formative information on the quality of their presentation and their depth of understanding of the content they are presenting.

To prepare students for handling dynamic presentations, students can engage in a Red Team protocol. As shown earlier (page 189), Red Teams are feedback groups that check students for several variables, including the following.

- **Accuracy:** How do you know that the background information you are using is valid?
- **Process:** Who did you involve? Where in the process did you involve others? How did you use that feedback in your decision making?
- **Perspective:** How have you ensured that you have listened to varying viewpoints and perspectives in this process and in your solution?
- **Range:** What other solutions did you consider? What other examples have you leaned on to make this decision?
- **Implementation:** How will you ensure high-quality implementation?
- **Accountability:** How will you ensure observable impact? How will you make adjustments along the way when things start to change?

During Red Teams, presenters give short five-minute presentations where individuals or groups pitch one or two minutes of a presentation and peers interject one or two questions and see how they respond. If they don't know the answer, then share with them that they should say that to the audience. "I don't have the answer to that question. I will investigate it and get back to you by _____."

Other strategies shown in table 6.7 (page 194) include preparing students for utilizing "the Situation Room." Scenario planning is critical in building adaptive problem-solving acumen. What if you are in the middle of presenting and a situation occurs that influences your decision? Imagine that you had just opened a new outdoor restaurant and smoke from fires far away is diminishing the air quality, or you find that your proposal for purchasing a fleet of electric cars for your company is disrupted by a military coup in Africa that is prohibiting cobalt from being exported (McDowell & Miller, 2022).

To prepare students for "what ifs," create a list of five to ten scenarios and write them on sticky notes. Hand out the notes, and ask students to prepare to adjust their presentations. Before they present, place students in pairs and have them give each other feedback. During formal presentations, you may provide a "what if" and observe how they handle the situation (McDowell & Miller, 2022). Here are a few scenarios for students.

- **Funding:** There has been an increase (or decrease) in funding for your solution. What will you do?
- **Popular sentiment:** Your idea, your organization, and/or you have fallen out of favor. What will you do?
- **Sudden change:** As you are preparing to present, a new issue emerges from seemingly out of nowhere that requires your attention.

Finally, teachers should consider using the Skunkworks protocol. During World War II, every manufacturing company in the United States was searching for substantial innovations to end the war. Lockheed Martin's Advanced Development Projects created a special independent laboratory experiment to develop new ideas, new products, and new actions. This special unit of people worked together to create solutions that were outside the current products and processes of the company. Moreover, this unit was next to a plastics factory in Burbank, California. The strong smells that made their way into the makeshift domicile made the Lockheed research and development workers think of the foul-smelling "Skunk Works" factory in Al Capp's Li'l Abner comic strip (Liang, 2014).

Schools need Skunkworks groups—groups that are independent of the collective beliefs and behaviors of the dominant culture. Such a separation would allow a group to truly experiment and rethink not only the problems to solve but how to solve those problems. Skunkworks groups need to be prepared to suspend their beliefs and take a deep dive into those innovations that are disruptive—those innovations that could fundamentally change the basic premise of traditional schooling and, as such, challenge the operating procedures of the school.

To begin, Skunkworks groups should focus more on learning than teaching and use evaluation of their impact on learning for all students as their driver for decision making. These suggested boundaries spark a need for understanding stakeholder perspectives, inspecting the underpinnings of educator actions, and tackling opportunity, student empowerment, and achievement issues. All disruptive innovative solutions will ultimately lead to the need to change teacher and administrative behavior, which is incredibly challenging in a system that typically changes everything around adults.

Big ideas start with small steps. Here are a few steps to kickstart the Skunkworks protocol.

1. **Begin with the 5 Whys:** Begin by attempting to find the foundational root to the problem or challenge and how such a problem is perceived by multiple stakeholders. Use at least 5 Why questions to get to the basis of the problem. For example: *Why do we do X as a means to enhance every learner's learning? Why is X important to us? Why is X being used as opposed to Y? Why are we focusing here?*

2. **Stay small; stay focused:** When you are questioning everything, tether it to learner progress across all subgroups, and when the team finds a question that is of interest, go for it and stick with it. Questions should be at the epicenter for equity and academic excellence; answers should connect to those strategies that have the probability of yielding a substantial impact on learning.

3. **Take a "bias to action and inspection" approach:** Once you have a driving question, begin implementing ideas and verify the impact of those ideas through various forms of data collection (surveys, pre/post, focus groups, and so on).

4. **Vote with your feet:** Find people who want to do this work and don't exclude anyone who is interested. Once you start, though, stick with that team. If you have more than seven people interested, you may want to create another Skunkworks team.

5. **Fishbowl (but don't feed the fish):** Let everyone see your work, but that's it. They get to listen, for now.

Jen Yonkers—New York Department of Education: Senior Director—Efficient Interdisciplinary Learning to Transfer Learning

I began my work with a group of sixty elementary schools in hope of piloting and eventually scaling a model that creates access to rich and rigorous learning experiences for all children. I quickly realized that in order to achieve this goal, we needed to start small with an intense focus on planning. Project-based learning was intended to be an aspect of this work, but I knew that project-based learning alone would not support us in achieving what we set out to accomplish. So instead of starting with a project, our first step was to start with high-quality curricular materials.

In beginning with high-quality curricular materials, I intentionally sought to address two barriers that often get in the way of students receiving a rich, rigorous, and meaningful education. First, we needed to ensure that all elementary school students were receiving enough instruction in social studies and science using high-quality, standards-aligned curricular resources for those disciplines. Second, we know that our curriculum comes to us segmented by discipline but this isn't the way our brains learn. We needed to tap into the science of how our brains learn by making connections to plan for interdisciplinary instruction. This was no small feat.

We took our curriculum across literacy, social studies, mathematics, science, and social-emotional learning, and began the task of interdisciplinary mapping using a knowledge-building approach and by highlighting key learning intentions and outcomes. In parallel to this, I designed resources for teams of teachers to engage in interdisciplinary mapping since maps are meant to be living documents where teams continuously make decisions grounded in the latest research and interrogate the quality of those decisions across the year.

Interdisciplinary mapping was only the first step since we know that our curriculum often sits at a surface and deep level. We needed to go beyond this so that our students had the opportunity to transfer their learning to new, real-world, authentic contexts. This is where the projects came in. Instead of retrofitting an already developed project from a bank, we used our curriculum, the connections across disciplines and the key learning intentions and outcomes to guide project development. In this way, our projects served as an umbrella connecting the surface- and deep-level learning students were doing in literacy, social studies, science, and mathematics to a real-world authentic context.

As we developed projects, we used an adapted version of the project planning template from *Rigorous PBL by Design* to map out our projects. Since this was a heavy lift for teacher teams, I gave them "half-baked" projects, which already outlined the curricular connections, key learning intentions and outcomes, success criteria at a surface, deep, and transfer level and to draft their ideas for entry and exit events. The teacher teams took it from there by digging into their curriculum for lessons that could promote the surface- and deep-level understanding needed so students could transfer their learning to new contexts. This not only helped instruction and planning become more tightly aligned but also solved another barrier to this work—TIME. Instead of teachers finding time to fit in project lessons that were sometimes disconnected from their curriculum and grade-level standards, they were using lessons directly from the curriculum that they were already planning to teach.

While we are still piloting this approach, we have learned a lot. A key to doing this work well is by leaning into the curricular resources we already have to support surface and deep

> learning. Doing this paired with an emphasis on key learning intentions and outcomes and success criteria at surface, deep, and transfer levels not only supported teachers with more intentional planning but also improved instructional coherence since teachers were tuned in to focusing on the most important learning intentions/outcomes and how to make instruction feel coherent across the day as they leveraged interdisciplinary connections. Best of all, it was fun. Teacher teams felt empowered to make instructional decisions, of course, grounded in research and guided by an inquiry process that helped them evaluate the quality of their decisions, and students were engaged in work that was meaningful, relevant, and connected to their everyday lives.

Conclusion

Transfer learning is a combination of lateral thinking across contexts and navigating dynamic situations in problem-based contexts. When students and teachers work together to leverage the learner qualities, the powerful strategies of surface and deep learning, and the habits of transfer learning, students are able to handle challenging situations. Ultimately, when such habits are in place, along with the other set of learning habits, students know what to do when they don't know what to do, and that is the ultimate work of educators.

Reflection Questions

1. What transfer-level habits (Habits 9 and 10) are students regularly engaging in?

2. With what transfer-level habits (Habits 9 and 10) are students requiring significant guidance from you and your colleagues?

3. To what extent are you finding trends and patterns with certain students in their development of transfer-level habits?

4. How are students infusing the transfer-level habits (Habits 9 and 10) into their behavior?

Rigor Redefined © 2024 Solution Tree Press • SolutionTree.com
Visit **go.SolutionTree.com/instruction** to download this free reproducible.

Next Steps

Go through the *Need It—See It—Start It—Show It* process. Work with colleagues to answer the following four questions.

1. **Need it: What is compelling to you and your team right now?** To address question 1, conduct a Learning Walk to observe the level of implementation and impact of these habits in your classroom. When observing, follow the What? So What? Now What? protocol.

    a. Write down only what was observed in class.

    b. Assign people to look at the interaction between two of the three elements of the instructional core.

       i. Teacher-student

       ii. Student-content

       iii. Teacher-content

    c. Debrief the observations by analyzing any patterns that emerge.

    d. Predict the kind of learning they might expect from the teaching they observed.

    e. Recommend the next level of work that could help the school better achieve their desired goal.

    Another option is to bring evidence of student work related to Habits 9–10 and discuss the findings using the What? So What? Now What? protocol (page 34).

2. **See it: How will you make what you want to improve observable in the next six weeks?** To address question 2, have staff complete an initial survey on the level of familiarity, employment, and inspection of teacher and student actions in the classroom as related to Habits 9–10. Debrief the survey data with department or grade-level groups (see survey in chapter 1. In addition, have staff identify a small and doable practice within one of the habits. Select the practice and identify what the practice would look like in the classroom in relation to teacher, the student, and the task now, in three weeks, and in six weeks.

3. **Start it: How can you lower the threshold to move from evidence and ideas into action and from action into evidence and ideas?** To address question 3, lower the threshold of implementation by using the following strategies to make habits more doable.

    a. Small—make it manageable

    b. Stack—link it to your current practice

    c. Sustain—make it routine

    d. Shelter—protect this work by not adding other changes

    e. Sprint—start with a small group before you scale

    f. Share—measure your impact, discuss findings, and determine next steps

4. **Show it: How will you demonstrate your impact to others?** To address question 4, use the Consultancy Dilemma (page 204) or Critical Friends (page 88) protocols to discuss key learning of implementing the dispositional habits discussed in this chapter.

Epilogue

All day, the world makes its demands.
There's so much of it, world, / begging to be noticed.
—*Leila Chatti*

When we wake up in the morning, there are millions of things that demand our attention. Our phones, filled with more apps and endless information than we could ever need, sit by our bedside table, pulling us away from any chance of remaining slumber. Megan Garber wrote that "Today's news moves as a maelstrom [of] information at once trifling and historic, petty and grave, cajoling, demanding, funny, horrifying, uplifting, embarrassing, fleeting, loud—so much of it, at so many scales" (as cited in Fattal, 2023). News, of course, demands one small fraction of our attention. Our children, our chores, and our responsibilities as a parent, spouse, caregiver, and educator pull our attention in different directions.

In the research literature, attention is considered the first of four major pillars of learning (Dehaene, 2020). Attention amplifies the information we focus on, which then promotes active engagement, which prompts our brain to ceaselessly test new hypotheses. This then enables us to seek feedback to see if our guesses fizzle or succeed in the real world. Finally, through our attention, we begin to consolidate our learning to where the learning becomes tacit. This is why student clarity is so important. Are they with us when we are teaching? Because if their attention is elsewhere, the other pillars likely fall away. You simply can't be curious and act on that curiosity if your attention is elsewhere.

When we enter our schools and classrooms, there are a number of experiences that fill our attention: checking in on colleagues, student feelings, the learning priorities of the day, the construction project in the schoolyard, the new lockdown drill, and so on. The idea of changing has always been stressful, but now the idea is overwhelming and off-putting and can leave us feeling uninterested, making us feel that others are being insensitive to our current plight of competing interests and demands.

Alas, the focused attention on the ten habits is challenging because of these seemingly endless demands on our attention. Like a seedling growing in an overcrowded redwood forest, everything is competing for sunlight. The challenge here is to focus our attention on rigorous teaching and learning.

The seedlings linked to deep and transfer learning have had a difficult time competing in the forest of school initiatives. As this book has shown, research illustrates that rigorous learning—and building student capacity to develop a set of skills to own their own learning—takes time and precision with a set of habits that must occur over and over and over. The difficulty is linked to determining the best fit for each strategy, implementing the strategy, and inspecting the impact of the strategy. These difficulties are associated with our degree of training, our ability to assess our own practice, and students' level of learning, all while other interests compete for our attention and that of our students. How do we circle this square? How do we get curious about this work?

When you close this book, there will be an impulse to do everything or get overwhelmed and do nothing. The former impulse will create a high degree of stress, and you will ultimately end up with a lot of planning without a thoughtful and sustained approach. The second will be a check on the book study group list and then a refocus on the other competing demands of your time.

The way forward is to engage in small and doable shifts in practice. In doing this, you and your team must determine what to observe in order to name and notice small and doable changes in student actions. Next, you will need to deprioritize other small habits by shifting your focus away from them. After this, you must start slowly, and the process should feel calm. When we wake up, we should say "1% percent better today for student learning—it doesn't have to be 100%, 1% each day is enough." Spending a bit of our attention on rigorous learning will enable students to grow in an overcrowded environment of competing demands. Like seedlings in an overcrowded forest, students will rise to high levels of rigorous learning and develop ownership over their learning over time. And, perhaps, you will find a sense of satisfaction as you control your attention and see the power of attention giving back to those who pay it both in emotional regulation and in a high degree of impact on student learning.

Appendix

Explicit conversational protocols enable classroom discussions to move across surface, deep, and transfer learning. Structured protocols provide scaffolding to promote focused, rigorous dialogue and create a framework that allows students to build on one another's ideas in a focused manner. When teachers employ thoughtful discussion protocols, they provide cognitive support that boosts critical thinking skills, scaffolding for students to construct understanding together, and equal opportunities for all students to participate and be heard. The protocols outlined in this appendix represent field-tested, high-leverage techniques for fostering the kinds of purposeful discussions that drive rigorous learning.

Consultancy Dilemma

1. *Setup*: Explain the purpose of the protocol and review the steps. (2 minutes)
2. *Present*: Overview (presenter) the dilemma and pose a focusing question. If documents are available, distribute and review. (7–12 minutes)
3. *Clarify*: Ask (group) clarifying questions, which the presenter answers. (5 minutes)
4. *Create probing questions*: Write (group) probing questions on sticky notes. (2 minutes)
5. *Ask*: Read (group) their probing questions aloud and pass sticky notes to the presenter. (3 minutes)
6. *Review and refine*: Share (presenter) which probing questions were most thought-provoking. (2 minutes)
7. *Refocus*: Restate or adapt (presenter) the focusing question. (1 minute)
8. *Separate*: Move (presenter) away from the group but stay within earshot, avoiding eye contact. (1 minute)
9. *Discuss*: Discuss (group) the dilemma with the focusing question and provocative questions in mind. (12 minutes)
10. *Recommend*: Offer (group) recommendations and suggestions. (3 minutes)
11. *Reflect*: Return (presenter) and share meaningful insights and discuss next steps. (5 minutes)
12. *Debrief*: Discuss (presenter and group) their experiences and reflections on the process. (5 minutes)

Source: Adapted from Dunne, F., Evans, P., & Thompson-Grove, G. (2021). Coalition of Essential Schools and the Annenberg Institute for School Reform.

Tuning Protocol

1. *Introduction:* The facilitator introduces the goals, guidelines, and schedule of the protocol. (5 minutes)
2. *Presentation:* The presenter shares context, supporting documents, student work, and a focusing question. Participants are silent. (10–15 minutes)
3. *Clarifying Questions:* Participants ask questions to understand the work better. Facilitator ensures questions are oriented toward the goals shared by the presenter. (3–5 minutes)
4. *Examining the Work:* Participants review the work, noting alignment with goals and potential disconnects. (3–5 minutes)

5. *Silent Reflection:* Participants silently review notes and prepare feedback. Presenter remains silent. (2–3 minutes)
6. *Warm and Cool Feedback:* Participants share warm (positive) feedback and cool (constructive) feedback while the presenter listens silently. (3–5 minutes)
7. *Reflection:* Presenter shares new insights gained from the feedback without defending their work. (3–5 minutes)
8. *Debrief:* Facilitator leads discussion about the tuning experience. (3–5 minutes)

Source: Adapted from McDonald, J. (n.d.). School Reform Initiative.

Affinity Mapping

1. *Setup:* Explain the protocol, reveal the question, and start silent brainstorming. (2–4 minutes)
2. *Place sticky notes:* Participants place their sticky notes on the chart paper in silence. (1 minute)
3. *Categorize:* Participants silently group sticky notes with similar ideas together. (5–7 minutes)
4. *Label:* Volunteers read and label each group of sticky notes, with input from the group. (15 minutes)
5. *Discuss:* Open discussion on emerging themes, surprises, and missing elements. (5 minutes)
6. *Next steps:* Decide next steps, timeline, resources, and responsibilities for each category. (8 minutes)
7. *Debrief and discuss:* Reflect on the protocol's effectiveness, the value of silence, and potential future use. (5 minutes)

Source: Adapted from Peterson-Veatch, R. (2006). Instructional Consulting. Indiana University Kelley School of Business.

References and Resources

Acar, O. A., Tarakci, M., & Knippenberg, D. V. (2019). *Why constraints are good for innovation.* Accessed at https://hbr.org/2019/11/why-constraints-are-good-for-innovation on July 15, 2023.

Agarwal, P. K. (2019). Retrieval practice & Bloom's taxonomy: Do students need fact knowledge before higher order learning? *Journal of Educational Psychology, 111*(2), 189–209.

Almarode, J., &Vandas, K. (2018). *Clarity for learning: Five essential practices that empower students and teachers.* Thousand Oaks, CA: Corwin.

Anderson, J., & Taner, G. (2023). Building the expert teacher prototype: A metasummary of teacher expertise studies in primary and secondary education. *Educational Research Review, 38.* Accessed at https://doi.org/10.1016/j.edurev.2022.100485 on February 20, 2024.

Apple Music. (n.d.). *American idiot.* Accessed at https://music.apple.com/us/album/american-idiot/1161539183 on August 28, 2023.

Argyris, C. (1999). Tacit knowledge and management. In R. J. Sternberg & J. A. Horvath (Eds.), *Tacit knowledge in professional practice: Researcher and practitioner perspectives* (pp. 123–140). Mahwah, NJ: Lawrence Erlbaum Associates.

Baddeley, A. D., & Longman, D. J. A. (1978). The influence of length and frequency of training session on the rate of learning to type. *Ergonomics, 21*(8), 627–635. https://doi.org/10.1080/00140137808931764

Barton, C. (n.d.). SSDD *problems.* Accessed at https://ssddproblems.com on June 18, 2024.

Biggs, J. (n.d.). *Solo taxonomy.* Accessed at https://www.johnbiggs.com.au/academic/solo-taxonomy/ on May 29, 2023.

Biggs, J., & Collis, K. (1982). *Evaluating the quality of learning: The SOLO taxonomy.* Cambridge, MA: Academic Press.

Bjork, R. A., & Bjork, E. L. (2020). Desirable difficulties in theory and practice. *Journal of Applied Research in Memory and Cognition, 9*(4), 475–479.

Blank, S. (2009). *Relentless: The difference between motion and action.* Accessed at https://steveblank.com/2009/11/09/relentless-–-the-difference-between-motion-and-action/ on May 29, 2023.

Bloom, B. S., Englehart, M. D., Furst, E. J., Hill, W. H., & Krathwohl, D. R. (1956). *The taxonomy of educational objectives, handbook I: The cognitive domain.* New York: David McKay Co.

Brackett, M. (2023, October 17). *The colors of our emotions.* Accessed at https://marcbrackett.com/the-colors-of-our-emotions on May 29, 2024.

Brown, B. (2020). *The gifts of imperfection* (10th anniversary ed.). Center City, MN: Hazelden.

California Air Resources Board. (2023). *Wildfires and climate change.* Accessed at https://ww2.arb.ca.gov/wildfires-climate-change on August 29, 2023.

California Department of Education. (2017, December). *Root cause analysis toolkit.* Accessed at https://www.lausd.org/site/handlers/filedownload.ashx?moduleinstanceid=45379&dataid=65270&FileName=Root%20Cause%20Analysis%20Toolkit.pdf on November 17, 2023.

Cepeda, N. J., Pashler, H., Vul, E., Wixted, J. T., & Rohrer, D. (2006). Distributed practice in verbal recall tasks: A review and quantitative synthesis. *Psychological Bulletin, 132*(3), 354–380. Accessed at https://www.doi.org/10.1037/0033-2909.132.3.354 on February 21, 2024.

Chapin, S. H., O'Connor, C., & Anderson, N. C. (2009). *Classroom discussions: Using math talk to help students learn, grades K–6.* Sausalito, CA: Math Solutions.

Chayka, D. (2020, June 18). The UN has too much on its plate. *The Economist.* Accessed at https://www.economist.com/special-report/2020/06/18/the-un-has-too-much-on-its-plate on August 29, 2023.

Christensen, C. M., & Shu, K. (2006). *What is an organization's culture?* (Rev.; Harvard Business School Background Note 399-104). Cambridge, MA: Harvard Business School.

City, E., Elmore, R. F., Fiarman, S. E., & Teitel, L. (2009). *Instructional rounds in education: A network approach to improving teaching and learning.* Harvard Education Press.

Claxton, G. (2021). *The future of teaching.* New York: Routledge.

Claxton, G. (2022). *Unfixing the growth mindset.* Accessed at https://www.guyclaxton.net/post/unfixing-growth-mindset on June 15, 2023.

Clear, J. (2018). *Atomic habits: An easy and proven way to build good habits and break bad ones.* New York: Avery.

Core Knowledge Foundation. (2017, November 15). *The baseball experiment.* Accessed at https://www.coreknowledge.org/blog/baseball-experiment-two-wisconsin-researchers-discovered-comprehension-gap-knowledge-gap/ on August 29, 2023.

Corrigan, C. (n.d.). *Open space technology.* Accessed at https://www.iisd.org/system/files/meterial/OST.pdf on February 4, 2024.

Corwin Visible Learning Plus. (2024). *Visible Learning Meta^x.* Accessed at https://www.visiblelearningmetax.com/ on February 21, 2024.

De Bono Group. (2023, December 23). *Six Thinking Hats.* Accessed at https://www.debonogroup.com/services/core-programs/six-thinking-hats on May 30, 2024.

de Jong, T., Lazonder, A. W., Chinn, C. A., Fischer, F., Gobert, J., Hmelo-Silver, C. E., et al. (2023, May). Let's talk evidence: The case for combining inquiry-based and direct instruction. *Educational Research Review, 39*, 100536.

Dehaene, S. (2020). *How we learn: Why brains learn better than any machine . . . for now.* New York: Viking.

Dempster, F. N., & Farris, R. (1990). The spacing effect: Research and practice. *Journal of Research and Development in Education, 23*(2), 97–101.

Donovan, S., & Bransford, J. (2005). *How students learn: History, mathematics, and science in the classroom.* Washington, DC: National Academies Press.

Duhigg, C. (2014). The power of habit: Why we do what we do in life and business. New York: Random House Trade Paperbacks.

Education Endowment Foundation. (n.d.). *Teaching and learning toolkit: An accessible summary of education evidence.* Accessed at https://educationendowmentfoundation.org.uk/education-evidence/teaching-learning-toolkit on August 29, 2023.

EL Education. (n.d.). *Reading informational texts: Researching freaky frogs.* Accessed at https://curriculum.eleducation.org/curriculum/ela/grade-3/module-2/unit-3/lesson-1 on August 29, 2023.

EL Education. (2024). *Educating for a better world. Accessed at* https://eleducation.org on February 21, 2024.

Epstein, D. (2019). *Range: Why generalists triumph in a specialized world*. New York: Riverhead Books.

Ericcson, K. A., Prietla, M. J., & Cokely, E. T. (2007, July–August). The making of an expert. *Harvard Business Review.* Accessed at https://hbr.org/2007/07/the-making-of-an-expert on February 21, 2024.

Erickson, H. L., & Lanning, L. A. (2014). *Transitioning to concept-based curriculum and instruction: How to bring content and process together.* Thousand Oaks, CA: Corwin.

Escaperoom.com. (2024). *FAQs.* Accessed at https://escaperoom.com/ on August 29, 2023.

ESPN cricinfo. (2023, December 11). *Meredith blow for Hurricanes as Hughes guides Sixers to second win.* Accessed at https://www.espncricinfo.com/series/big-bash-league-2023-24-1386092/hobart-hurricanes-vs-sydney-sixers-5th-match-1386098/match-report on February 20, 2024.

Facing History and Ourselves. (2020, May 12). *Socratic Seminar.* Accessed at https://www.facinghistory.org/resource-library/socratic-seminar on July 5, 2023.

Fattal, I. (2023, May 27). The art of paying attention. *The Atlantic.* Accessed at https://www.theatlantic.com/newsletters/archive/2023/05/attention-mary-oliver-technology/674227/ on August 29, 2023.

Ferlazzo, L. (2020). Author interview with Dr. Gholdy Muhammad: 'Cultivating genius.' *Ed Week.* Accessed at https://www.edweek.org/teaching-learning/opinion-author-interview-with-dr-gholdy-muhammad-cultivating-genius/2020/01 on June 18, 2024.

Fisher, D., & Frey, N. (2013). *Better learning through structured teaching: A framework for the gradual release of responsibility* (2nd ed.). Alexandria, VA: ASCD.

Fogg, B. J. (2021). *Tiny habits: The small changes that change everything.* Harvest.

Ganz, M. (2009). *What is public narrative: Self, us & now* (*public narrative worksheet*) [Working paper]. Accessed at https://dash.harvard.edu/handle/1/30760283 on August 29, 2023.

Gilovich, T. (1993). *How we know what isn't so: The fallibility of human reason in everyday life.* New York: The Free Press.

Gould, S. J. (1990). *Wonderful life: The Burgess Shale and the nature of history.* New York: W. W. Norton & Company.

Grieff, S., Graesser, A., Iliescu, D., Rouet, J.-F., Scheiter, K., & Scherer, R. (2021). *4. PIAAC cycle 2 assessment framework: Adaptive problem solving*. Accessed at https://www.oecd-ilibrary.org/sites/3a14db8b-en/index.html?itemId=/content/component/3a14db8b-en on February 4, 2024.

Greiff, S., Scheiter, K., Scherer, R., Borgonov, F., Britt, A., Graesser, A., et al. (2017). Adaptive problem solving: Moving towards a new assessment domain in the second cycle of PIAAC. *OECD Education Working Papers, 156*. Accessed at https://dx.doi.org/10.1787/90fde2f4-en on August 29, 2023.

Grissmer, D., White, T., Buddin, R., Berends, M., Willingham, D., DeCoster, J., et al (2023). *A kindergarten lottery evaluation of core knowledge charter schools: Should building general knowledge have a central role in educational and social science research and policy?* (EdWorkingPaper 23-755). Annenberg Institute at Brown University. Accessed at https://doi.org/10.26300/nsbq-hb21 on February 20, 2024.

Halliday, M. (1993). Towards a language-based theory of learning. *Linguistics and Education, 5*, 93–116. Accessed at https://lchc.ucsd.edu/mca/Paper/JuneJuly05/HallidayLangBased.pdf on August 29, 2023.

Harvard Graduate School of Education. (2022). *Project Zero's thinking routine toolbox*. Accessed at https://pz.harvard.edu/thinking-routines on June 9, 2023.

Hattie, J. (2003, October). *Teachers make a difference: What is the research evidence?* [Conference presentation]. Australian Council for Educational Research Conference, Melbourne, Australia. Accessed at http://research.acer.edu.au/research_conference_2003/4/ on August 29, 2023.

Hattie, J. (2009). *Visible learning: A synthesis of over 800 meta-analyses relating to achievement*. New York: Routledge.

Hattie, J. (2021, March 22). *We need to get better at learning transfer*. World Education Summit. Accessed at https://www.tes.com/magazine/archived/john-hattie-we-need-get-better-learning-transfer on February 20, 2024.

Hattie, J. (2023a). *How great teachers think*. Accessed at https://www.edutopia.org/article/great-teachers-engage-evaluative-thinking on December 28, 2023.

Hattie, J. (2023b). *Visible learning: The sequel: A synthesis of over 2,100 meta-analyses relating to achievement*. New York: Routledge.

Hattie, J., & Donoghue, G. M. (2016). Learning strategies: A synthesis and conceptual model. *Science of Learning, 1*. Accessed at www.nature.com/articles/npjscilearn201613 on June 3, 2024.

Hattie, J., & Timperley, H. (2007). The power of feedback. *Review of Educational Research, 77*(1). Accessed at https://journals.sagepub.com/doi/10.3102/003465430298487 on February 21, 2024.

Heifetz, R. A., Linsky, M., & Grashow, A. (2009). *The practice of adaptive leadership: Tools and tactics for changing your organization and the world*. Cambridge, MA: Harvard Business Press.

Hendrick, C., & Macpherson, R. (2019). *What does this look like in the classroom? Bridging the gap between research and practice*. Woodbridge, Suffolk, United Kingdom: John Catt Educational.

High Tech High. (n.d.). *Empathy interviews*. Accessed at https://schoolguide.casel.org/resource/empathy-interview-protocol/ on August 29, 2023.

Hochman, J. C., & Wexler, N. (2017). *The writing revolution: A guide to advancing thinking through writing in all subjects and grades*. San Francisco: Jossey-Bass.

Hogarth, R. M., Lejarraga, T., & Soyer, E. (2015). The two settings of kind and wicked learning environments. *Current Directions in Psychological Science, 24*(5), 379–385.

Hook, P., & Casse, B. (2013). *SOLO taxonomy in the early years: Making connections for belonging, being and becoming*. Invercargill, New Zealand: Essential Resources.

Huberman, A. (Host). (2022a, January 2). *The science of making and breaking habits* [Audio podcast episode]. Huberman Lab. Accessed at https://podcastnotes.org/huberman-lab/episode-53-the-science-of-making-breaking-habits-huberman-lab on June 3, 2024.

Huberman, A. (Host). (2022b, January 30). *Build or break habits using science-based tools* [Audio podcast episode]. Huberman Lab. Accessed at https://www.hubermanlab.com/newsletter/build-or-break-habits-using-science-based-tools on February 20, 2024.

Icard, M. (2021). *Fourteen talks by age fourteen: The essential conversations you need to have with your kids before they start high school*. Albuquerque, NM: Harmony Books.

Kelemanik, G., Lucenta, A., & Creighton, S. J. (2016). *Routines for reasoning: Fostering the mathematical practices in all students*. Portsmouth, NH: Heinemann.

Kim, J. S., Burkhauser, M. A., Relyea, J. E., Gilbert, J. B., Scherer, E., et al (2023). A longitudinal randomized trial of a sustained content literacy intervention from first to second grade: Transfer effects on students' reading comprehension. *Journal of Educational Psychology, 115*(1), 73–98.

Knight, J. (2022). *The definitive guide to instructional coaching: Seven factors for success*. Alexandria, VA: ASCD.

Korinek, A., Schindler, M., & Stiglitz, J. (2021). *Technological progress, artificial intelligence, and inclusive growth* (Working Paper No. 2021/166). Washington, DC: International Monetary Fund.

Johnson, S. (2011). *Where good ideas come from: The natural history of innovation*. Riverhead Books.

Lee, K. (2017, February). *10 tips for speaking like a Ted Talk pro*. American Psychological Association. Accessed at https://www.apa.org/monitor/2017/02/tips-speaking on August 29, 2023.

Liang, B. C. (2014). Risk = management (as does uncertainty). In B. C. Liang (Ed.), *Managing and leading for science professionals* (pp. 57–66). Elsevier. Accessed at https://www.sciencedirect.com/science/article/abs/pii/B9780124166868000062?via%3Dihub on February 21, 2024.

Liljedahl, P. (2020). *Building thinking classrooms in mathematics, grades K–12: 14 teaching practices for enhancing learning*. Thousand Oaks, CA: Corwin.

Lipnevich, A. A., Panadero, E., & Calistro, T. (2023). Unraveling the effects of rubrics and exemplars on student writing performance. *Journal of Experimental Psychology: Applied, 29*(1), 136–148.

Lortie, D. C. (2002). *Schoolteacher: A sociological study* (2nd ed.). Chicago: University of Chicago Press.

Martella, A., Schneider, D., O' Day, G., & Karpicke, J. (2024). Investigating the intensity and integration of active learning and lecture. *Journal of Applied Research in Memory and Cognition*.

Marzano, R. J. (2010). *Formative assessment and standards-based grading*. Bloomington, IN: Marzano Resources.

Marzano, R. J. (2017). *The new art and science of teaching*. Bloomington, IN: Solution Tree Press.

Marzano, R. J. (2018). *The handbook for the new art and science of teaching*. Bloomington, IN: Solution Tree Press.

Marzano, R. J., & Heflebower, T. (2012). *Teaching and assessing 21st century skills*. Bloomington, IN: Marzano Resources.

Mason, L., & Otero M. Just how effective is direct instruction. *Perspectives on Behavioral Science, 44*(2-3), 225-244.

Mayer, R. E. (2008). Applying the science of learning: Evidence-based principles for the design of multimedia instruction. *American Psychologist, 63*(8), 760–769.

McDonald, J., & Allen, D. (n.d.). *Turning protocol examining adult work.* Accessed at https://www.schoolreforminitiative.org/download/tuning-protocol-examining-adult-work/?wpdmdl=12766&refresh=64ef3b5f76b4d1693399903 on August 30, 2023.

McDowell, M. (2020). *Teaching for transfer: A guide for designing learning with real-world application.* Bloomington, IN: Solution Tree Press.

McDowell, M., & Miller, K. S. (2022). *The project habit: Making rigorous PBL doable.* Mimi and Todd Press.

McTighe, J. (2021, January 28). *8 quick checks for understanding.* Edutopia. Accessed at https://www.edutopia.org/article/8-quick-checks-understanding/ on August 30, 2023.

McTighe, J., Silver, H., Perini. (2020). *Deep learning is doable: Five strategies for supporting deep learning in virtual environments.* Accessed at https://jaymctighe.com/wp-content/uploads/2020/12/Deep-Virtual-Learning-article-12.9.10.pdf on February 21, 2024.

McTighe, J., & Wiggins, G. (2013). *Essential questions: Opening doors to student understanding.* Alexandria, VA: ASCD.

Meta, J., & Fine, S. (2019). *In search of deeper learning.* Cambridge, MA: Harvard University Press.

Moats, L. C. (2020). *Speech to print: Language essentials for teachers* (3rd ed.). Baltimore, MD: Brookes Publishing.

Muller, D. A. (2008). Saying the wrong thing: Improving learning with multimedia by including misconceptions. *Journal of Computer Assisted Learning, 24*(2), 144–155.

Murphy, D. H., Little, J. L. & Bjork, E. L. (2023, September 8). The value of using tests in education as tools for learning—Not just for assessment. *Educational Psychology Review, 35*(89). Accessed at https://link.springer.com/article/10.1007/s10648-023-09808-3 on February 21, 2024.

National Center for Education Statistics. (2012, September). *Writing 2011: National assessment of educational progress at grades 8 and 12.* Washington, DC: U.S. Department of Education. Accessed at https://nces.ed.gov/nationsreportcard/pdf/main2011/2012470.pdf on August 30, 2023.

National School Reform Faculty. (n.d.a). *Framing consultancy dilemmas and consultancy questions.* Accessed at https://www.nsrfharmony.org/wp-content/uploads/2017/10/consultancy_dilemmas_0.pdf on February 21, 2024.

National School Reform Faculty. (n.d.b). *Pocket guide to probing questions.* Accessed at https://www.nsrfharmony.org/wp-content/uploads/2017/10/probing_questions_guide.pdf on August 30, 2023.

Nelsestuen, K., & Smith, J. (2020, October). Empathy interviews. *The Learning Professional, 41*(5), 59–62. Accessed at https://learningforward.org/wp-content/uploads/2020/10/tool-empathy-interviews.pdf on August 29, 2023.

Nicholls, J. (1989) *The competitive ethos and democratic education.* Cambridge, MA: Harvard University Press.

Nottingham, J. (2017). *The learning challenge: How to guide your students through the learning pit to achieve deeper understanding.* Thousand Oaks, CA: Corwin.

Oppland, M. (2017, April 28). *13 most popular gratitude exercises and activities.* Positive Psychology. Accessed at https://positivepsychology.com/gratitude-exercises/ on August 30, 2023.

Organisation for Economic Co-operation and Development. (2018). *PISA 2015: Results in focus.* Accessed at https://www.oecd.org/pisa/pisa-2015-results-in-focus.pdf on August 30, 2023.

Organisation for Economic Co-operation and Development. (2021). *The assessment frameworks for cycle 2 of the Programme for the International Assessment of Adult Competencies.* Accessed at https://www.oecd.org/skills/piaac/publications/PIAAC-Frameworks-Cycle2-en.pdf on August 29, 2023.

Pellegrino, J. W., & Hilton, M. (2012). *Education for life and work: Developing transferable knowledge and skills in the 21st century.* Washington, DC: National Academies Press.

Pierre-Louis, K. (2019, August 22). How to rebound after a disaster: Move, don't rebuild, research suggests. *The New York Times.* Accessed at https://www.nytimes.com/2019/08/22/climate/sea-level-managed-retreat.html on August 30, 2023.

Quigley, A., Muijs, D., & Stringer, E. (2018). *Metacognition and self-regulated learning: Guidance report.* Education Endowment Foundation. Accessed at https://files.eric.ed.gov/fulltext/ED612285.pdf on February 14, 2024.

Recht, D. R., & Leslie, M. (1988). Effect of prior knowledge on good and poor reader memory of text. *Journal of Educational Psychology, 80*(1), 16–20.

Reeves, D. B. (2010, January 7). *The myth of buy-in.* Creative Leadership Solutions. Accessed at https://www.creativeleadership.net/resources-content/the-myth-of-buy-in on August 30, 2023.

Ritchhart, R. (2012). *Making thinking visible: 10 apps for parents.* Accessed at https://www.berkleyschools.org/downloads/rogers_elementary/10_apps_for_parents_to_make_thinking_visible.pdf on August 28, 2023.

Rosenshine, B. (2012). Principles of instruction: Research-based strategies that all teachers should know. *American Educator.* Accessed at https://www.aft.org/sites/default/files/Rosenshine.pdf on February 4, 2024.

Schleicher, A. (2019, May 22). *A new tool for navigating through a complex world.* OECD Education and Skills Today. Accessed at https://oecdedutoday.com/education-skills-learning-compass-2030/ on August 30, 2023.

Schmoker, M. (2011). *Focus: Elevating the essentials to radically improve student learning.* Alexandria, VA: ASCD.

Schmoker, M. (2018). *Focus: Elevating the essentials to radically improve student learning* (2nd ed.). Alexandria, VA: ASCD.

Schwarz, R. (2013). *Eight behaviors for smarter teams: How you and your team get unstuck to get results.* San Francisco: Jossey-Bass.

Segre, P. S., Cade, D. E., Calambokidis, J., Fish, F. E., Friedlgender, A. S., Potvin, J., et al. (2019). Body flexibility enhances maneuverability in the world's largest predator. *Integrative and Comparative Biology, 59*(1), 48–60.

Seifriz, J. J., Duda, J. L., & Chi, L. (1992). The relationship of perceived motivational climate to intrinsic motivation and beliefs about success in basketball. *Journal of Sport and Exercise Psychology, 14*(4), 375–391.

Sherrington, T., & Goodwin, D. (n.d.). *Five ways: A series of short posts and one-pagers summarizing some everyday classroom practices.* Accessed at https://headguruteacher.files.wordpress.com/2022/09/five-ways-one-pagers-booklet-1.pdf on August 28, 2023.

Smith, R. E., Cumming, S. P., & Smoll, F. L. (2008). Development and validation of the Motivational Climate Scale for Youth Sports. *Journal of Applied Sport Psychology, 20*(1), 116–136.

State of Debate. (n.d.). Accessed at https://www.smashboom.org/page/state-of-debate on August 30, 2023.

Sternberg, R. J., & Horvath, J. A. (Eds.). (1999). *Tacit knowledge in professional practice: Researcher and practitioner perspectives.* Mahwah, NJ: Lawrence Erlbaum Associates.

Stonefields School. (2024). *Our vision.* Accessed at https://www.stonefields.school.nz/our-school-vision on June 20, 2023.

Takala, M. (2006). The effects of reciprocal teaching on reading comprehension in mainstream and special (SLI) education. *Scandinavian Journal of Educational Research, 50*(5), 559–576.

Taylor, D. (2023, November 3). *Backward Faded maths.* Accessed at https://taylorda01.weebly.com/uploads/4/2/3/8/42387051/backward_faded_calculations_with_bounds.pdf on February 2, 2024.

Terada, Y. (2023). *A research-backed tool kit of what works—and doesn't work—in education.* Accessed at https://www.edutopia.org/article/research-backed-tools-what-works-in-education on May 5, 2023.

Thompson-Grove, G. (2012). *What? So what? Now what?* Center for Leadership & Educational Equity. Accessed at https://www.schoolreforminitiative.org/download/what-so-what-now-what on August 30, 2023.

Toossi, M. (2002). *A century of change: The U.S. labor force, 1950–2050.* Accessed at https://www.bls.gov/opub/mlr/2002/05/art2full.pdf on February 14, 2024.

Turkle, S. (2021). *The empathy diaries: A memoir.* New York: Penguin.

U.S. Surgeon General. (2023). *Social media and youth mental health.* Accessed at https://www.hhs.gov/sites/default/files/sg-youth-mental-health-social-media-advisory.pdf on August 30, 2023.

Wang, H., & Troia, G. A. (2023, July 19). How students' writing motivation, teachers' personal and professional attributes, and writing instruction impact student writing achievement: A two-level hierarchical linear modeling study. *Frontiers in Psychology, 14*, 1213929. Accessed at https://www.doi.org/10.3389/fpsyg.2023.1213929 on February 21, 2024.

Wexler, N. (2023, April 9). Dramatic new evidence that building knowledge can boost comprehension and close gaps. *Forbes.* Accessed at https://www.forbes.com/sites/nataliewexler/2023/04/09/dramatic-new-evidence-that-building-knowledge-can-boost-comprehension-and-close-gaps/?sh=5a8092727725 on February 4, 2024.

Wiliam, D. (2011). *Embedded formative assessment.* Bloomington, IN: Solution Tree Press. Wiliam, D. (2017). *Embedded formative assessment (strategies for classroom formative assessment that drives student engagement and learning)* (2nd ed.). Bloomington, IN: Solution Tree Press.

Wiliam, D. (2018). *Creating the schools our children need: Why what we're doing now won't help much, and what we can do instead.* Bloomington, IN: Solution Tree Press.

Wiliam, D. (@dylanwiliam). (2023, March 26). *Bloom and his committee proposed a taxonomy of educational objectives, not a hierarchy. If you read the original report, it is also clear that what the committee regarded as knowledge was far-ranging* [Post]. X (formerly Twitter). Accessed at https://twitter.com/dylanwiliam/status/1639904973830987777 on August 30, 2023.

Willingham, D. T. (2023). *Outsmart your brain: Why learning is hard and how you can make it easy.* New York: Gallery Books.

Winter, J. (2023, July 16). The parent of a teenager is an emotional-garbage collector. *The New Yorker.* Accessed at https://www.newyorker.com/culture/the-new-yorker-interview/the-parent-of-a-teen-ager-is-an-emotional-garbage-collector on August 28, 2023.

Wolf, M. (2018). *Reader, come home: The reading brain in a digital world.* New York: HarperCollins.

Zwiers, J., Dieckmann, J., Rutherford-Quach, S., Daro, V., Skarin, R., Weiss, S., et al. (2017, February 28). *Principles for the design of mathematics curricula: Promoting language* and *content development.* Accessed at https://ul.stanford.edu/sites/default/files/resource/2021-11/Principles%20for%20the%20Design%20of%20Mathematics%20Curricula_1.pdf on June 3, 2024.

Index

A

ABCD/1234, 37, 39, 111–112
academic vocabulary
    development, 39, 103, 105–106
    responses, 108
accountability, 91
    upper- and lowercase, 48
Achieve the Core, 102
acting on corrective feedback, 112–113
    deliberative practice, 113
    example course schedule, 114
    four-quarter marking, 113
    quizzes and correcting, 113–115
    sticky note technique, 113
action habits, 96
adaptive problem solving, 5, 193–194
additional information, 104

addressing setbacks and changes, 193–198
    curveball strategies, 194
    red team protocol, 194–195
    scenarios, 195
    skunkworks, 194–196
"adjacent possible" thinking (Johnson), 171
affinity mapping, 38, 42, 189–190, 205
Agarwal, P. K., 17, 25
agree/disagree, 39, 111–112
agreements, 160
Akbar, K., 138
Allen, D., 205
Almarode, J., 29
American Idiot (Green Day), 63
analogies and metaphors, 41
    generating, 172, 178
analysis vs. synthesis, 121

anchor solutions to agreed-on criteria, 84

Anderson, J., 11

Apple Music, 63

Applying a solution, 191

applying conceptual knowledge

    success criteria, guideposts, and teacher routines, 40–41

applying conceptual understanding, 10–11, 14, 122, 151

    competency habits, 30

    creating and inspecting claims, evidence, and reasoning, 152–159

    developing, discussing, and challenging ideas with others, 159–161

applying understanding, 18, 20–21

appositives, 39

appreciation, apology, aha, 38, 84

approximate feedback protocol examples, 162

arguments, 160

ask students to think about their thinking, 38, 83

aspirations, 160

assessment scramble, 37, 71, 172–173

assessments

    obtrusive, 57

    student constructed, 57–58

    unobtrusive, 57

assumptions, 160

attention, 201–202

autonomy, 91

B

backward fading, 38–39, 87, 99–101

    sample mathematics problem, 100

    sentence development, 39

backward fading sentence structure, 124, 130–131

    steps, 130

balance, 3, 12–13, 15, 25

balancing ten key habits, 14

Barton, C., 148

behavioral engagement, 28

Biggs, J., 95

Bjork & Bjork, 88

Blank, S., 35–36

Bloom, B. S., 5, 19, 22

Bloom's taxonomy, 19, 22

"Bohemian Rhapsody" (Queen), 64

Botox Brow (Icard), 87

box induction, 145

    example, 145

bridging levels of learning, 90

bridging questions, 38

Brown, B., 78

build upon strategy, 38, 84–85

building a collection of stories of shared growth, 65–66

    questions that drive the three stories, 66

building background knowledge, 14

building conceptual understanding, 10–11, 170–171

    addressing setbacks and changes, 194–198

    comparing contexts, 171–178

    competency habits, 30

    employing problem-solving processes, 182–191

    engaging with authentic audiences, 191–194

    making predictions, 171, 178–181

solving complex problems, 181–182

    success criteria, guideposts, and teacher routines, 41

building knowledge, 18, 20–21

building knowledge together, 11

    competency habits, 30

    interacting with new information, 97–107

    making surface learning a habit, 96

    success criteria, guideposts, and teacher routines, 39

building systems to engage students in rigor-refined habits, 11–13

C

California Dept. of education, 192

calm process, 15

camera 1/camera 2, 37

carousel brainstorm, 42, 188

Cepeda, N. J., 87

CER.
    See claim, evidence, reasoning (CER) turn and talks

chalk talks, 40, 42, 135, 141–142., 185

challenging ideas with others, 151

challenging instead of rescuing, 67

changing AI-generated fronted adverbials, 129
- sample, 129

Charette protocol, 42, 191

chat station, 40, 135–137

ChatGPT, 53, 58

check assumptions, 84

checking and responding to understanding together, 10–11
- competency habits, 30
- making surface learning a habit, 96, 109–115
- success criteria, guideposts, and teacher routines, 39

checking for understanding, 14

checking the quality of the argument, 161
- Issaquah routine, 161
- red team, 161

choral and echo reading, 39, 102–105

Christensen, C. M., 64

chunking, 97–98
- surface-level questions, 111

circle of viewpoints, 40

circles of action, 41, 185

claim, evidence, reason (CER) turn and talks, 152–154
- claim types and examples, 154
- examples, 153
- five-interval transfer-level examples, 176–177
- general questions, 154–155
- leveraging, 172, 175–178
- logical error questions, 156–157
- perceptive and scenario questions, 156
- turn and tasks, 40

claim, support, question method, 40, 152, 157

clarifying questions, 49

clarity checks, 72–73
- for outcomes, 72

Clarity for Learning (Almarode & Vandas), 28

classification charts, 172

Claude, 58

Claxton, G., 25, 78, 170

clear and muddy protocol, 39, 107–108

Clear, J., 8, 65

close read, 39, 103, 105

cloze activities, 39, 103–104, 124, 130–131
- additional information, 104
- omitted information, 104

clues approach, 37, 71

Coalition of Essential Schools (Allen), 205

co-constructing expectations of learning, 69–72
- content, 70
- context, 70
- settings, 70
- strategies, 70–71
- task, 70

co-construction, 41, 172–173
- strategies, 172–173

co-crafting questions and problems, 42

cognitive dissonance, 70

Cokely, E. T., 86

collaboration.
See working with others

Collaborative for Academic, Social, and Emotional Learning (CASEL), 192

The Color of Water (Thomas), 138

comparing and contrasting concepts, 123
- gradually building complex dialogue, 123–142
- infusing thinking routines, 123, 142–151

comparing contexts, 170–172
- co-construction, 172–173
- generating analogies and metaphors, 172, 178
- graphic organizers, 172–173
- leveraging CER turn and talks, 172, 175–178
- leveraging deep learning strategies, 172
- semantic analysis, 172–175
- whip-around, 178

compass points, 37, 79

competency-based habits, 11
- applying conceptual understanding, 30
- building conceptual understanding, 30
- building knowledge together, 30

checking and responding to understanding togethers, 30
deep learning, 9, 99
developing conceptual understanding, 30
making them habitual, 29–30
solving complex problems, 30
surface learning, 9–11
transfer learning, 9–11
complex learning, 2–3
concept maps, 40, 173
conducting debates, 160
friendly controversy, 160
Lincoln–Douglas debates, 161
town hall meetings, 160
conjunctions, 39
connect to context, 67
connect, extend, and challenge (Project Zero), 40, 152, 158
connected to other ideas, 67
considering the rigorous learning process, 18–21
examining categories of knowledge and skill, 24–28
shifting from hierarchies to taxonomies, 22–24
consolidating learning, 7–11, 14, 19–20, 86
dispositional habits, 29
rehearsing and reflecting on learner qualities and the learning process, 86–90
success criteria, guideposts, and teacher routines, 38
constructing curveballs, 50, 54, 62
constructing learning intentions, 49–51, 62
tagging the categories of knowledge and skill, 50
consultancy dilemma, 37–38, 41, 81, 191, 204
content-rich curricula, 25
contextual knowledge, 25–27
across surface, deep, and transfer learning, 27
defined, 25
description and examples, 26
convergent thinking. 135
affinity mapping, 190
problem cause chart, 186
sample protocols, 184

vs. divergent thinking, 183
when defining a problem, 186–187
conversation norms, 84
corrective feedback, 106–115
COVID-19 pandemic, 64
creating a range of assessments, 56–58
obtrusive, 57
student constructed, 57–58
unobtrusive, 57
creating a schedule for habits, 46–47
creating and inspecting claims, evidence, and reasoning, 151
CER turn and talks, 152–157
claim, support, question, 152, 157
connect, extend, and challenge, 152, 158
imagine if … routine, 152, 158
kick the tires, 152, 159
think-puzzle-explore, 152, 158–159
creating roles for process, 38, 83
creating tasks, 50, 54, 62
reading, writing, and talking tasks across surface, deep, and transfer learning, 54
creative comparisons, 42, 189
credibility observer, 84
critical friends protocol, 38, 40, 42, 88, 191
cue transfer prompts, 38
cues, 8
cultivating curiosity, 81–83
cups technique, 37, 79
curveball questions, 38, 42, 90
curveball strategies
addressing setbacks and changes, 194

D

Damour, L., 77
de Jong, T., 96
de Vergara, P. R., 165–166
declarative knowledge, 25–27
across surface, deep, and transfer learning, 27
defined, 25
description and examples, 26
deep learning
curveball questions, 89

elements of, 3

percentage of student work, 12

habits, 14

competency habits, 30

declarative, procedural, and contextual knowledge, 27

learning process, 20–21

pathways for ensuring, 23–24

pinwheel vs. pendulum thinking, 17–18

to transfer learning, 90

developing the habits of, 119–168

defining, 120–121

defined, 2–3, 5–6, 11–14

defining the problem, 182, 184–185

chalk talks, 185

circles of action, 185

convergent thinking, 186–187

divergent thinking, 185–186

fishbone, 184

five whys, 184

gap analysis, 185

open space technology, 185

portable surprises, 185

realm of concern, 184

seminars, 185

skunkworks, 185

step in, step out, step back, 185

Dehaene, S., 76, 96, 172

deliberate practice, 38, 113

Dempster, F. N., 87

determining next steps, 74–75

determining rigor sequences, 56–57

developing a growth mindset, 67

developing conceptual knowledge, 10–11, 14

developing conceptual understanding, 123

compare and contrast concepts, 123–151

competency habits, 30

success criteria, guideposts, and teacher routines, 39–40

developing deep learning habits, 121–122

developing dispositional habits, 63–64

consolidating learning, 86–90

embracing change, 77–83

engaging metacognition, 68–77

incorporating into a *we do* culture, 90–91

making-thinking-visible routines (Ritchhart), 66–67

next steps, 93

reflection questions, 92

six competency-based habits, 67–68

starting with a culture of *we do*, 64–68

taking action to improve learning, 74–77

working well with others, 83–86

developing learner qualities, 65–68

developing leveled success criteria, 50–54, 62

crafting driving questions, 53

learning intentions and success criteria across multiple goals, 51

questions types and examples, 53

success criteria verb rhetoric, 51

developing relationships, 83–85

establishing and implementing expectations for collaborative work, 83–84

developing the complex sentence structure, 124

backward fading sentence structure, 124, 130

cloze activities, 124, 130–131

fronted adverbial drills, 124, 126–129

picture worth 1,000 words, 124, 130

three-interval turn and talk, 124–126

developing the habits of deep learning, 119–120

applying conceptual understanding, 122, 151–161

defining deep learning, 120–121

developing conceptual understanding, 122–151

developing deep learning habits, 121–122

making deep learning feedback routine, 165–166

making deep learning feedback social, 161–165

next steps, 168

reflection questions, 167

developing transfer learning habits, 169–170

building contextual understanding, 171–181

learning to transfer, 170

next steps, 200

reflection questions, 199

solving complex problems, 181–198
developing, discussing, and challenging ideas with others, 159
    checking the quality of the arguments, 161
    conducting debates, 160–161
    prepare for challenging ideas, 159–160
Dickens, C., 138–139
direct modeling, 39, 98–99
discovery-based learning, 96
discussion mapping.
    See Harkness protocol
dispositional habits, 11, 14
    building a system, 14
    consolidating learning, 9–11, 29
    developing, 63–93
    engaging metacognition, 9–11, 28
    making them habitual, 28–29
    navigating challenge, 9–11, 29
    working with others, 9–11, 29
dispositional skills that enhance rigorous learning, 7–8
    consolidating learning, 7
    engaging metacognition, 7
    navigating challenge, 7
    working with others, 7
divergent thinking, 135
    defining a problem, 185–186
    open space technology, 141
    sample protocols, 184
    SWOT, 190–191
    vs. convergent thinking, 183
    when defining a problem, 185–186
Donoghue, G. M., 30–31, 42–43, 169
dots strategy, 41, 76, 165
dynamic presentations, 42, 194

E

echo reading.
    See choral and echo reading
effective habits, 2
    competency-based, 9–11
    dispositional, 9–11
    learning, 10
    three-step process, 8
EL Education, 26
elaborate interrogation, 160
elaborating on and summarizing new information, 107–108
    strategies, 107
elaborative interrogation, 40, 132
    sample questions, 133
embracing change, 77
    cultivating curiosity, 81–83
    managing negative thinking, 77–81
embracing commitment, 192
embracing community, 192
embracing not knowing, 191
embracing radical differences, 192
emotional appeal, 91
emotional engagement, 28
empathy, 191–193
The Empathy Diaries (Turkle), 191
empathy interviews, 42, 193
Employing problem-solving processes, 182–184
    applying a solution, 183
    defining the problem, 182
    sample divergent and convergent protocols, 184
    searching for information, 182
encouraging questions, 67
engaging in clarity checks, 69, 73–73
engaging metacognition, 7, 9–11, 14, 68–69, 87
    dispositional habits, 28–29
    finding the gap, 69
    success criteria, guideposts, and teacher routines, 37
    taking action to improve learning, 69
    using evidence of learning to inform next steps, 69–74
engaging with authentic audiences, 191–193
    embracing commitment, 192
    embracing community, 192
    embracing not knowing, 191
    embracing radical differences, 192
    protocols for, 193
enhancing conversations, 90

ensuring tasks incorporate reading, writing, and talking across surface, deep, and transfer learning, 56, 58

entrance/exit tickets, 37

entry events, 37

Epstein, D., 4

Ericcson, K. A., 86

error analysis, 37, 71

Escaperoom.com, 4

Eureka moments, 161

evaluation, 121

examining categories of knowledge and skill, 24–28
    contextual knowledge, 25–26
    declarative knowledge, 25–26
    examples, 26–27
    procedural knowledge, 25–26

examples and nonexamples, 39, 98, 102

expanding complex sentences to paragraphs, 131–135
    sustaining complex thinking across multiple ideas, 135–142

F

Farris, R., 87

feedback
    acting on, 106–115
    following through via, 56, 58–60

feelings and options, 38, 84

final word protocol, 39, 134

fishbone, 41, 184, 186

fishbowl, 196

5 whys, 41, 184
    beginning with, 196

Five Ways (Sherrington & Goodwin), 108

five-interval transfer-level examples, 176–177

five-interval turn and talks, 39, 41, 131–13
    examples, 132–133
    sample questions, 133

flat affect, 38, 86–87, 110

fluidity, 3, 15, 21

focusing on learning instead of work, 67

following through via feedback, 56, 58–60

For Whom the Bell Tolls (Hemingway), 119, 139

the four As routine, 40, 160
    agreements, 160
    arguments, 160
    aspirations, 160
    assumptions, 160

four corners, 37–39, 82, 111–112

four-quarter marking (Wiliam), 39, 113

Fourteen Talks by Age Fourteen (Icard), 86–87

Frayer model, 40, 142–144
    samples, 143–144

friendly controversy routine, 40, 42, 160, 189

fronted adverbial drills, 39, 124, 126–127, 131
    changing AI-generated fronted adverbials, 129
    matching fronted adverbial types with sample sentences, 127–128
    matching fronted adverbials with sample sentences, 127
    sentence creation from fronted adverbials, 128
    sequencing fronted adverbials, 128–129

full-sentence and academic vocabulary responses, 39, 107–108

G

gallery walk, 40, 42, 135, 191
    conducting, 140
    opening moves, 139–140
    reflections and next steps, 140

Ganz, M., 65–66

gap analysis, 37, 41, 185

Garber, M., 201

Gemini, 58

general CER questions, 154–155

generate–sort–connect–elaborate (Project Zero), 40, 146–147

generating analogies and metaphors, 172, 178

generating hypotheses, 41, 178–179

getting on the balcony, 68, 76–77

getting the gist, 39, 107–109

Gilovich, T., 5

goals, 8

Goodwin, D., 108

Gould, S. J., 22

gradually building complex dialogue, 123

developing the complex sentence structure, 124–131

expanding complex sentences to paragraphs, 131–135

strategies, 124

sustaining complex thinking across multiple ideas, 135–142

grain size of habit development, 45

graphic organizers, 40–41, 150–151, 172–173

arcs, 150

boxes, 150

concept maps, 150

examples, 150

nodes, 150

pictographs, 150–151

T-charts, 150

Venn diagrams, 150–151

Grashow, A., 68

gratitude prompts, 37, 79–81

Great Expectations (Dickens), 139

Green Day, 63–64

Grissmer, D., 25

group protocols for leveraging voice and choice, 85

Grove, G. T., 34

Guernica (Picasso), 119

guided practice, 97–98

backward fading, 99–101

direct modeling, 98–99

examples and nonexamples, 98, 102

surface-level questions, 111

zoom in, zoom out, 99, 101

guilt vs. shame, 78

H

habit science, 13

leveraging, 14

habit stacking. *See* stacking

Harkness protocol, 41, 162

examples, 163

The Hate U Give (McBride), 138

Hattie, J., xi–xiv, 30–31, 42–43 62, 196

Heifetz, R. A., 68

Hemingway, E., 139

hexagonal approach, 37, 71

hierarchies

defined, 18–19

shifting to taxonomies, 22–24

vs. taxonomies, 18

high-quality dialogue, 121–142

Hochman, J. C., 123

Horvath, J. A., 86

Hosseini, K., 138

How We Learn (Dehaene), 76, 96

Huberman, A., 46

I

I describe, you draw routine, 39, 103, 106–107

I used to think … Now I think … routine, 37–38, 67, 87–88, 112

Icard, M., 86–87

imagine if … thinking routine, 40, 152, 158

implementation, inspiration, and impact questions, 48

implementing structured protocols, 81

for mastery-oriented feedback, 81

importance of rigorous learning, 4–7

in2out protocol, 38, 40, 82, 134

inclusion, 3, 15

incorporating dispositional habits into a *we do* culture, 90–91

incorporating small changes in routines, 86, 88–90

bridging levels of learning, 90

change in the context, 88

change in the setting, 88

change in the task, 88

curveball questions, 89

influences on student learning across levels of rigor, 43

infusing thinking routines, 123, 142

box induction, 145

Frayer model, 142–144

generate-sort-connect-elaborate, 146–147

graphic organizers, 150–151

parts, purpose, and complexity, 147

+1 routines, 146

sentence stems, 146

SSDD problems, 148–150

strategies, 142

inside-out process, 183

inspecting the motion work, 55–56

creating a range of assessments, 56–58

determining rigor sequences, 56–57

following through via feedback, 56, 58–60

incorporating reading, writing, and talking across levels of learning, 56, 58

tagging categories of knowledge, 56

interacting with new information, 97

chunking, 97–98

guided practice, 97–102

interactive activities with surface knowledge and skill, 102–107

repetition, 97–98

variation, 97–98

interactive activities with surface knowledge and skill, 102

academic vocabulary development, 103

choral and echo reading, 102

close read, 103

cloze activities, 103

I describe, you draw, 103

making predictions, 102–103

mnemonics, 103

numberless word problems and slow reveal graphs, 103

interleaving, 38, 87

The Invisible Man (Wells), 138

Issaquah routine, 40, 161

J

jigsaw method, 40, 135, 139

Johnson, S., 171, 185

K

Karaka, M., 114–115

keep-inquiry-going prompts, 38, 82

cue transfer prompts, 82

kick the tires routine, 40, 152, 159

kind environments, 4

navigating challenge, 8

kind problems, 4, 6

feedback links outcomes to actions, 4

King, M. L. Jr., 58

The Kite Runner (Hosseini), 138

know, want to know, learned (KWL) chart, 37

know/need to know (K/NTK), 37

Known/Nuance/Novel protocol, 37, 72–73

Korinek, A., 4

L

launch entry events, 70

launching the work, 50, 55, 62

across surface, deep, and transfer learning, 55

The Learning Challenge (Nottingham), 28

learning for understanding. *See* deep learning

Learning GPS, 37, 75

learning habits

competency, 29–30

deep learning, 119–168

dispositional, 28–29

making them habitual, 28

surface learning, 99–117

transfer learning, 169–200

learning process, 20–21

applying understanding, 20–21

building knowledge, 20–21

defined, 19

making meaning, 20–21

learning taxonomy, 19

learning to transfer, 170

Leslie, L., 25

Letters from a Birmingham City Jail (King), 58

leveled success criteria, 69–70, 73–74

leveraging CER turn and talk, 172, 175–178

leveraging deep learning strategies, 172

leveraging habit science, 14

light bulb moments, 161

Lincoln–Douglas debates, 40, 161

Linsky, M., 68

logical error questions, 156–157

lowercase accountability, 48

M

making deep learning feedback routine, 165–166
    sample approximate feedback strategies, 165
making deep learning feedback social, 161–165
    approximate feedback protocol examples, 162
    consultancy dilemma process, 165
    Harkness protocol examples, 163
    talk detective process, 164
    talk detective discussion guidelines, 164
    what? so what? now what? protocol, 164
making meaning, 18, 20–21
making motion matter, 49–50
    constructing curveballs, 50, 54
    constructing learning intentions, 49–51
    creating tasks, 50, 54
    developing leveled success criteria, 50–54
    launching the work, 50, 55
"The Making of an Expert" (Ericcson et al.), 86
making predictions, 39, 102–103, 178
    generating hypotheses, 178–179
    planning scenarios, 178, 181
    predict and verify, 178–179
    SCCG framework, 178
    the 3 Cs routine, 180–181
making rigorous learning doable, 35–36
    inspecting motion work, 55–60
    making motion matter, 49–55
    next steps, 62
    reflection questions, 61
    starting and sustaining a habit, 36–49
making surface learning a habit, 95–96
    building knowledge together, 97–109
    checking and responding to current understanding together, 109–115
    mutual learning, 96–97
    next steps, 117
    reflection questions, 116
making the ten rigorous learning habits habitual, 28–30
    competency habits, 29–30
    dispositional habits, 28–29

making-thinking-visible routines (Ritchhart), 66–67
managing negative thinking, 77–78
    implementing structured protocols, 81
    monitoring orientation, 78–81
    strategies, 79
Martella et al., 65
Martyr (Akbar), 138
Marzano, R. J., 22–23, 43, 132
matching fronted adverbial types with sample sentences, 127–128
    types with samples, 127–128
matrix and assessment scramble, 41
matrix approach, 37, 71, 172
McBride, J., 138
McDaniel & Butler, 88
McDonald, J., 23, 205
McTighe, J., 120
metaphors
    generating, 172, 178
mnemonics, 39, 103, 106
    acronyms, 106
    enhance understanding and application, 106
    facilitate recall and retention, 106
    promote collaboration and communication, 106
    spark creativity and engagement, 106
monitor your mood, 37, 79
monitoring orientation, 78–81
monitoring progress using leveled success criteria, 69–70, 73–74
motion habits.
    See making motion matter; planning habits
Muijs, D., 7
Murphy, D. H., 113–114
mutual learning, 96–97
    growth flow chart, 97

N

name generator, 39, 110
National Assessment of Educational Progress, 122
navigating challenge, 7–11, 14, 87
    dispositional habits, 29

success criteria, guideposts, and teacher routines, 37–38

need it-see it-start it-show it process, 62, 93, 117, 168, 200

next steps
  developing dispositional habits, 93
  developing the habits of deep learning, 168
  developing transfer learning habits, 200
  making rigorous learning doable, 62
  making surface learning a habit, 117
  redefining rigor, 33

nominal group techniques, 42, 189

nonvolunteer strategies, 39

Nottingham, J., 28

numberless word problems and slow reveal graphs, 103–105

numbers on chairs, 39, 110

O

obtrusive assessments, 57

Occam's razor, 35

odd one out, 41

OECD.
  See Organisation for Economic Co-operation and Development (OECD)

omitted information, 104

on the move, 37, 41

open space technology (OST), 41, 135, 141, 185–186

open the success criteria, 42, 194

option explosion revise, 42, 184, 188

Orange, T., 138

orchard cove, 42, 188

Organisation for Economic Co-operation and Development (OECD), 5, 182–183, 193
  OECD Learning Compass, 5

orientation reflection on progress, 37, 79

out of many, 165

outside-in process, 183

P

"The Parent of a Teenager Is an Emotional Garbage Can" (Damour & Winter), 77

parts, purpose, and complexity, 40, 147

Pashler, H., 87

pass the questions around, 38, 82

pendulum thinking, 12, 17, 31–32, 96, 115

perceptive and scenario questions, 156
  potential, 157

Perplexity, 58

perspective analysis, 40

persuasion, 91

Picasso, P., 119

pictographs, 40, 173

picture worth 1,000 words, 39, 124, 130–131

pinwheel thinking, 1–2, 10, 12, 15, 17, 22, 27–32, 96, 115, 166

Planning scenarios, 178, 181

+1 routines (Project Zero), 40, 146

pointing out and noticing thinking, 67

popsicle sticks, 39, 110

portable surprises, 41, 185

practice habits.
  See action habits

The Practices of Adaptive Leadership (Heifetz et al.), 68

praise the pause, 37, 82

predict and clarify, 41

predict and verify routine, 178–179

preparing for challenging ideas, 159
  elaborate interrogation, 160
  the four As, 160

present-deepening projects, 38, 82

Prietula, M. J., 86

probing and process questions, 39, 110

problem solving, 14

problem-based approach, 22, 43

procedural knowledge, 25–27
  across surface, deep, and transfer learning, 27
  defined, 25
  description and examples, 26

process observer, 84

process.
  See learning process

Project Zero, 146, 158

project-based approach, 22, 35, 43

protocols for engaging with authentic audiences, 193

Q

question stems, 53–54
    comparisons, 40
questions
    clarifying, 49
    encouraging, 67
    for discussion, 136–137
    general CER, 154–155
    implementation, inspiration, and impact, 48
    logical error, 156–157
    measuring your impact, 48–49
    perceptive and scenario, 156
    probing and process, 39, 110
    surface-level, 111
    talk detective discussion, 164
    that drive the three stories, 66
questions before comments routine, 41, 165
quick checks, 41
Quigley, A., 7
quizzing and correcting, 38–39, 87, 113–115

R

The Ramones, 64
Reader, Come Home (Wolf), 81
reading skills, 14, 25
Ready, M., 59–60
realm of concern, 41, 184
Recht, D. R., 25
Red team technique, 40, 42, 161, 189
    addressing setbacks and changes, 194–195
redefining rigor, 17–18, 31
    considering the rigorous learning process, 18–28
    making the ten habits habitual, 28–30
    next steps, 33
    reflection questions, 32
    what? so what? now what? protocol, 34
reflection questions
    developing dispositional habits, 92
    developing the habits of deep learning, 167
    developing transfer learning habits, 199
    making rigorous learning doable, 61

making surface learning a habit, 116
rehearsal, 38, 87
rehearsing and reflecting on learner qualities and the learning process, 86
    incorporating small changes in routines, 88–90
    slowing things down, 86–87
    spacing things out, 87–88
repetition, 97–98
    surface-level questions, 111
research, 91
responding to surface-level questions, 110–112
    ABCD or 1234, 111–112
    agree or disagree, 111–112
    four corners, 111–112
    name generator, 110
    numbers on chairs, 110
    popsicle sticks, 110
    probing and process questions, 110
    surface-level questions linked to active engagement strategies, 111
    true or false, 111–112
revisiting cloze activities, 39
rewards, 8
rigor
    redefining, 17–31
    traditional thinking about, 1–2
Rigor Redefined
    habits, 11–13, 36, 43, 62
    survey, 32, 33–34, 116
rigorous learning
    balance, 3
    building systems to engage students in rigor-refined habits, 11–13
    considering the process, 18–27
    defined, 2–3
    developing dispositional habits, 63–93
    developing the habits of deep learning, 119–168
    developing transfer learning habits, 169–200
    dispositional skills to enhance, 7–8
    fluidity, 3
    fostering, 8–11

importance of, 4–7
inclusion, 3
is fluid, 13
making it doable, 35–62
making surface learning a habit, 95–117
making the ten habits habitual, 28–30
Ritchhart, R., 66–67
Rohrer, D., 87
Rosenshine, B., 96–97
routines, 8, 12
rubrics
hierarchy-centered vs. taxonomy-centered, 23
scoring, 22–23

S

same surface, different depth (SSDD) problems (Barton), 40, 148–150
examples, 148–149
sample approximate feedback strategies, 165
sample course schedule, 114
sample divergent and convergent protocols, 184
scaffold the start, 37, 82
scaffolds
developing the complex sentence structure, 124–131
expanding complex sentences to paragraphs, 135–142
sustaining complex thinking across multiple ideas, 135
SCCG.
See sequence, cause, consequences, and motivation (SCCG) framework
scenario planning, 41–42, 188
schema, 18
Schindler, M., 4
Schleicher, A., 5
Schmoker, M., 54
scoring rubrics, 22–23
searching for information, 187–189
affinity mapping, 189–190
carousel brainstorm, 188
convergent thinking, 190
creative comparison, 189
divergent thinking, 190–191

friendly controversy, 189
nominal group techniques, 189
option explosion revise, 188
orchard cove, 188
red team, 189
SCCG, 188–189
scenario planning, 188
SWOT, 189–191
SWOT analysis, 190
town hall meetings, 189
semantic analysis, 41, 172–175
defined, 173–174
subtypes and signal words for basic relationships, 174–175
symbol relationships, 174
seminars
(*see also* Socratic seminars), 185
sentence creation from fronted adverbials, 128
sentence stems, 40, 146
comparisons, 40
samples, 146
sequels, 42, 194
sequence, cause, consequences, and motivation (SCCG) framework, 41–42, 178, 180, 188–189
sequencing fronted adverbials, 128–129
sample, 128
setting up and using arguments, 38, 83
shame, 77–78
sharing, 45, 48–49
sheltering, 44, 47
Sherrington, T., 108
shifting from hierarchies to taxonomies, 22–24
pathways for ensuring surface, deep, and transfer learning, 23–24
rubrics, 23
show me the evidence, 67–68
Shu, K., 64
silent protocol, 37, 70–72
situation room, 42, 194–195
six key questions, 14
skunkworks, 41–42, 185, 194–196
begin with the 5 whys, 196

fishbowl, 196
    stay small, stay focused, 196
    take a "bias to action and inspection" approach, 196
    vote with your feet, 196
slow reveal graphs.
    See numberless words and slow reveal graphs
slow things down, 86–87
    flat affect, 86–87
    quizzing, 87
    rehearsal, 87
    wait for an answer, 86
small, 44–45
Socratic seminars, 40–41, 135, 137–138
    steps to, 138
solving complex problems, 10–11, 170
    competency habits, 30
    success criteria, guideposts, and teacher routines, 41–42
solving problems together, 85–86
    group protocols for leveraging voice and choice, 85
sort it out protocol, 165
space things out, 87
    backward fading, 87
    critical friends, 88
    I used to think … now I think … routine, 87–88
    interleaving, 87
    success analysis protocol, 87–88
    take away, take back, and tension, 88
    what? who what? now what? protocol, 88
spaced practice, 38, 87, 162
speak like you are right and listen like you are wrong, 84
sprinting, 45, 47–48
SSDD problems.
    See same surface, different depth problems
stacking, 44, 46–47
starting and sustaining a habit, 36–44
    influences on student learning across levels of rigor, 43
    sharing, 45, 48–49
    sheltering, 44, 47

small, 44–45
sprinting, 45, 47–48
stacking, 44, 46–47
success criteria and teacher routine checklist, 37–42
sustaining, 44–45
starting with a culture of *we do*, 64–65
    building a collection of stories of shared growth, 65–66
    developing learner qualities, 65–68
stay small, stay focused, 196
step in, step out, step back, 42, 185
Sternberg, R. J., 86
sticky note technique, 39, 41, 113
Stiglitz, J., 4
Stonefields School (New Zealand), 20–21
strategies for elaborating on and summarizing new information, 107
strengths, weaknesses, opportunities, and threats, 42, 189
    analysis, 190
Stringer, E., 7
structured protocols, 131, 134
    for scaffold level 2, 134–135
student buy-in, 90–91
    to action, 91
    to motion, 91
student-constructed assessments, 57–58
subordinating conjunctions, 39
subtypes and signal words for basic relationships, 174–175
success analysis protocol, 38, 87–88
success criteria
    acting on corrective feedback, 112–115
    addressing setbacks and changes, 194–198
    building contextual understanding, 170–198
    co-constructing expectations of learning, 70–72
    comparing and contrasting concepts, 123–152
    comparing context, 172–178
    creating and inspecting claims, evidence, and reasoning, 152–159
    developing relationships, 83–85
    developing the habits of deep learning, 123–151

developing, discussing, and challenging ideas with others, 159–161

elaborating on and summarizing new information, 107–109

employing problem-solving processes, 182–191

engaging in clarity checks, 72–73

engaging metacognition, 69–70

engaging with authentic audiences, 191–194

interacting with new information, 97–107

making predictions, 178–181

making surface learning a habit, 97

managing negative thinking, 77–83

monitoring progressing using leveled success criteria, 73–74

rehearsing and reflecting on learner qualities and the learning process, 86–90

responding to surface-level questions, 110–112

solving complex problems, 181–182

solving problems together, 85–86

taking action to improve learning, 74–77

success criteria and teacher routine checklist, 37–42

summarizing key learning, 37

summarizing on new information, 108

    getting the gist, 108–109

    summarizing the story so far, 109

    think-pair-share, 109

summarizing the story so far, 39, 107, 109

support, 91

surface learning, 5–6, 11–14

    competency habits, 30

    curveball questions, 89

    declarative, procedural, and contextual knowledge, 27

    defined, 2–3

    elements of, 3

    learning process, 20–21

    making it a habit, 95–117

    pathways for ensuring, 23–24

    percentage of student work, 12

    pinwheel vs. pendulum thinking, 17–18

    to deep learning, 90

sustaining complex thinking across multiple ideas, 135

    chalk talk, 135

    chat station, 135

    gallery walk, 135

    jigsaw, 135

    open space technology, 135

    Socratic seminar, 135

    text-to-text, text-to-self, text-to-world, 135

    world café, 135

sustaining complex thinking across multiple ideas, 135–142

    five-interval turn and talks, 131

    structured protocols, 131

sustaining, 44–45

SWOT. *See* strengths, weaknesses, opportunities, and threats

symbol relationships, 174

synthesis

    defined, 121

    vs. analysis, 121

T

TAG protocol, 37, 81

tagging categories of knowledge, 56

take a "bias to action and inspection" approach, 196

take away, take back, and tension protocol, 38, 88

taking action from feedback, 74–76

    camera 1/camera 2, 75

    on the move, 75

    30:5, 75

taking action to improve learning, 69, 74–77

    determining next septs, 74–75

    taking action from feedback, 74–76

    using differentiated feedback, 74, 76–77

talk detectives process, 41, 163–165

    consultancy dilemma process, 164–165

    discussion guidelines, 164

    guideline questions, 164

talking skills, 14

Taner, G., 11

taxonomies

    Bloom's, 19, 22

learning, 19
shifting to, 22–24
vs. hierarchies, 17
Webb's Depth of Knowledge, 19

Taxonomy of Educational Objectives (Bloom et al.), 22

T-charts, 40–41, 172–173

Teaching for Transfer (McDowell), 23

tell me more, 67

text-to-text, text-to-self, text-to-world, 39, 135, 138–139

think again, 37, 82

think and wonder, 38, 83

think, feel, care routine, 38, 42, 83, 193

thinking hats protocol, 42, 193

think-pair-share, 39, 107, 109

think-puzzle-explore process, 40, 152, 158–159

third teacher references, 37

30:5, 3730:5, 75
camera 1/camera 2, 75
on the move, 75

Thomas, A., 138

3 Cs routine, 41, 180–181

3 read, 39

3-2-1, 37

three stories protocol, 42, 193

three-interval turn and talks, 39, 41, 124–126, 131
examples, 125–126

to and through, 37, 41

town hall meetings, 40, 42, 160, 189

transfer learning, 5–6, 11–14
competency habits, 30
curveball questions, 89
declarative, procedural, and contextual knowledge, 27
defined, 2–3
developing learning habits, 169–200
elements of, 3
learning process, 20–21
pathways for ensuring, 23–24
pinwheel vs. pendulum thinking, 17–18

true for whom? protocol, 42, 193

true or false, 39, 111–112

tuning protocol, 37–38, 41, 58, 81, 85–86, 191, 204–205

Turkle, S., 191–192

2 box induction, 40

U

unobtrusive assessments, 57

uppercase Accountability, 48

using differentiated feedback, 74, 76–77

using evidence of learning to inform next steps, 69–70
co-constructing expectations of learning, 69–72
engaging in clarity checks, 69, 73–73
monitoring progress using leveled success criteria, 69–70, 73–74

V

"The Value of Using Tests in Education as Tools for Learning—Not Just for Assessment" (Murphy et al.), 113

Vandas, K., 29

variation, 97–98
surface-level questions, 111

Venn diagrams, 40–41, 172–173

viewpoint coach, 84

visual thinking maps, 172

vocabulary.
See academic vocabulary development

vote with your feet, 196

Vul, E., 87

W

wagon wheel protocol, 40, 135

wait for an answer, 38, 86

wait time, 110

Wandering Stars (Orange), 138

we do culture.
See starting with a culture of *we do*

Webb, N., 19

Webb's Depth of Knowledge (Webb), 19

Wells, H. G., 138

Wexler, N., 25, 123

What Is an Organization's Culture? (Christensen & Shu), 64

what makes you say that? protocol, 39, 107–108

what? so what? now what? protocol (Grove), 38, 41–42, 88, 162–164, 191
    redefining rigor, 34

whip-around protocol, 41, 178

wicked environments, 5
    navigating challenge, 8

wicked problems, 4–6
    defined, 5

Wiggins, G., 120

Wiliam, D., 22, 47, 113

Winter, J., 77

Wizted, J. T., 87

Wolf, M., 80–81

Wooden, J., 58

work sample scramble, 37, 70

working with others, 7–11, 14, 83
    developing relationships, 83–85
    dispositional habits, 29
    solving problems together, 85–86
    success criteria, guideposts, and teacher routines, 38

world café strategy, 135, 140–141
    open space, 40

The Writing Revolution (Hochman & Wexler), 123

writing skills, 14

Y

Yonkers, J., 196–198

Z

zones of learning, 37, 79

zoom in, zoom out, 39, 99, 101

Teaching for Transfer
Michael McDowell

Empower K–12 learners to transfer their current knowledge to new contexts, navigate real-world problems, and more. This resource contains instructional strategies educators can use to build 21st century skills in learners and increase student engagement.
BKF950

Raising the Rigor
Eileen Depka

Discover questioning techniques proven to enhance critical thinking and 21st century skills, deepen student engagement, and improve college and career readiness. This user-friendly guide provides templates, surveys, and checklists for planning instruction, unpacking standards, and increasing rigor in the classroom.
BKF722

Ambitious Instruction
Brad Cawn

In *Ambitious Instruction*, author Brad Cawn offers a blueprint for how to make rigor visible, accessible, and actionable in grade 6–12 classrooms. Educators can improve students' cognitive function and ensure college and career readiness through problem-based learning examples and rich content.
BKF842

Deconstructing Depth of Knowledge
Erik M. Francis

If your understanding of depth of knowledge (DOK) is a little cloudy, you're not alone. This resource is your one-stop-shop for learning what it is and how to use it to provide learning experiences that are academically rigorous, socially and emotionally supportive, and student responsive.
BKF960

Stick the Learning
Eric Saunders

Research shows that desirable difficulties as achieved with spaced repetition, interleaving, and retrieval (SIR) have positive long-term impacts on student learning because the learning sticks. This book guides you through these three techniques for a more brain-compatible classroom geared toward student success.
BKG083

Visit SolutionTree.com or call 800.733.6786 to order.

Global PD teams
Collaborative Learning for School Improvement

Quality team learning **from authors you trust**

Global PD Teams is the first-ever **online professional development resource designed to support your entire faculty on your learning journey.** This convenient tool offers daily access to videos, mini-courses, eBooks, articles, and more packed with insights and research-backed strategies you can use immediately.

GET STARTED
SolutionTree.com/**GlobalPDTeams**
800.733.6786